Finance: Servant or Deceiver?

Also by Paul H. Dembinski

THE LOGIC OF THE PLANNED ECONOMY
The Seeds of the Collapse

ECONOMIC AND FINANCIAL GLOBALIZATION
What the Numbers Say

ENRON AND WORLD FINANCE
A Case Study in the Ethics (*editor*)

Finance: Servant or Deceiver?

Financialization at the Crossroads

Paul H. Dembinski

Translated from French by Kevin Cook

© Observatoire de la Finance 2009
Foreword © Ernesto Rossi di Montelera 2009
English translation © Kevin Cook 2009

All rights reserved. No reproduction, copy or transmission of this publication may be made without written permission.

No portion of this publication may be reproduced, copied or transmitted save with written permission or in accordance with the provisions of the Copyright, Designs and Patents Act 1988, or under the terms of any licence permitting limited copying issued by the Copyright Licensing Agency, Saffron House, 6-10 Kirby Street, London EC1N 8TS.

Any person who does any unauthorized act in relation to this publication may be liable to criminal prosecution and civil claims for damages.

The author has asserted his right to be identified as the author of this work in accordance with the Copyright, Designs and Patents Act 1988.

First published in French 2008
English edition published 2009 by
PALGRAVE MACMILLAN

Palgrave Macmillan in the UK is an imprint of Macmillan Publishers Limited, registered in England, company number 785998, of Houndmills, Basingstoke, Hampshire RG21 6XS.

Palgrave Macmillan in the US is a division of St Martin's Press LLC, 175 Fifth Avenue, New York, NY 10010.

Palgrave Macmillan is the global academic imprint of the above companies and has companies and representatives throughout the world.

Palgrave® and Macmillan® are registered trademarks in the United States, the United Kingdom, Europe and other countries

ISBN-13: 978-0-230-22037-9   hardback
ISBN-10: 0-230-22037-1   hardback

This book is printed on paper suitable for recycling and made from fully managed and sustained forest sources. Logging, pulping and manufacturing processes are expected to conform to the environmental regulations of the country of origin.

A catalogue record for this book is available from the British Library.

A catalogue record for this book is available from the Library of Congress.

10 9 8 7 6 5 4 3 2 1
18 17 16 15 14 13 12 11 10 09

Printed and bound in Great Britain by
CPI Antony Rowe, Chippenham and Eastbourne

Contents

List of Figures and Boxes viii

Foreword x

Introduction 1
Background 1
Good timing 2
Theoretical background 3
How financialization is changing society 5
Structure of the report 7

Part I The Financial Iceberg 11

Chapter 1.1 The Historical Development of Finance 13
The euphoric years 13
Money: from servant to master 18
ICT euphoria 23
The break-up of money 27

Chapter 1.2 Players and Institutions 33
Markets as trust-building mechanisms 33
Mega-players 41
Custodians of the market temple 48
Public deficits and how they are financed 50

Chapter 1.3 The Financial World View 54
The efficiency ethos 55
Risk and return: a neat paradigm 58
Risk – fear of risk – a risk-free future 62
From interest to greed: unbridled passion 63

Part II A New Pattern 73

Chapter 2.1 Financing Relationships and Financial Transactions 74
Financing relationships 74
From financing relationships to financial transactions 78
Financial transactions 80

Chapter 2.2 The Spread of Transactions — 83
The institutional process — 83
Financial markets as sounding boards — 87
Finance as intermediary — 89
Relationships and transactions: statistical orders of magnitude — 91
Finance and the rest of the economy — 99

Chapter 2.3 Very Large Corporations: The Vehicles of Financialization — 105
Very large corporations (VLCs) — 105
A global marketing economy — 110
Enterprises' value: new forms of capital — 111
Shareholder value: the mantra of the new foremen — 113
ROE rules — 115
Procedures as a vehicle for efficiency — 119

Chapter 2.4 Financialization of the Economic Fabric — 121
VLCs' subcontractors — 121
SMEs: private equity on the prowl — 122

Chapter 2.5 Tying Customers to Enterprises — 125
Planned obsolescence — 125
'Personalized' customer relations — 127
Dissolving products into services — 129
The alienation of the anaesthetized consumer — 130

Chapter 2.6 Other Aspects of Financialization — 132
The age of anticipation: banks and their customers — 132
Humanity in the grip of financialization — 134
Finance: a metaphysical response — 136

Chapter 2.7 Implications of the New Pattern — 138

Part III Finance – What Kind of Society Do We Want? — 145

Chapter 3.1 Limits Inherent in the Process Itself — 148
The spectre of sterility — 148
Complexity — 150
Concentration of economic power — 151

Chapter 3.2 Limits Inherent in Human Nature — 153
Transactions: beyond conflicts of interest — 153
Ethical alienation — 155
A sense of helplessness — 156

Chapter 3.3 What is to be Done? 159
Challenge financial ethics 159
Encourage long-term relationships 160
Change the system of remuneration 162
Revisit financial process 162

Appendix 167

References 171

Index 180

List of Figures and Boxes

Figures

1.1	Messages delivered by the SWIFT system	26
1.2	Expansion of 'savings silos'	45
1.3	Half a century of inflation	51
1.4	Public debt and interest burdens in the OECD countries	52
2.1	Outstanding bonds and world product	92
2.2	Average stock-market capitalization by country and world product	93
2.3	Stock-market growth in terms of capitalization and transactions between 1995 and 2005 (fast-moving countries)	94
2.4	Stock-market growth in terms of capitalization and transactions between 1995 and 2005 (slow-moving countries)	95
2.5	Annual volume of transactions in derivatives	96
2.6	Annual volume of foreign-exchange transactions	97
2.7	Economic and financial rates of return in the American economy	102
2.8	Ten-year rates of cumulative return (mobile average)	103
2.9	Very large corporations and the poorest countries: a comparison (2000)	106
2.10	Economic influence of the 1,000 largest European corporations	107
2.11	Economic influence of the 1,000 largest Japanese corporations	108
2.12	Economic influence of the 1,000 largest American corporations	109
2.13	Distribution of added value in the largest quoted corporations	117

Boxes

1.1	SWIFT	25
1.2	Too big to fail? Long-Term Capital Management (1998–9)	38
3.1	The fecundity of money	146
3.2	The Observatoire de la Finance	164

Foreword

It is some fifteen years since the author of this book, Paul H. Dembinski, and his colleague and associate Alain Schoenenberger wrote a brief essay in response to a question raised by Professor Maurice Cosandey, Chairman of the Board of the Swiss Federal Institutes of Technology and a member of the Board of the Charles-Léopold Mayer Foundation for Human Progress (FPH). The essay was entitled 'Financial markets: mission impossible?'.

The need to pursue what were clearly key avenues of research led to the establishment of the Observatoire de la Finance, which was to receive support and encouragement from leading academics, economists and financiers.

A series of initiatives (meetings, working groups, research projects, publications, personal conversations, etc.) over the past fifteen years has culminated in this report – the outcome of a constant exchange of ideas, experiences and questions.

The technological development of finance, its growing complexity and its inaccessibility to the public – who are its ultimate users and supposed beneficiaries – have created a sense of uncertainty, distrust and anxiety which recent events have done little to dispel.

Taking a moral stance is not enough. It is vital to understand what is happening and what issues are at stake. What impact will this seemingly uncontrolled groundswell have on society as a whole? This book highlights the difference between *relationships* and *transactions* – the key to a proper understanding of finance. The book shows how a basically technical analysis can end up touching on questions of human coexistence and cooperation, and hence of *trust*.

In presenting this publication on behalf of the Board of the Observatoire de la Finance, I would like to pay tribute to the author and his colleagues for drawing together all these years of effort into a single book. Far from claiming to be the last word on the subject, this report is an invitation to continue and expand the research carried out so far.

Ernesto Rossi di Montelera
Chairman of the Board, Observatoire de la Finance

Introduction

Background

In the early 1990s, in response to a request from the Charles-Léopold Mayer Foundation for Human Progress (based in Lausanne and Paris), we drew up a report on the role of financial markets in today's economy and society.[1] The report indicated that finance in the broad sense of the term had now moved far beyond its classic macroeconomic role of converting savings into investment, and had instead become a coherent pattern of techniques, institutions and behaviours that were profoundly altering the economy and society as a whole. These findings led to the establishment of the Observatoire de la Finance in Geneva in 1996 and the launch of the journal *Finance & the Common Good/Bien Commun* in 1998.

Following on from the initial report, the work of the Observatoire de la Finance over the past decade has shown that the continuing spread of financial thinking through society is the result of a converging set of factors. These include: (i) the development of technology and, more generally, of wealth-creating capacity; (ii) a growing fear of risk and the unforeseen as living standards rise; (iii) finance's scientifically-based claim to guarantee – at least to the West – a carefree future; and (iv) the problems and implications of economic and social development in the Southern half of the world. In the course of the Observatoire's research it has become clear that the psychological, philosophical and moral dimensions of finance are as vital to a proper understanding of it as its economic, technical and institutional aspects. These are the avenues that the Observatoire has explored over the past decade. The result is a single conceptual framework that has served as the basis for the broad diagnosis set out in this report. The diagnosis is that the rapid expansion of finance is profoundly changing society, through a process known as 'financialization'.

Good timing

The financial crisis which began in 2007 with doubts as to the soundness of American subprime mortgage loans has unexpectedly made clear just how relevant the Observatoire's work is. This report will attempt to explain why, in 2008, something so relatively insignificant continues to threaten not only the financial sector but the entire global economy. However, the 2007–2008 financial crisis is not the central topic of this report. It merely serves to illustrate a broader diagnosis – one with far more serious implications. Over the last quarter-century the West has experienced an inversion of ends and means. There has been a shift away from relationships (as a mode of human social and economic interaction) towards transactions (which allow relationships to be unilaterally and abruptly terminated). Increasingly, relationships are established to exploit a temporary opportunity and then reap the profits by performing a transaction. This entails a sudden reversal of alliances and loyalties, sometimes at the partner's expense. As such behaviour becomes more widespread, partners are less and less willing to trust each other. To avoid losing out, they hedge their decisions from the outset. This cramps their relationship and destroys some of its creative – and economic – potential. Their permanent fear of being stabbed in the back distracts them from the actual relationship, making it hollow and meaningless. Finance is not the only factor responsible for this change in patterns of social and economic interaction, but – as this book will show – it has spearheaded it and done a great deal to make it possible.

This ambitious attempt to grasp the many different aspects of financialization could not have been undertaken without the vigorous intellectual exchanges that have taken place at the Observatoire de la Finance over the past ten years. Several versions of this report have been discussed and presented at the Observatoire as well as at symposia and conferences. Over the years it has greatly benefited from the criticism, comments and suggestions offered by Pierre Calame, Henri-Claude de Bettignies, Andrew Cornford, Patrick de Laubier, Philippe de Weck, Ernesto Rossi di Montelera, Mohammad Farrokh, the late Emilio Fontela, Jean-Claude Lavigne O.P., Bertrand Legendre, François-Marie Monnet, Etienne Perrot S.J., Mohsen Sohrabi and many others. The report would never have seen the light of day without almost daily assistance from Alain Schoenenberger, who relieved the author of many of his tasks at Eco'Diagnostic while the text was being finalized, and from Jean-Michel Bonvin, who came up with the idea in the first place. I am deeply grateful to all these people, to my two dedicated colleagues at the Observatoire de la Finance, Sibilla Guidotti and Claudio Bologna, and to all those who have contributed to the discussion at one point or another. Despite all these efforts, the report will doubtless contain inaccuracies or indeed errors, for which I apologize to readers in advance, and for which I assume full responsibility.

Theoretical background

Recent years have seen an outpouring of reports and analyses on the growing importance of finance in today's world. These publications, which have varied in their approach and their literary form, have been written by practitioners as well as observers, and by economists as well as sociologists and social psychologists.[2] Despite their differences, they have at least two features in common. First, they all display concern – expressed and justified in different terms – about where the economy and society are heading, and about the very future of civilization. To some, the present situation heralds the downfall of capitalism, while to others, who are more fatalistic, it is simply the fulfilment of Marxist laws of history. Second, they all more or less explicitly admit that the models, theories and concepts normally used in the social sciences fail to provide a convincing picture of the new situation, or identify the new challenges. There is evidently a gap between academic analysis and intuitive diagnosis.

This is compounded by a growing sense of frustration among economists, more and more of whom are aware that the statistical and modelling tools which until recently were the pride of their profession are unable to grasp, let alone satisfactorily explain, the process which is only too clearly taking place.

This situation has caused a rift between economists which may herald a new 'Methodenstreit', like the one that raged between the German historical school and the theoretical, abstract school in the late nineteenth century. Today the choice is between a comforting loyalty to the dominant but self-referential paradigm, and openness to reality. However, the second of these options would require economics to give up at least some of its claims to epistemic autonomy and move closer to social sciences such as sociology, anthropology, psychology or even political science.

The prevailing economic paradigm treats direct evidence of reality as irrelevant, and stays locked in a world of abstract models whose increasing sophistication and logical consistency make them appealingly neat and tidy. This paradigm has acquired a degree of institutional power that ultimately makes it tyrannical. The ceaseless pressure on academics to 'publish or perish' nips most criticism in the bud. Safe behind its institutional ramparts, the dominant paradigm can easily withstand the assaults of mavericks whose very subversiveness ensures they remain on the sidelines.[3]

The alternative to this theoretical monolith is inevitably less dazzling and more fragmented, for it focuses on relevance rather than blind loyalty to established ideas. The work of such writers as Drucker, Galbraith, Guitton, Hayek, Minsky, North, Perroux, Polanyi, Sauvy, Schumpeter, Shackle or Veblen has combined criticism of mainstream thinking with 'local theories' or methods of interpretation that can explain certain readily observable phenomena. Despite what are often significant contributions to our understanding of the world, not one of these monuments of twentieth-century economic thinking has been fully acknowledged or assimilated by mainstream economics, quite simply because they are too realistic, and hence not abstract enough. The unity and elegance of the dominant theory contrast starkly with the disordered mass of efforts to find 'local relevance' – disordered because they depend on inductive rather than deductive reasoning, on anecdote and on fragmented information.

There is no need to go back as far as the 'Methodenstreit'. Much more recently, mainstream economists' inability to grasp the shortcomings of Soviet planning raised some theoretical issues that went largely unnoticed. A quarter-century ago, Alain Besançon expressed his amazement at the gap between economists' reassuring claims about the Soviet economy and the palpable evidence of its failure. It took János Kornai to open economists' eyes even slightly.[4] Subsequent history has left the pundits' analyses in tatters and confirmed what was obvious at the time, even though it could not be grasped by classic methods.

Mainstream economists' current attitude to financialization is curiously reminiscent of their earlier views on planned economies – they simply refuse to acknowledge it as a specific phenomenon. The similarity is so great that Alain Besançon's words of warning are well worth quoting verbatim: 'There has been a considerable amount of academic writing on the Soviet economy .... Yet those .... who have become familiar with the Soviet system through history, literature, travel or stories told by emigrants fail to recognize it when described by economists – as though there were an unbridgeable gulf between the system of the economists, recorded in terms of measurements and figures, and their own instinctive understanding of the system, without measurements or figures of any kind, based entirely on their own immediate experience.'[5]

A similar gap is emerging in the current debate on financialization. Despite the depth and acuity of many of the analyses mentioned earlier, there has not yet been any coherent, across-the-board assessment of financialization that points out its full implications for society. This report by the Observatoire de la Finance, to which current events have unexpectedly lent additional relevance, is an attempt to fill this gap. It is new in two respects. First, it uses a research method, largely based on systems analysis, that enables it to examine the external causes and internal mechanisms of financialization. Second, this deliberately multi-disciplinary analysis extends well beyond the traditional bounds of economics, revealing the socioeconomic and ethical implications of financialization and the challenges it poses to civilization.

How financialization is changing society

Society never stands still. It is the scene of a never-ending confrontation – sometimes latent and sometimes overt – between the various 'organizing principles' that simultaneously operate within it, and that seek to extend their control over society at their main competitors' expense.[6] This confrontation can take various forms. Principles may be absorbed by others, may merge, or may coexist, with clearly demarcated spheres of influence. The processes involved are not linear, but are peculiar to specific moments in history.[7]

These 'organizing principles' are not just abstract categories, but become tangible when two developments coincide: (i) a pattern of behaviour or 'rationality' (referred to by some authors as an 'ethos') finds a social group that can put it into practice, and (ii) the group finds institutions and structures that can act as vehicles for its actions and hence, indirectly, its rationality. Both are essential if an organizing principle is to extend its control over society. The various components interact closely and influence one another, with no obvious hierarchy or order of precedence. So interwoven are the processes involved that the replacement of one dominant organizing principle by another has a truly profound impact on society.

Finance, in its theoretical and abstract form, is a rationality that allows social and economic realities to be grasped and acted upon. It becomes an organizing principle when a set of conventions, techniques and professional practices, underpinned by legal and institutional arrangements, enables it to form a basis and justification for people's actions and decisions. These conventions, techniques and institutions in turn reinforce and validate the underlying rationality and increase its control over human behaviour. This dual shift – first from 'finance as rationality' to 'finance as pattern of behaviour' and then to 'finance as organizing principle' – leads to far-reaching psychological, social, economic and political changes.[8]

This report sets out from the premise – which has to be verified in the light of reality – that precisely such changes have taking place for the last three or four decades. Taking advantage of this fertile breeding ground, financial thinking has gradually permeated and transformed behaviour patterns, mechanisms and structures, and extended its control over society to the point where it is now one of its main organizing principles, or indeed the dominant one.

The term 'financialization' is used here to describe this process, which is profoundly altering the way in which the two primary elements in all societies – relationships and transactions – relate to one another. 'Financialization' has a very different meaning in English-language and other Marxist literature, namely the emergence of 'financial capitalism' as opposed to 'industrial capitalism'. Some authors, such as Gerald Epstein, have used the term to mean 'the increasing role of financial motives, financial markets, financial players and financial institutions in the operation of the domestic and international economies.'[9]

Analysing the financialization process as a profound social transformation has four advantages and one drawback. The drawback is a theoretical one: a systemic approach is formally and from the epistemic point of view less satisfying than classic methods of analysis. This is because systemic analysis merely assesses whether the various phenomena are coherent among themselves, whereas classic analysis sets out to reveal the internal structure of each. Thus a systemic approach merely identifies interactions, whereas classic analysis looks for causes. Systemic analysis simply provides a rough framework to be refined and fleshed out later by more detailed studies.

However, the theoretical limitations of a systemic approach are offset by its advantages in diagnosing the implications of financialization:

- A systemic approach focuses on the internal coherence of society, and hence on the arena in which rival organizing principles compete.
- A systemic approach assesses coherence at all three levels: the macro level (the structures of the system), the meso level (mechanisms or subsystems) and the micro level (individual behaviour).

- The expansion of one organizing principle at the expense of – or quite simply in place of – another is a multidimensional rather than a linear process that involves causes external to the system as well as amplifying mechanisms within it. Some aspects of the process are tangible, others are psychological. A systemic approach allows input from various disciplines to be combined into an *ad hoc* interpretation, without any claim to be a general theory.
- In focusing on 'local relevance', a systemic approach is especially suitable for diagnosing processes (such as financialization) that are still going on, for in rejecting any claim to a general theory it also rejects determinism. It merely outlines the possible outcomes and so can suggest ways of behaving, without having to comply with expectations or predictions. In some ways, such an approach can thus serve as a guide to behaviour.

Structure of the report

The first part of the report outlines the main features of society and the economy that are being reshaped and transformed by financialization. It reviews the historical background, the players that are the main vehicles of the process, the underlying motives and perceptions, the social forms the process takes, the rationality models that fuel it, and its implicit aims. A method of interpretation based on Aristotle's 'multimodal causality' is used to reveal the hidden mechanisms of financialization – the submerged parts of the financial iceberg. After Aristotle, this method of assessing changes in reality was adopted by the scholastic tradition, and more recently it has been given a new lease of life by authors such as Jean-Loup Dherse and André Comte-Sponville.[10]

The second part of the report deals with the actual transformation process, and more specifically the way in which financialization is permeating and taking control of the various parts of the economy and society and so imposing a new pattern on them. Since this process is still going on, the new shape of the system is only gradually becoming apparent. Only the initial stages can as yet be seen – what the final outcome will be is largely a matter of conjecture. It is this second part, which deals with the emerging new pattern, that contains the main thrust of the analysis. It examines the processes that have enabled financialization to expand at the expense of other organizing principles, and identifies the institutional, economic and psychological mechanisms that have allowed transactions to predominate over relationships.

The third part looks to the future and examines the issues raised by financialization, as well as the intrinsic limits to the process. These are of two kinds: limits inherent in the process itself (the strains or indeed contradictions that the process creates within society, such as sterility, complexity and social unrest triggered by excessive concentration of wealth), and external limits. This part of the report attempts to distinguish between 'good' and 'bad' financialization, which obviously involves a value judgement. The criterion used here is an anthropological one, based on the notion of the common good. It is only meaningful from an anthropological point of view which acknowledges that human beings' individual and social dimensions are inextricably linked.

This part of the report briefly examines issues such as growing distrust, ethical alienation and the predominance of transactions over relationships. This brings us to the alternative title of this report, which was *Finance: Servant or Deceiver?* Behind this seemingly innocent dichotomy lies a crucial inversion of ends and means. As a servant, finance is merely a technique, an instrument that serves other purposes. As a deceiver, it becomes and end in itself. The closing section is therefore devoted to the question 'What is to be done?' Should financialization be allowed to run its course until it reaches its limits – or should it be curbed by deliberately introducing a different organizing principle and so guiding society in another direction?

The diagnosis set out in this report is at the same time an appeal for a debate and exchange of views on the subject. A discussion forum has therefore been set up on the Observatoire de la Finance website (www.obsfin.ch). Reactions to the book should be sent to rapport@obsfin.ch.

In the Appendix, the reader will find the Observatoire de la Finance manifesto 'For Finance that Serves the Common Good', issued in April 2008, and updated at the end of 2008.

Notes

1 Paul H. Dembinski and Alain Schoenenberger, *Financial markets: mission impossible?*, Paris, Charles-Léopold Mayer Foundation for Human Progress, 1993, 94 pp. (originally published in French as *Marchés financiers: vocation trahie?*, Paris, Charles-Léopold Mayer Foundation for Human Progress, 1993, 110 pp.). The book has also been translated into Spanish.
2 Among these recent works are: Michel Aglietta and Antoine Rebérioux, *Dérives du capitalisme financier*, Paris, Albin Michel, 2004, 394 pp.; Christian Arnsperger, *Critique de l'existence capitaliste*, Paris, Le Cerf, 2006, 205 pp.; Claude Bébéar, *Ils vont tuer le capitalisme*, Paris, Plon, 2003, 222 pp.; Randy

Martin, *Financialization of Daily Life*, Philadelphia, Temple University Press, 2002, 220 pp.; Bernard Perret, *Les nouvelles frontières de l'argent*, Paris, Seuil, 1999, 296 pp.; Jean Peyrelevade, *Le capitalisme total*, Paris, Seuil, 2005, 95 pp.; John Plender, *Going off the Rails*, London, John Wiley & Sons, 2003, 282 pp.; George Soros, *The Crisis of Global Capitalism*, New York, Public Affairs, 1998, 288 pp.; George Soros, *The New Paradigm for Financial Markets: The Credit Crash of 2008 and What It Means*, New York, Public Affairs, 2008, 208 pp.; Joseph Stiglitz, *Globalization and its discontents*, London, Penguin Books, 2002, 288 pp.; and Paul Windolf (ed.), *Finanzmarkt-Kapitalismus*, Wiesbaden, VS Verlag für Sozialwissenschaften, 2005, 516 pp.

3 Among the winners of the 2004 Nobel Prize in Economics was Edward Prescott, for his work on business cycles. In 2000 he used economic theory and econometrics to 'prove' that financial markets were as rational as ever. Within a matter of months the 'dot-com bubble' burst and share prices were 'corrected' by 50 per cent, a shock from which financial markets such as NASDAQ have still not fully recovered. See, *inter alia*, Edward Prescott and Ellen R. McGrattan, 'Is the Stock Market Overvalued?', in *Federal Reserve Bank of Minneapolis Quarterly Review*, Vol. 24, No. 4, 2000, pp. 20–40.

Although the winner of the 2001 prize, Joseph Stiglitz, is publicly known for his critical views on mainstream thinking, there is nothing radical about his criticism. He does not challenge the dominant paradigm, which seeks a general theory based on deductive reasoning. His criticism is levelled at the content of the theory rather than its scientific basis. For an analysis of his views, see the book review in *Finance & the Common Good/Bien Commun*, No. 15, summer 2003, pp. 60–3.

4 János Kornai, *Economics of Shortage*, Amsterdam, Elsevier, 1980, 316 pp.
5 Alain Besançon, *Anatomie d'un spectre: l'économie politique du socialisme réel*, Paris, Calmann-Lévy, 1981, p. 9, quoted in Paul H. Dembinski, *The Logic of the Planned Economy: the Seeds of the Collapse*, Oxford, Oxford University Press, 1991, p. 1.
6 One is reminded here of works of literature devoted to systems' theory such as Joseph Bochenski, 'Pour une ontologie du système', in Maja Svilar, *Concepts of human freedom: Festschrift in honour of André Mercier on the occasion of his 75th birthday*, Frankfurt am Main, Lang, 1988, 227 pp., or Jean-Louis Le Moigne, *Théorie du système général*, Paris, Presses Universitaires de France, 1990, 330 pp.
7 Most theories of evolution encompass the confrontational view, from Marx's historical materialism and Fukuyama's 'end of history' to the processes described by John Kenneth Galbraith, Joseph Schumpeter and Karl Polanyi or, on another level, by Samuel Huntington in *The Clash of Civilizations and the Remaking of World Order*, New York, Simon & Schuster, 1996, 367 pp.
8 In some ways this analysis recalls Jacques Ellul's analysis of the 'technological system'. Ellul saw Technology with a capital T as the emerging, dominant organizing principle in present-day society. However, he did not look at how society was actually changing as a result, i.e. was being permeated by technological patterns of behaviour. See Jacques Ellul, *The technological system*, New York, Continuum, 1980, 362 pp. (cf. page 23 below).
9 See *Financialization and the World Economy*, edited by Gerald A. Epstein, Cheltenham & Northampton, Edward Elgar, 2005, 425 pp., p. 3; for the Marxist connotation see the contributions to this book by Gerald Epstein, Gérard Duménil, Dominique Lévy and James Crotty. See also the article

by Greta Krippner, 'The financialization of the American economy', in *Socio-Economic Review*, No. 2, Vol. 3, 2005, pp. 173–208. Here the term 'financialization' is used in a less 'loaded' manner to describe the expansion of the role of banks and other financial institutions in today's economy.

10 Jean-Loup Dherse and Hugues Minguet, *L'éthique ou le chaos?*, Paris, Presses de la Renaissance, 1999, 381 pp., and André Comte-Sponville, *Le capitalisme est-il moral ?*, Paris, Albin Michel, 2004, 237 pp.

Part I
The Financial Iceberg

Like the part of an iceberg that is above water, visible, measurable finance rests on a base that is submerged and hence more difficult to analyse. Leaving metaphor aside, finance is the result and the tangible expression of a 'spirit of finance' that is shaping and structuring present-day society via institutions, players, techniques and motives. The hidden mechanisms of this multidimensional process – the submerged base of the iceberg – will be analysed as accurately as possible in this first part of the report.

Understanding change has always been a challenge to philosophers, especially those who, like Aristotle and his many commentators and disciples (such as the Thomists), took reality as their sole frame of reference. To fathom the mysteries of dynamic change, the Aristotelian tradition recommends that every emerging reality be approached on the basis of four 'causes', four types of sequences which together can account for its existence.[1] We can abandon the now confusing traditional terminology and refer to the Aristotelian method of analysis as 'multimodal causality'. Causality acts simultaneously through at least four 'modes', each of which refers to a different level of reality: (i) emerging reality seen in terms of its raw material (traditionally known as the 'material cause') – this raw material is seldom directly perceptible, for it is 'covered' and contained within the emerging form; (ii) reality seen in terms of the form that conditions, shapes and models the material (the 'formal cause'); (iii) reality seen in terms of the players whose action has shaped the raw material (the 'efficient cause'); and (iv) the same reality seen in terms of the goal pursued by the players (the 'final cause'). In addition to the actual goal, some authors refer to the vision, model or perception that presides over the players' action (the 'exemplary cause').[2]

Multimodal causality will be the method used here to examine the financial iceberg in an attempt to grasp the mechanisms of financialization. The various sections of this part will deal in turn with the profound historical forces that have culminated in a period favourable to the development of finance (the material cause), the players and institutions that have helped finance extend its influence (the efficient cause), and finally the perceptions and visions that reveal these players' motives, aims and ethos (the final and exemplary causes). The remaining mode of causality, whereby financialization is gradually reshaping social reality and the socioeconomic system, will be discussed in Part II.

1.1
The Historical Development of Finance

Financialization is taking place at a specific point in world history, and in this sense it is part of what Pierre Renouvin, without going into further detail, called 'the profound forces of history'. Since the 1970s, changing political ideals and technological and institutional capabilities have created conditions conducive to the expansion of finance by the process in this report. Finance has managed to gain control of entire sections of society because of other, more profound developments which it has in turn reinforced. A distinction needs to be made here (as suggested by the late Fernand Braudel[3]) between the various 'speeds' of history: the slow history of structural change, the history of social processes and finally the fast history of a single human life.

The euphoric years

Jean Fourastié coined the phrase *les Trente glorieuses* – 'the Thirty Golden Years' – to describe the years of prosperity between the end of the Second World War and the first oil crisis (a period some American authors have dubbed 'the Golden Age of Capitalism'). What name should we give the period that has followed those thirty years of uninterrupted growth? Since we cannot know exactly how long this period will be, we will simply refer to 'the euphoric years'. The period, which extends from the mid-1970s to the present, is remarkable not for its economic performance – which has in fact been mediocre – but for its increasingly euphoric infatuation with the idea of an economy-based society. Distrust of politics has continued to grow throughout this period, and the fall of the Berlin Wall seemed the ultimate proof that free market forces were the only social institution capable of ensuring both collective and individual happiness.

The ideological victory of the idea of an economy-based society was not an instant process, but the culmination of slow but profound changes in the hierarchy of values which paved the way for its rapid rise after the end of the Thirty Golden Years. The lasting political crisis in the United States (especially the Vietnam quagmire) and the cultural shock of May 1968 in Western Europe were unmistakable evidence of the doubts that began to erode the West's morale in the late 1960s. Though still present, the threats of the Cold War were no longer enough to halt the collapse of former certainties. The slogan 'Better red than dead' crystallized the change in the mindset of the West, once unshakable in its resistance to the communist threat but now ready to make any compromise for the sake of material comfort. At the same time, the oil crises made it aware of its economic vulnerability and the inability of its political leaders to tackle unemployment and social exclusion.

The turning point was the rise to power of Britain's 'Iron Lady', Margaret Thatcher – whose categorical slogan TINA ('There Is No Alternative') was echoed in France by the concept of *la pensée unique* ('one-way thought') – and, shortly afterwards, of Ronald Reagan across the Atlantic. The idea of an economy-based society ceased to be a mere pragmatic recipe and was turned into a veritable doctrine – not to say ideology – whose simplicity and efficiency seemed appealing. This doctrine swept across the globe, rousing the Asian Tigers and others as it did so. Even left-wing governments had no answer to the wave of liberalization and privatization that followed a profound reassessment of the place of government in society and the economy, especially its role in redistributing resources and pooling risks. The West's economic revival enabled it to throw down an ultimate challenge to the USSR in the form of 'Star Wars', which was to bring about the downfall of the Soviet empire.[4] Western economic performance was there for all to see: inflation was under control, productivity was rising, and public deficits seemed to have been curbed. Yet, as economic indicators improved, Western anxiety became a matter for individuals, and the pursuit of meaning became a private rather than a public affair. The 'euphoric years' were also the years in which Western society lost – perhaps forever – the notion of shared meaning.[5] As society faded into the background – Margaret Thatcher went to so far as to say there was 'no such thing' as society – markets emerged as the lowest common denominator among individuals freed from collective control.

On the other side of the Iron Curtain, the period corresponding to the 'euphoric years' was very different. There, 1968 was marked by a powerful upsurge in shared hopes of 'socialism with a human face', which were quickly repressed, only to revive from 1975 onwards. The Helsinki agreements unintentionally gave dissidents an unexpected platform and allowed intellectual and other forces to regroup around the notions of mutual support, solidarity and pursuit of truth. Although there were to be twenty more years of struggle and confrontation with the regime, a wind of freedom began to blow from the late 1960s onwards, with the first glimmers of hope that countries might one day escape from the totalitarian tunnel.[6]

As the West grew increasingly secular, in the East the erosion of totalitarianism was marked by the spread of religious practices. These two contrasting movements came together with the election of John-Paul II in 1978. The famous cry 'Do not be afraid!', uttered by a pope tried and tested in the struggle against the two totalitarianisms of the twentieth century, echoed very differently on each side of the Berlin Wall, with the West fearing for its material possessions and the East thirsting for freedom and consumption. In both halves of Europe, this cry was to revive and rehabilitate the Christian view of social issues.[7]

From an economic point of view, the euphoria of the economy-based society eased the difficulties the West was facing as its way of growth changed. During the previous Thirty Golden Years, Europe had resumed the industrial growth interrupted by the war, and America had spread its consumption model and way of life across the globe. Demand for cars and household appliances seemed inexhaustible, allowing firms to offer unlimited paid employment (Fordism). This type of economic organization became established in people's minds – in agreement on this point with the Marxist Vulgate – as the ultimate way of organizing economic and social relations. The oil shocks of the 1970s that coincided with the saturation of some industrial markets sounded the death knell of an industrial society sustained by plentiful energy and strong demand for infrastructure and consumer durables.[8] Just as the economic structure of industrial society began to totter, the ranks of job seekers were swelled by women released from household chores by technology and freed from family ties and the constraints of motherhood by sexual 'liberation'. The service sector expanded, cushioning the structural impact in terms of jobs. By the early 1970s, Western economies were clearly entering the post-industrial era and becoming increasingly tertiary. The service sector was now also a key factor in international trade negotiations. The thorny question of liberalization of international trade in services was tackled for the first time by the General Agreement on Tariffs and Trade (GATT) Tokyo Round (1973–9).

At international level, the 'euphoric years' were the years of rapid economic globalization. The breakdown of protectionist barriers encouraged the consolidation of large corporations and transnational groups which, by the end of the twentieth century, were to become mega-players in the world economy. As they internationalized their methods of production and distribution, these transnational firms did a great deal to increase trade and so make countries economically more interdependent, especially in Europe. The catchword was free trade, expanded by successive rounds of international negotiations.

It was against this socially and economically favourable background that an updated notion of the market-based society gradually became established as a doctrine. Markets were now seen as a social institution. Idealized markets – carefully conceptualized by neoclassical economists such as Pareto, Walras and Marshall – now appeared the best means of regulating the production and distribution of goods and services so as to maximize satisfaction. Authors such as Hayek, Von Mises and Popper, who became newly popular during the euphoric years, assigned markets a role – a political one, by definition – as the shapers of the public interest.[9] This implied a fundamental change in the purpose of politics, which was now expected to keep a very low profile and act as a kind of night watchman, making sure nothing impeded the smooth workings of the market-based society. The unexpected fall of the Berlin Wall seemed to validate this doctrine, which was to be rationalized by the 'prophet' Francis Fukuyama in his famous, or notorious, proclamation of 'the end of history'.[10] Henceforth this would no longer be just one doctrine among many, but a demonstrated truth. Markets would be the ultimate in human capability. As public opinion and most experts flocked to espouse this view, it was received not as revelation but as the purest product of self-evident scientific reason, backed up by economists' mathematical proof. Behind the euphoria of the market-based economy was a sense of relief that, after centuries of wandering in the ideological and religious wilderness, humanity had finally found its way back to reason, of which markets were the supreme embodiment.[11]

The strength of this doctrine was that it was an extension of both positivistic rationalism and materialism. It was thus perfectly in keeping with the intellectual landscape that prevailed at the start of the euphoric years. This increasingly rejected all metaphysical ideas and was more and more infatuated with technology. However, the doctrine depended on an over-simplified picture of man. Neoclassical economic theory was based on an extremely reduced view of man as an individualized algorithm for maximizing utility or satisfaction, a.k.a. *homo oeconomicus*.[12] His needs and wishes had to be satisfied at the expense of all other concerns in order to ensure his individual welfare and happiness. This seemingly rational reduction implied that human nature had now yielded up its ultimate secrets – those of Economic Man – and, by extension, that an ideal society founded on reason was now within reach. All this seemed to confirm the ancient philosophical intuition that markets could unfailingly turn private vices into public virtues.[13]

In many ways, the euphoric years were an extension of Auguste Comte's rationalistic positivism. Yet, like Comte's system, they were based on a view of man which was unmistakably metaphysical. Towards the end of his life Comte was led to found a 'positivist religion' in order to bridge this increasing gap in his rational system. Without such an extension into metaphysics, positivism could not be self-contained. There is some similarity to the closing years of the twentieth century – a hundred years after Comte – when the metaphysical underpinnings of the economy-based society began to appear, revealing the limitations of its positivistic claims. Some of the hitherto most fervent believers in the doctrine began to feel qualms. This will be discussed at length in the final part of this book.

With the market doctrine now totally unchallenged, there was an unusually favourable intellectual, economic and social climate for the economy to become the linchpin of society – and finance the linchpin of the economy. West societies launched themselves unreservedly into the future, confident in their ability to control it through technology. Conditions were particularly conducive to the development of finance:

- The shortages and uncertainties of wartime were a thing of the past. Despite the oil crises, the West was prosperous and comfortably ensconced in an almost universal social welfare system. It was thus able to move beyond day-to-day survival and focus instead on the medium and long term, releasing resources as it did so. Finance now seemed the ideal way to build and secure its material future.
- The West had faith in its long-term survival, the stability of its public institutions and the way it was organized. This favourable climate enabled it to extend its horizons and so smoothed the way for the development of finance – of what was later, in a happy turn of phrase, to be called 'trade in promises'.[14] In the new climate of freedom and material prosperity, traditional solidarity was waning. The village, the clan and the family were changing, shrinking, indeed disintegrating. Left to fend for themselves, individuals were now

building their futures on an 'actuarial utopia'[15] of mathematical promises which was guaranteed by institutions and validated the fundamental choices on which these were based.
- On the threshold of the post-industrial era, the Western economy was becoming more and more service-oriented. The same was true of jobs, a growing number of which involved 'manipulation of symbols'[16] rather than handling of tangible matter – a perfect breeding ground for finance, which was entirely forward-looking and based on intangibles.

A precise diagnosis of the factors that led the West to embrace the economy-based society is beyond the scope of this book. Suffice it to say that financialization fuelled the very factors that had enabled it to emerge in the first place. This positive feedback loop enabled the process to spread until it became the most striking phenomenon of the late twentieth century. Besides the 'slow' history of politics and society mentioned earlier, there are two other aspects of financialization that deserve particular attention, although these were driven by faster processes: the crisis in regulation of the global economy, and the development of information and communication technology.

Money: from servant to master

In 1943, the question of how the international economy should be governed was a key topic of discussion among the Allies, particularly the United States and Britain. In summer 1944 a conference was held at Bretton Woods to create an institutional framework for the post-war world economy. After weeks of theoretical and political debate, the forty delegations returned home having accomplished their task – a comprehensive agreement on an international institutional and regulatory framework known as 'the Bretton Woods system'.

From now on, the international economic order was to be founded on three principles: coordinated reduction of trade barriers, convertibility of currencies based on a system of fixed exchange rates, and aid for reconstruction and development. These principles would be applied by three sister institutions that were to form the backbone of the system: the International Monetary Fund (IMF), the International Bank for Reconstruction and Development (which later became the World Bank) and an International Trade Organization which did not actually come into being until half a century later, when the GATT was replaced by the World Trade Organization (WTO) in 1995.

In accomplishing this unprecedented task, the delegates were spurred on by keen memories of the Great Depression of the 1930s, which led to the rise of Nazism, and the cataclysm of the Second World War, which was then nearing its end. As the resulting Bretton Woods system showed, this was a favourable historical context for ambitious projects that held out promises of peace and prosperity to an exhausted human race, promises based on the 'gentle commerce' principle so beloved of Montesquieu.[17]

Profoundly liberal in its tenets, but at the same time respectful of national sovereignty, the system focused on developing international trade (by gradually eliminating protectionist barriers) and setting up an effective system of international payments and settlements. It was an intergovernmental system in the sense that it merely coordinated the external action of governments while respecting their internal sovereignty, which remained the cornerstone of the international system set up by the UN. In creating a system that would stabilize international payments by means of convertible currencies and fixed exchange rates, its architects hoped to curb monetary instability and so sustain international trade in the long term. Countries that joined the IMF undertook to make their currencies convertible as soon as possible. Under the terms of the IMF's articles of agreement, convertibility, once achieved, was irreversible. However, the same articles of agreement restricted the convertibility requirement to payments relating to current account transactions (trade and transfers), leaving capital account transactions unaffected. With regard to capital flows, governments were theoretically still free to choose how exchange rates would be set.

Drawing lessons from the spiral of devaluation and protectionism that had proved so fatal to international trade between the wars, the architects of Bretton Woods provided 'circuit breakers' that would allow the monetary and commercial spheres to be decoupled if there was any risk of disruption. To ensure flexibility, the convertibility principle and the system of fixed exchange rates were backed up by two 'safety valves' that could be used to contain any disequilibrium in payments in the monetary sphere and keep trade flows unaffected. The first was a set of advances and loans that the IMF could make available to any country suffering from temporary disequilibrium in its balance of trade. The second allowed governments to renegotiate exchange rates under the auspices of the IMF in the event of lasting balance-of-trade disequilibrium. However, this was a last resort, to be used only if balance-of-trade support failed to overcome the difficulties and these proved more than just temporary. Thus, although the architects of the system realized that payment flows might also be seriously disrupted, their main priority was to protect trade flows.

In choosing to leave the capital account, and hence financial flows, out of the Bretton Woods system, its architects were acting as though international finance were merely a secondary phenomenon that posed no threat to world trade – a grave misjudgement which was to bring the system crashing down within twenty-five years. In their defence, it should be remembered that at the time – at the end of the war, and after the Great Depression – the present-day expansion of finance was hard to imagine. The only major international payments other than current-account payments and transfers were either intergovernmental payments (such as those linked to reparations after the First World War) or occasional bond issues which were usually guaranteed by governments. It is therefore not so surprising that finance was excluded from international regulation at Bretton Woods. It was simply taken for granted that finance, like monetary policy and bank supervision, was a national affair with no international implications, and hence should be governed entirely by national authorities and legislation.

The Bretton Woods system introduced fixed exchange rates, which meant that the value in US dollars of the various currencies that were part of the system was laid down in intergovernmental agreements. At the same time, the value of the dollar was set once and for all by the US government at 35 dollars an ounce of fine gold. The US dollar thus became the international means of exchange and reserve currency. More convenient to use than gold, the dollar circulated widely outside the borders of the USA throughout the period. The two leading Bretton Woods negotiators, Britain's John Maynard Keynes and America's Harry Dexter White, clashed over the issue of the international means of exchange. As White saw it, the US monetary authorities had incurred an implicit moral obligation in exchange for the privilege of having the dollar play the key role in the world monetary system. Their monetary policy should therefore ensure that the volume of dollars in circulation not only met the needs of the US economy, but provided the liquidity required for international commercial payments. As history was to show, the American government did not take this moral obligation very much to heart.

What kept the Bretton Woods system going was the strictly intergovernmental nature of world economic governance. Exchange rates were managed by governments, which – through negotiation – could ensure that all the partners enjoyed lasting balance-of-trade equilibrium. After the war, it was only gradually that the main currencies became convertible within the meaning of the IMF's articles of agreement. It thus took over fifteen years for the system's monetary arrangements to take full effect and reach cruising speed. No sooner had they done so than the system started running into phenomena it was totally unequipped to deal with. From eurodollars to gold arbitrage, these were all linked to the development of international finance.

As major currencies became fully convertible once more – by 1961 all the industrialized countries had fulfilled the IMF requirements – and with international trade continuing to grow, the central banks in leading countries gradually lifted exchange controls on international capital movements, for purely economic as well as political reasons. This liberalization of capital movements led to a vast expansion in international debt relationships, especially in the wake of the first oil crisis.[18]

From the late 1950s onwards, the leading commercial banks either set up branches abroad or established correspondence relationships with foreign banks. Today this process has culminated in the emergence of global financial mega-players such as Citi or Union Bank of Switzerland, the result of more than a quarter-century of mergers and takeovers. As they developed their international financial activities, the commercial banks opened up cracks in the Bretton Woods system, and the cracks gradually widened.

From the early 1960s onwards, the commercial banks introduced a radical financial innovation, a new kind of private liquidity instrument: first eurodollars, and later eurocurrency. This enabled them to take full advantage of their international expansion. Eurodollars were dollars which were held by active banks – and could be used by them to grant loans – outside the USA. Eurodollars and eurocurrency emerged in a regulatory vacuum, for at the time no central bank could control either foreign-currency operations by resident banks or domestic-currency operations by non-resident ones. Taking advantage of these regulatory gaps, banks were able to increase their foreign-exchange commitments without any restrictions, other than their own assessments of the risks involved.[19]

By allowing large-scale lending and borrowing of foreign currency (i.e. currency foreign to the place of operation), this 'euromarket' allowed arbitrage operations to expand, increased international mobility of capital and created a private and uncontrolled by central banks source of liquidity. Eurocurrency gave world finance an abundant supply of cheap liquidity for investment, particularly to finance public deficits, which were skyrocketing at the time.

Besides the eurodollar, another factor that destabilized the Bretton Woods system was the gold market. This did not reopen after the war until 1954, when gold was the basis – through the dollar – for the Bretton Woods system. In 1961, the leading governments agreed to intervene on the gold market in order to maintain the fixed dollar-gold parity of 35 USD per once. From 1968 onwards, however, central banks found it increasingly difficult to cope with the growing volume of private transactions. To solve this problem, the gold market was split into two: the private market, in which the exchange rate was free to float, and the market for inter-bank transactions, in which it was more or less fixed. This opened up prospects for gold-dollar arbitrage which private capital would use to mount attacks on the fixed gold-dollar parity – the linchpin of the Bretton Woods system.

President Nixon's surprise announcement on 15 August 1971 that the dollar was no longer convertible to gold wrecked the Bretton Woods system and plunged the governance of global finance into a state of confusion from which, over thirty-seven years later, it has yet to emerge. The American authorities took this step to avert the immediate risk of their gold reserves being drained away by their growing trade deficit, which was largely due to arms expenditure and the Vietnam war. At the same time, they were implicitly admitting they were unable to control their trade deficit, and effectively yielding to the power of innovative private financial players. From now on, global economic governance would be forced to take account of private finance – a new force whose existence had not even occurred to the architects of Bretton Woods.

With the dollar no longer convertible to gold, fixed exchange rates almost instantly made way for more or less flexible ones, and a global foreign-exchange market sprang up. This turned domestic currencies into 'financial assets' that non-residents could hold for speculative purposes, and it posed new challenges to domestic monetary policy. Under the system of fixed exchange rates, the balance of capital flows, together with that of current payments, had influenced each country's gold stocks and hence its money supply and domestic rate of interest. When the Bretton Woods system collapsed, exchange rates were no longer fully controlled by national or international monetary authorities, and central banks were forced to change their attitude towards financial markets. The domestic purchasing power of currencies – the only legal means of payment within their respective countries – would henceforth partly depend on how their exchange rates were affected by international finance. This is borne out by all the financial crises of the past few decades, especially the most recent ones – in Asia, Russia and Argentina.

By shattering the Bretton Woods system, Nixon freed money from the 'straitjacket' of gold stocks and from its previous meek role as a mere means of payment in international trade. His watershed decision replaced external regulation of domestic currencies (through gold stocks) with internal regulation in the light of domestic economic data. Although the system of floating exchange rates allowed domestic monetary policy to become more independent, it also increased the risk that money would become self-referential, and indeed subservient to politics.[20] Ever since 1971, international monetary and financial governance has thus been in a state of disarray, although there have been some signs of improvement, particularly the 'Basle II' agreement on banking supervision.[21] Moreover, three-and-a-half decades after the collapse of Bretton Woods, there are still attempts to protect money from political influence, either by making central banks more independent of politics (as is the case with the European Central Bank) or by assigning monetary policy goals relating to inflation levels (consumer price indexes). The aim is to find an external anchor for money – like its traditional anchor in gold stocks – that can protect it against both political and market fluctuations.

Freed from international regulatory constraints, and taking advantage of a general climate that was favourable to markets and the service sector, finance was now able to extend its control over society thanks to the emergence of an uniquely powerful vehicle for its spread – modern information and communication technology.

ICT euphoria

One of the main factors that has unquestionably helped finance to expand is information and communication technology (ICT). The years of euphoric infatuation with the economy-based society have also been the years of infatuation with ICT. This is just one more reflection of the rationalist faith of our times. ICT has fundamentally transformed today's socioeconomic structure and has brought about a revolution comparable to the industrial revolution of the nineteenth century. In an unparalleled analysis, Jacques Ellul stated that the technological system (now spearheaded by ICT) had two tendencies: a 'totalizing' tendency and a 'universalizing' tendency. As a result of its totalizing tendency, Technology – i.e. technologies as a whole, for which Ellul used a capital T – was permeating every area of individual, economic and social life, and becoming a membrane, an interface, a mediator which prevented direct contact between man and his environment (social as well as natural). As for the universalizing tendency, this meant the ability of the technological system (Technology) to spread right across the globe.[22]

One of the first sectors to take advantage of the new tools was finance, which not only used them but also adapted them to its own particular needs and capabilities so as to obtain the greatest benefit from them. The development of ICT over the last quarter-century unquestionably led financial systems – both national and international – to become more market-oriented (cf. Part II below). Finance benefited not only from the spread of communication and transmission techniques but also from the explosive growth in information storage and processing capacity. Although these two elements are now starting to converge, they made separate contributions to the expansion of finance and hence need to be looked at separately.

The speed at which information could be transmitted was always a key aspect of both warfare and enterprise. The techniques varied, but the speed was limited either by the range of human senses (sight or hearing) or by the vehicles used (pigeons or messengers). The breakthrough came in the nineteenth century, when Samuel Morse first used changes in the intensity of electric current to transmit information. It is thus more than 150 years since the speed at which information could be transmitted ceased to depend on the speed at which its physical vessel could move. In order for telecommunications to change society, two problems had to be solved – one of them technical, the other socioeconomic. It took several decades of invention and improvement for the telephone and telegraph to permeate society and become an essential part of the everyday lives of both people and enterprises. By extending players' range of action, expansion of the network changed their relationship to space and allowed activities that were physically distant from one another to be coordinated in real time. This link-up in real time increased the hierarchical coordinating power and the efficiency of the decision-making centres where information began to converge, which in turn encouraged the concentration of economic power triggered by globalization.

Finance was one of the first sectors to use the new technologies made possible by facsimile transmission lines. These came into service in France from 1870 onwards and were mainly used by financial brokers. The same was true of the first transatlantic links and the first underwater telephone cable between London and New York, inaugurated in 1956. Thus the creation of long-distance communication facilities coincided with the international expansion of the banking network and came just a few years before the large-scale emergence of eurodollars discussed earlier.[23]

In a world built around the premise that trade was a civilizing influence, the continuing fall in the cost of transmitting information nullified distance and thus had eminently positive connotations. A combination of technological and political breakthroughs boosted the expansion of activities whose raw material was information. Among financial activities, transactions – the purchase and sale of securities – were almost entirely based on the processing of standardized information. Once technical progress and standardization led to a substantial fall in processing and transmission costs, the number of players able to take part in standardized real-time transactions, anywhere in the world, could theoretically increase to infinity. However, the reliability of this greatly expanded market could only be maintained by ensuring that transactions were only performed by solvent, trustworthy players. Accordingly, only a small number of qualified players were permitted to deal directly, and anyone else was obliged to use them as intermediaries (see also below).

Greatly increased access to financial intermediaries and, indirectly, to the markets themselves, especially after the Internet boom in the 1990s, was followed by a period of consolidation. Organized financial markets also began to change. Originally cooperatives whose members were

---

Box 1.1 SWIFT

The establishment in 1973 of the Society for Worldwide Interbank Financial Telecommunication (SWIFT for short) by 240 of the world's banks was a far-sighted move. To forestall what they feared might become an uncontrollable flood of telexed money transfers, they decided to computerize interbank payments. The system was eventually planned to deliver 300,000 messages a day, with a transmission time of thirty minutes.

Today, thirty-five years on, SWIFT delivers just under three billion messages a day to its 2,400 members, with a transmission time of just a few seconds. Between 1991 and 2006, the number of messages multiplied by a factor of eight, whereas nominal gross world product doubled over the same period. In 2006, just over a third (34 per cent) of the messages concerned securities transactions, a percentage that had expanded very rapidly since the mid-1990s.

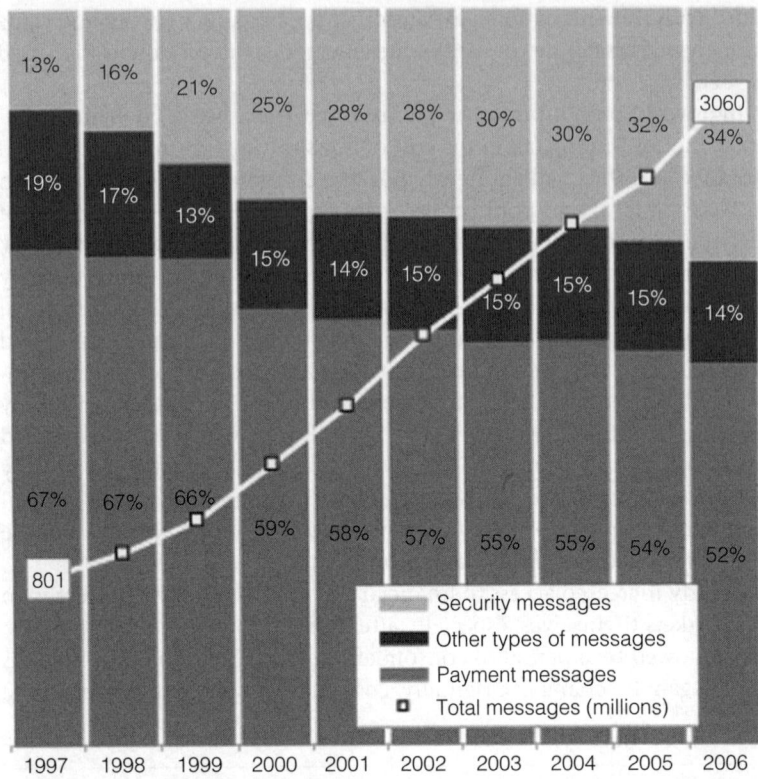

Figure 1.1 Messages delivered by the SWIFT system
© Observatoire de la Finance, 2008 [www.obsfin.ch]
Primary data: SWIFT annual reports

qualified intermediaries, they mostly became quoted enterprises like any other. This paved the way for a process of mergers and consolidation. Today, global financial markets have regrouped round a small number of transaction centres, as witness the merger (which took effect in 2007) between Euronext – itself the result of mergers between the Amsterdam, Brussels, Paris and Portuguese stock exchanges between 2000 and 2002 – and the prestigious New York Stock Exchange.

The example of SWIFT (which is just one of many) suggests that ICT was initially grafted onto the financial sector and only later began to transform and restructure it in depth. Financial institutions thus made the new technologies an intrinsic part of their development (on-line customer access, computerized branch offices, debit cards, automatic teller machine – ATM, cash dispensers and so on). New players emerged in the wake of this, especially – but not only – on-line brokers.

Financial institutions' use of ICT enabled the biggest ones to achieve economies of scale that gave them a considerable competitive advantage. The sums required in order to maintain and develop their computerized information systems and keep them secure were colossal, and not everyone could afford them. The amount of investment involved was probably comparable to the volumes of assets immobilized in the past by traditional heavy industry. Yet such expenditure was only partially reflected in balance sheets, for much of it was operational expenditure and was recorded as such.

Their extraordinary data processing and storage capacity enabled financial institutions to develop completely new services and skills in such areas as payment, customer account management, investment strategy models, asset management and so on. ICT allowed many financial institutions, particularly traditional banks, to diversify their sources of income. Nowadays all major banks obtain a large and growing part of their income from commissions on services they provide on a fee-for-service basis. This has reduced their dependence on their traditional activities, which are remunerated by the difference between debtor and creditor interest.

Increased computer and data storage and transmission capacity, together with the fall in unit costs and international liberalization, boosted financial innovation, particularly in the form of 'financial products' – more or less standardized packages of entitlements and obligations in respect of underlying assets or transactions. There was a proliferation of transactions and financial products such as hybrid, synthetic or conditional instruments (swaps, options, warrants, convertibles, CDOs and so on). Financial innovation is a key aspect of the financialization process, and will be discussed in Part II. For the time being, suffice it to say that unrestrained financial innovation, boosted by new technological capabilities, enabled finance to merge with money and so become part of monetary policy.

The break-up of money

Although entire libraries have been written about it over the centuries, money remains an enigma. Of the many books on the subject, Georg Simmel's are particularly valuable. At the end of the nineteenth century Simmel investigated the nature, or rather the essence of money – what it was about it that remained invariable through time and space

– as well as its more fortuitous features which were dependent on context and circumstances. He concluded two things. First, the essential function of money was to establish exchange relationships between objects. Second, money did not need necessarily a material substance to perform this function – it could be a pure sign. However, this struck Simmel as unrealistic, for such a substanceless money was barely conceivable under the technical conditions that prevailed at the time.[24]

Simmel's contribution was crucial, for it identified two complementary aspects of what enabled money to function: (i) its form (object or sign), and (ii) the social institution within which it circulated, and which helped to give it meaning. Whatever form money took, said Simmel, its use showed that all payments involved a third party. Though, this third party (the issuer or guarantor of the money – the ruler, or society) guarantees money purchasing power. This turned trade – which *prima facie* involves just two partners – into a social phenomenon. The third party's presence made money fully transferable and hence a 'general equivalent', thanks to the equally general trust in purchasing power created by the presence of the third party. According to Simmel, trust in monetary systems always had two anchors: the form of the money, and the social institution. This intuitive discovery, now more than a century old, can be used to formulate the 'dual anchor of trust in money' hypothesis, which helps explain the profound changes that money is now undergoing as a result of financialization. These changes are due to the spread of ICT (through financial innovation) and the fact that money is no longer linked to any external standard.

According to the 'dual anchor' hypothesis, monetary regimes can only be viable if they succeed in controlling three fears that surround the use of any means of payment: (i) fear that it may be counterfeit, (ii) fear that it may lose some or all of its value, and (iii) fear that it may not be accepted (redeemed) by third parties. Monetary regimes can rely on either their 'form' anchor or their 'social institution' anchor to help them do this. What distinguishes one monetary regime from another is the way in which they use the two anchors to deal with the public's fears.

Over the centuries, monetary regimes became increasingly sophisticated, and trust in the form of money was gradually replaced by trust in the social institution as enshrined in legislation. Monetary signs now circulate in dematerialized form – as information – within legally and technologically organized areas. As a result, fear of traditional forgery was replaced by fear of trickery, bank fraud or illicit access to bank accounts. Trust became based on how effectively payment traffic was supervised and bank fraud was tackled, rather than the material form of the money. Similarly, trust in lasting purchasing power was now based on how effectively monetary policy protected the standard of value against macroeconomic fluctuations (inflation), rather than the metal content of the coins. Finally, trust that money would be accepted was now based on the concept of legal tender, rather than the intrinsic value of the coinage.

The 'dual anchor' hypothesis reveals how trust operates in present-day monetary regimes. As society has grown more complex, technologically and otherwise, trust in the procedures that govern monetary regimes has become a good deal more important than trust in the tangible form of money. This was well illustrated by the switch-over to the euro in January 2002.[25] Trust in monetary regimes is thus now based almost entirely on governments' ability to regulate and supervise technological circuits and maintain the value of money through appropriate monetary policies.

However, as the social institution became the sole source of trust in monetary regimes (thanks to technology and procedures), they became more sophisticated, with a number of specialized but interdependent areas, each responsible for transactions corresponding to the 'classic' functions of money. Two specialized areas are now becoming increasingly prominent within present-day monetary regimes. In the first, money functions as a 'means of payment'; in the second, as a 'store of purchasing power'. Increasingly, payments take place within a spider's web of technological link-ups whereby money-as-information is moved from one account to another. As for maintaining the value of idle cash (savings) over time, money's function as a store of purchasing power has increasingly been taken over by the various types of financial assets.

The section on technology has shown how payment traffic has gradually become integrated into finance. As with SWIFT, statistics on other modes of payment have shown a continuous increase in the volume of non-cash transactions. The economies of scale generated by ICT, the fall in transaction costs and the geographical expansion of activities have speeded up this dematerialization process. By creating direct links between the transaction partners' accounts, dematerialization has reduced the amount of cash in circulation. Taken to the extreme, in an economy in which individual players' accounts were perfectly interlinked, all payments would be made by book entry and there would no longer be any need for cash. All that would then remain would be money-as-information, an integral part of the social institution from which it derives its meaning and reason to exist – in Keynesian terms, 'accounting money'.

The dematerialization of money and its confinement to hermetic technological areas changed the very nature of payment. This now became a chargeable service which could only be carried out by intermediaries with access to the appropriate technological area. Economic players are increasingly encouraged to use technological payment systems. Specialized intermediaries have at least two good reasons to keep these areas technologically hermetic. First, they could perform clearing operations within them, and by doing so saving liquidity that they could invest outside of the area. Second, they have an interest in developing fee-for-access technological payment areas, because of the commissions they could earn and the economies of scale generated by the size of the network.

The new technologies thus make the payment area less uniform than in the days when settlements were still made in cash. It is now a hierarchy of interlinked payment networks to which access is controlled by two things: the fee charged for the payment service, and the payer's reputation and quality. Economic players are granted access to higher and higher compartments of the payment area as their paying agents consider them more financially sound and trustworthy (on the evidence of credit cards, for instance), are less reluctant to grant them loans and are more willing to reduce their charges for services.[26]

The transfer of payments to a special technological area has deprived cash of some of its traditional functions and hence reduced its holders' freedom of manoeuvre. One obvious example is on-line payment, where cash is useless. Another result of this situation is financial exclusion – people without access to banking services are effectively excluded from society. Not surprisingly, there are some politicians who claim everyone should be entitled to a bank account.[27]

Just as the payment area has been taken over by the private sector, another area is taking over money's classic function as a store of wealth. Any temporarily idle unit of accounting money – information recorded in a technologically hermetic area – can readily be converted into a yield-earning or risk-bearing asset, provided it is traded for or traded as a financial asset. As this process of converting idle cash balances into financial assets becomes more efficient, there is less and less reason, or opportunity, for money to act as a store of wealth. This function is being taken over by the second specialized area – finance. Financial innovation, boosted by technological capabilities, has encouraged the spread of relatively liquid types of financial assets that can perform near-monetary functions. This has led to the emergence of a whole range of assets which are not money in the classic sense of the term. In fact, the boundary between what is money and what is not is now so blurred that some central banks actually refer to 'near-money'. The sudden drying of inter-bank credit market and of the money market in Autumn 2008 stressed the almost forgotten difference between cash and all the near-money instruments.

In today's monetary regimes there is thus no longer any such thing as idle cash, for any temporarily unused sums deposited with financial institutions instantly become financial assets. It is all these assets and the fluctuations in their relative value that nowadays function as a store of wealth. The resulting fusion between money and finance has effectively made finance part of the monetary regime. This fusion, which at times seems more like *con*fusion, raises serious questions as to the status of the emerging monetary-financial system. Traditionally, trust in the monetary system was maintained by government, whereas finance was an entirely private affair. In contrast, what is now emerging is a mixed monetary-financial regime which, by definition, straddles the public and private domains. The public policy quandrum of Autumn 2008 as to how and when to intervene in the financial domain clearly is a consequence of the above-mentioned confusion.

Traditionally, maintaining the purchasing power of money by controlling the amount of it in circulation has been one of the main functions of central banks. However, this presupposes a clear distinction between what is money and what is not. When this boundary becomes blurred – as is now the case, conceptually as well technically – monetary policy loses its quantitative bearings. This is reflected in ever-changing statistical definitions of monetary aggregates.[28] Central banks have responded by changing their goals. They have stopped trying to quantify the money supply and have focused instead on fighting inflation. The emergence of the new monetary-financial regime puts inflation in a new light: does it only reflect changes in consumer prices, or does it also include fluctuations in the prices of financial assets? Central banks have not yet made up their minds about this, but the question is there to be answered and is raising every day higher on the central banks' agenda.[29]

At the same time, supervision of financial regimes and the techniques used by the main players and markets is now more clearly than ever a government responsibility,[30] reflecting the fact that they have become increasingly important parts of the monetary-financial system. Governments began to increase their control over finance in the 1990s – firm evidence that money and finance had irreversibly merged and that central banks' political responsibility for money in the strict sense of the term now extended to finance. It would be only a slight exaggeration to say that, in the days of Bretton Woods, money and its internal and external stability were a public matter, whereas finance was essentially a private one. Today, in the final analysis, governments are politically entitled to supervise finance just as they supervised traditional monetary systems. The events that have rocked world finance since August 2007 have left central bankers in a quandary. Should they maintain financial stability by bailing out certain players or market segments threatened by lack of liquidity and risk a bout of inflation (Northern Rock or Bear Stearns rescues force mergers or bankruptcies as Lehman Brothers), or should they concentrate instead on the classic risks of inflation and risk triggering a financial crisis? Curiously answers to this dilemma seems in October 2008 to be still different on both sides of the Atlantic. This very dilemma is proof that finance and money have indeed merged in recent decades.

Before examining the actual financialization process in Part II, we must look at the profiles of the main players and institutions that have spearheaded it and then, in the third and final section of Part I, analyse their motives and, more generally, their world view. This will take us further and further away from economics and closer to social philosophy.

1.2
Players and Institutions

The euphoric years saw the gradual development of conditions in which finance could rapidly emerge as one of society's main organizing principles. In the course of this process, specialized firms run by people with a specific world view and philosophy of action helped the 'spirit of finance' and financial techniques to spread throughout society. A favourable political, regulatory and technological climate triggered a self-perpetuating process fuelled by the growing efficiency of enterprises and the spread of a world view that justified financialization.

Markets as trust-building mechanisms

The history of organized markets in Western civilization goes back a long way. Before the theory of pure, perfect competition was formulated in the late nineteenth century, businessmen and traders knew from experience that markets, as a social institution, could perform two complementary functions. They could inform potential partners of the conditions of supply and demand, and they could set an equilibrium price that would result in the greatest number of transactions. In order for markets to perform these two functions, they had to be treated carefully. It was a matter of great importance to both merchants and rulers just where, when and how periodic fairs and markets were held. Merchants made very sure that their routes across the world intersected on specific dates and in specific places so that markets could be held.

By the end of the nineteenth century, standards of quality, weight and composition were so sophisticated, and commodity markets so specialized, that there was less and less need for buyers to be physically present. What now mattered most was that prices should be set in a transparent, impartial manner. Once commodities were standardized, the only information that was still required concerned price and quantity. Better procedures and closer supervision enabled some commodity markets to expand and become financialized, first through futures contracts and later through derivatives.

Unlike markets for tangible goods and services, financial transactions concern intangibles – promises and commitments. All such contracts derive their meaning and value from a context of interpretation which is guaranteed by the legal system. Thus trust depends not only on the markets where the transactions take place, but also on what happens beforehand and afterwards. Besides the way in which markets are organized and regulated, it is the behaviour of market players that gradually builds – or destroys – trust. There is a delicate equilibrium between formal and informal financial markets, and, in a historic speech delivered on 15 July 2002, the then chairman of the US Federal Reserve, Alan Greenspan, very clearly expressed his fears about how long this equilibrium could last: 'Well-functioning markets require accurate information to allocate capital and other resources, and market participants must have confidence that our predominately voluntary system of exchange is transparent and fair. Although business transactions are governed by laws and contracts, if even a modest fraction of those transactions had to be adjudicated, our courts would be swamped into immobility. Thus, our market system depends critically on trust – trust in the word of our colleagues and trust in the word of those with whom we do business. Falsification and fraud are highly destructive to free-market capitalism and, more broadly, to the underpinnings of our society.'

During the euphoric years, new or modernized financial markets were set up in many transitional or developing countries, often at the instigation of the International Financial Corporation (IFC), a subsidiary of the World Bank. These countries made regulatory and legal arrangements based on international best practices. Yet, despite their apparent sophistication, few of them gained the lasting trust of foreign investors, and foreign capital fled the country at the slightest hint of trouble. During the past decade, Russia, Turkey, Ukraine and Thailand have all had the bitter experience of crises that were aggravated when positions were abruptly sold by foreign investors.[31]

Like monetary regimes, financial markets must be anchored in trust if they are to function and develop properly. During the euphoric years, the anchors of trust in financial markets shifted slightly and became somewhat stronger, as had happened with monetary regimes. These changes were a response to three potential fears about organized markets.

These matched the three fears that all monetary regimes have to deal with.

The first fear, as we have seen, is fear of counterfeiting. In financial markets, this means the fear that securities of uncertain or even zero value may be quoted. Market authorities – which in most Western countries are private bodies operating under strict government supervision – deal with this by imposing very strict information standards on all quoted securities. These standards concern the frequency, validation and degree of detail of accounting information, which in turn is standardized. Exemplary penalties are imposed to dissuade potential offenders, as in the case of Arthur Andersen following the Enron affair.[32]

This 'primary' information is used by a whole range of specialized players – rating agencies, advisers, experts and so on – to produce secondary information that is explicitly aimed at less professional clients. Organized markets thus only deal in securities that meet the relevant information standards. All other financial assets and contracts are traded 'over the counter', between professionals, or are aimed at 'qualified investors' rather than the general public, who by definition are less knowledgeable and more gullible. This is the case, for instance, with hedge funds, private equity funds, foreign currency and most derivatives or structured products.[33]

The second fear about financial markets concerns the conditions under which quoted securities are sold. This corresponds to the fear of non-redemption (non-acceptance) in the case of money. Unlike monetary systems, which use the concept of legal tender to deal with this, financial markets can only limit the risks by maintaining a minimum level of liquidity. This reassures security holders that they can 'get out' without too much difficulty. There are no miracle ways of maintaining liquidity, but there are some factors that help provide security, by providing the market with minimal depth. This is one reason why the leading world financial centres are so eager to merge. In consequence, market organizers (market makers) are required – up to a point – to use their own funds to offset disparities between orders to buy and sell. Finally, when trouble looms, market authorities may suspend quotation of certain securities or, in emergencies, even shut markets down temporarily. In Summer 2007, then in Autumn 2008, the financial world experienced how disastrous can be the consequence of suddenly drying liquidity in certain markets.

A related issue is the 'quality' of the prices set by markets. In theory, markets are the single point where *all* orders to buy or sell securities converge. This concentration of information ensures that market prices are perfect, for they take account of all the available information. In practice, however, things are less simple, for some operators may be tempted to make over-the-counter transactions or perform pre-market clearing operations. While such clearing operations may be attractive to the operators concerned, they pose a twofold threat to organized markets.[34] First, they remove a large volume of transactions from markets, reducing their liquidity. Second, they deprive them of some of the information on supply and demand, reducing the 'quality' of market prices. To boost liquidity, and to ensure that all the information is reflected in real time by changes in prices, market authorities have gradually extended trading hours and introduced continuous quotation.

The third fear, which corresponds to the fear of loss of value in the case of money, raises two different issues. The first is how to make sure all the players are on an equal footing as regards changes in prices, and to avoid favouring some at the expense of others. The second is more general: how to prevent financial crises, i.e. sudden, prolonged falls in the prices of *all* securities.

To make sure all the players are on an equal footing as regards information, regulations on insider trading have been tightened up and the penalties have been increased. At the same time, technical resources for tracking down possible offenders have been greatly expanded. The regulations make it an offence for anyone to take advantage of privileged information on a security, enterprise or project by placing an order to buy or sell. The main targets of such regulations are the senior management of quoted companies and those close to them, bankers and auditors and anyone else who may, for professional reasons, have access to confidential information. Yet even increasingly long lists of prohibited acts and exemplary penalties have failed to ensure market integrity. The tempting prospect of easy gain will always be a threat to public trust in markets as a social institution.

Fear of financial crises of the kind described by Minsky or Galbraith[35] can be compared to fears of inflation in the case of money. Unlike trust in monetary systems, which is based on 'guaranteed results' (no counterfeiting, no inflation, legal tender), trust in financial markets is based on 'guaranteed means' which are used to ensure that the markets function almost like machines. Thus operators' trust depends not on price levels or on the volume of trade, but on the ability of markets to function transparently, stably and correctly. Yet the spectre of prices collapsing or markets suddenly drying up is seldom far from people's minds. The sudden disappearance of inter-bank lending in late 2007 and then in Autumn 2008 was an example that took the world by surprise of how quickly otherwise liquid markets can dry up.

Organized financial markets, however global, are therefore not equipped to prevent financial crises, nor is that their purpose. At most – in the light of the lessons learned from the 1987 financial crisis – they nowadays have several circuit breakers that will supposedly allow players to recover and regain control. In emergencies, however, governments have no choice but to intervene. The recent spread of finance and its fusion with money puts the question of government responsibility for preventing financial crises in a completely new light. Today such crises have an unprecedented capacity to wreak socioeconomic havoc. Judging by the attitudes of central banks, financial markets (and even some segments of them) are now quite simply 'too big to fail' in times of trouble – such as the period that began in August 2007. The only fear being that some of them may ultimately prove 'too big to be saved' without heavy collateral damage.

The rescue of the Long-Term Capital Management (LTCM) hedge fund, orchestrated by the US Federal Reserve in 1998, is described in the box. This textbook case illustrates the dilemma governments face when risks taken by one financial player pose a threat to the financial system or indeed the whole economy. As of early 2008, the wider implications of the American subprime mortgage crisis are confronting central banks with the same dilemma as they faced ten years earlier in the case of the LTCM, and the measures proposed by G7 in spring 2008 resemble those advanced but not introduced after the LTCM crisis. On the one hand, government intervention 'socializes losses' and also has the pernicious medium-term effect of encouraging moral hazard type behaviours on behalf of operators who are tempted to take ill-considered risks. On the other hand, if a financial crisis is allowed to persist, the entire economy may be thrown into recession. Central banks are trying to find a middle way – not to rescue financial markets at all costs, but to cushion the economic impact of abrupt changes in stock-market prices (to the extent that they can afford to, and taking account of other constraints).[36]

The market mechanism, of which financial markets are the most sophisticated version, is based on an ideal of efficiency. Market economies achieve optimum allocation of resources by functioning efficiently. However, a rapid review of markets and their mechanisms of trust shows them to be delicate sets of weights and counterweights that supposedly serve the public interest by functioning properly, at the expense of private interests which seek to distort or manipulate them. The recent past is full of examples of such attempts, including price manipulation, dissemination of inaccurate or even deliberately falsified information, issuance

Box 1.2   Too big to fail? Long-Term Capital Management (1998–9)

Long-Term Capital Management (LTCM) is a hedge fund set up by John Meriwether in Greenwich, Connecticut, in February 1994, after he had been forced to step down as vice-president of the Salomon Brothers investment bank following a scandal involving manipulation of the Treasury bond market. A senior official who had investigated the case later joined LTCM. By joining forces with partners such as Merton Miller and Myron Scholes (winner of the 1997 Nobel Prize in Economics), the LTCM team threw down a challenge to Salomon Brothers and the entire financial industry. The team's scientific, professional aura attracted and reassured investors, including private individuals (Wall Street bank directors, LTCM partners and staff), institutional investors and some early sovereign wealth funds (the Bank of Italy and Asian central banks). The minimum investment was ten million US dollars, committed for three years. Soon after it was set up, LTCM already had some four billion dollars' worth of equity capital.

LTCM's strategy was to use powerful leverage to exploit price differences between highly similar financial products and so take advantage of 'market imperfections'. For example, LTCM sold short liquid assets such as thirty-year US Treasury bonds forward and announced its intention to buy $29^{1}/_{2}$-year ones (which were proportionally cheaper), thus hoping to earn the 'liquidity premium' paid on the thirty-year bonds, which were considered more liquid. LTCM had also taken advantage of mergers and acquisitions by acquiring strong positions in potential targets. In 1997–8, the financial turmoil caused by the Asian and Russian crises not only limited opportunities for arbitrage, thus weakening these positions, but at the same time led to a considerable slow-down in mergers and acquisitions.

The return on LTCM's equity capital, after commission, was 29 per cent in 1994, 43 per cent in 1995, 41 per cent in 1996 and 17 per cent in 1997. In late 1997, to prevent too great a fall in its return on equity, 2.7 billion of the seven billion dollars held by LTCM was refunded to shareholders. In 1998, with rather less than five billion dollars' worth of equity capital (1.9 billion of it controlled by the sixteen partners), LTCM built up a total exposure of around 200 billion dollars through bank loans and the use of derivatives. At the end of 1998, the Bank for International Settlements estimated the notional

Box 1.2 *Continued*

gross position of all the derivative contracts opened by LTCM at around a trillion dollars. On 2 September 1998, John Meriwether warned shareholders that LTCM had lost 44 per cent of its equity capital, but this did not worry them. They were gambling either on market situations changing back in favour of LTCM's contracts or on an influx of new shareholders. Like other hedge funds, LTCM had a very restrictive information policy: its net estimated value was made known only once a month, and only to shareholders.

Although banks like working with hedge funds because of the large volume of transactions they generate, it was a bank that eventually sounded the alarm. Bear Stearns, an investment bank and LTCM's clearing agent, said it had issued a 500 million dollar margin call to LTCM so that it could continue to perform clearances despite the unfavourable development of its positions. Margin calls can prove fatal when liquidity is short, for recipients are forced to liquidate positions at short notice in an unfavourable market. By September 1998 LTCM was looking round desperately for solutions. Warren Buffet made a takeover bid which would have led to LTCM's management losing its entire investment and being dismissed. The bid was rejected.

At the end of September 1998, the Federal Reserve Bank of New York called an emergency meeting of the fifteen leading Wall Street institutions that were linked to or held shares in LTCM. Recapitalization to the tune of 3.625 billion dollars was organized under government supervision, increasing LTCM's equity capital to 4.5 billion. Following this forced increase in capital, the share owned by former shareholders – including the management team – was reduced to 10 per cent, the other 90 per cent going to the rescue consortium. It ultimately took help from thirty-five other financial institutions to save LTCM.

The purpose of this coordinated arm's-length intervention by the US government was to allow LTCM's positions to be liquidated in a tidy manner, so as to prevent market panic and contain the risks to the whole system. Because of its size and the individual positions it held, particularly in Britain's national debt, LTCM was simply 'too big to fail'. This view was not shared by the previous chairman of the Federal Reserve, Paul Volcker, who strongly criticized his successor's intervention. As a result, the matter was taken up by Congress, and

Box 1.2 *Continued*

President Clinton set up a working group to determine what lessons should be learned from the crisis.

A few days after the rescue meeting, Union Bank of Switzerland wrote off 750 million dollars of its exposure. The price of its shares fell by over 30 per cent, and the chairman, Mathis Cabiallavetta, and two other senior officials left the bank with golden parachutes. Merrill Lynch, which had been exposed to the tune of 1.4 billion in LTCM, cut its staff by 5 per cent (3,400 jobs), and Citigroup and Bank of America saw their profits fall by half. ING Bank cut 1,200 jobs, and Dresdner Bank wrote off 142 million dollars.

Congress's criticism of the Federal Reserve Bank's rescue operation sheds light on the position of hedge funds, which are not subject to bank supervision and hence are not bound by the same transparency standards. It also shows just how little information the authorities have about over-the-counter transactions.

Four months after the rescue, in February 1999, the banks that had supported LTCM met to conclude that the funds they had advanced would certainly not be lost, although they were unable to state either when or how they would be recovered. The next day, the *Financial Times* came close to deploring this happy ending: '… the opportunity to teach financial players a much needed lesson about the dangers of hedge funds has been lost.' At the end of December 1999, the consortium that had come to LTCM's aid announced that between the end of September and the end of November it had seen a net return of 11 per cent on the capital it had invested.

What lessons were learned from the LTCM crisis?

(1) In its 1999 annual report, the Bank for International Settlements (BIS) pointed to gaps in the statistical coverage of derivatives traded over the counter. The LTCM crisis had shown that central bank data grossly underestimated the amounts involved.

(2) The BIS decided not to call for the creation of a 'central credit registry' that would give partial creditors an overall picture of the exposure of their debtors, such as hedge funds.

(3) Twelve of the largest banks that had taken part in the rescue set up a Counterparty Risk Management Policy Group to draw up standards for the financial industry that would prevent shocks of this kind. The group's avowed goal was to make sure, through self-regulation, that Congress would not lay down stricter rules.

> **Box 1.2** *Continued*
>
> (4) At Congress's request, President Clinton set up a working group to investigate the affair and propose supervisory and regulatory measures. The group submitted two reports to Congress: *Hedge Funds, Leverage, and the Lessons of Long-Term Capital Management* (April 1999) and *Over-the-Counter Derivative Markets and the Commodity Exchange Act* (November 1999). The latter report merely recommended that regulators be given better information on positions acquired by hedge funds, particularly in derivatives, because of their potential impact on the entire system.
>
> Perusal of this report, almost ten years on, shows that all the wider implications of the 2007–8 crisis were identified and known by the late 1990s.

of worthless securities and failures in performing audit and rating functions. Such practices are an everyday occurrence. Market integrity depends not only on the courage, willpower and technical capabilities of the supervisory authorities, but also on players' respect for these fragile mechanisms – in other words, the extent to which they treat them as shared goods. Like financial systems, organized markets are social institutions that constantly seek the optimum level of regulation. On the one hand, if the regulatory apparatus is too heavy, it may increase trust but will also make markets cumbersome and inflexible; on the other hand, inadequate supervision and regulation will undermine trust and the ability of markets to allocate resources properly. If the rules prove inadequate or inappropriate, and if players stop treating markets as shared goods to be respected and cared for, they will be weakened as social institutions, and this may eventually disrupt the entire monetary-financial regime.[37]

Mega-players

The profound changes that have made finance one of the main organizing principles in Western society are due not only to increasingly efficient, better-organized markets, but also to the rise of financial 'mega-players'. The prosperity of the Thirty Golden Years enabled Western society – and especially households – to save a great deal of money, year after year. These savings were increasingly channelled into financial circuits, fuelling the growth of specialized institutions. At the same time, as borders opened up, truly global banks began to emerge. The financial system now had an unprecedented mission: to maintain value in a relatively liquid form (an extension of the function of money as a store of purchasing power) and to make most of the world's savings yield a return.

One of the main factors that encouraged this development was a change in both individual and societal attitudes towards the funding of pensions. One main trend in developed countries in the late twentieth century was greater use of 'capitalization' – a set of public and private initiatives which induced households to accumulate financial 'pension capital' by setting aside part of their disposable income to be managed by institutions that would pay them pensions in their old age or if they became ill or incapacitated. This shift towards capitalization was due to the erosion of political support for the welfare state, which during the Thirty Golden Years had covered these risks in a highly egalitarian way through taxation. This rapidly led to more individualistic attitudes. Nourished by demutualization of risks, capitalization was also seen as a good way to cope with the problem of longer-lived, ageing populations. The spread of compulsory or optional pension funds, such as life insurance, was in keeping with this idea of 'forced savings'. The forced nature of the savings was particularly evident in defined-benefit schemes.

Pension funds – together with life insurance companies – were the main financial institutions to benefit from the trend towards demutualization of risks. Pensions had first become a key element in industrial relationships at the start of the twentieth century, but it was especially in the second half of the century that the idea of individualization through capitalization of contributions and benefits began to spread. Individualization of pensions through capitalization creates a link between the contributions paid by individuals and their employers throughout their lives and the amount of their pensions. This link is based on the capitalization principle, which, through return on the accumulated savings, enables the benefits paid to be financially linked to contributions.[38] This creates a cyclical savings-dissavings relationship between the individual and the insurer over a period which in most cases exceeded a quarter-century. In the course of this relationship, the gradually accumulated capital is invested in financial markets to generate a return and a profit. When contributors retire, the amount due is normally a multiple (in purchasing-power rather than merely nominal terms) of the contributions paid. Dazzling actuarial calculations, together with the frothy promises of financialization, induced many Western countries to make capitalization an integral part of their pension systems, sometimes at the expense of traditional redistribution. This is not the place for a technical debate on the advantages and disadvantages of the various methods of cover. Suffice it to say that the rise of capitalization inevitably meant greater use of financial assets, and hence of transactions and markets.

The trend towards making capitalization the main legal basis for pension cover relies on the macroeconomic hypothesis that the costs of managing financial assets will always be less than the resulting gains. This hypothesis takes economic growth and constantly rising productivity for granted. Were the relationship between management costs and increased productivity to be inverted for any length of time, this could pose a serious threat to the viability of pension promises – which are among the most striking political and social achievements of the recent wave of financialization in Western society. The far-reaching social implications of such a failure would leave governments with no option but to intervene.

Half of all British, American and Canadian wage-earners now rely on pension funds for their retirement. In countries such as Switzerland and the Netherlands the proportion is a good deal higher, whereas in other European countries it is increasing but is so far no more than 10 per cent. The resources thus accumulated are vast, equivalent to some 50 per cent of GDP in the OECD countries, where they account for a similar proportion of stock-market capitalization. Over the past ten years, resources entrusted to pension funds have been growing at an average rate of almost 20 per cent a year, which is four or five times the rate of economic growth. The resources accumulated in pension funds and other social welfare institutions are estimated at fifteen trillion dollars and account for some 30–60 per cent of households' gross savings.[39]

Insurance (especially life insurance and reinsurance) companies also benefited greatly from the expansion of 'forced savings' which began during the Thirty Golden Years. In traditional society, risks associated with death were mainly covered by the family and the clan. It was in the nineteenth century, in the English-speaking countries, that accounting became more sophisticated and friendly societies and cooperatives were set up, mainly to help the poorest – in other words, to mutualize these risks. Today's life insurance companies are their distant heirs. Like pension funds, life insurance companies establish relationships with their clients, at the end of which they undertake to provide benefits if the clients die or their health becomes impaired before they reach a given age. In return, the companies receive regular payments which they invest to make a profit. This is 'forced savings', but not in the legal sense as in the case of pension fund contributions, for once the policies are signed households are under a contractual obligation to contribute over a long period. Life insurance premiums now account for almost 5 per cent of GDP in Western countries, and property insurance premiums for almost 4 per cent – a total of some 3,300 dollars per capita per annum. Since 1980, the volume of life premiums has increased twice as fast as global GDP.[40]

The flow of premiums has consistently helped swell the balance sheets of insurance companies around the world. Between 1996 and 2006, according to the Thomson Financial database, the balance sheets of the fifteen largest insurance companies expanded fourfold, while nominal world product grew by a factor of 1.6 (see Figure 1.2). These figures are only indicative and should be treated with great caution, for they reflect not just the undoubted expansion in insurance as such, but also takeovers by the leading players in the insurance sector. Nevertheless, in 2005 the balance sheets of the world's fifteen largest insurance companies accounted for 16 per cent of world product, compared with just 6 per cent ten years earlier.

The increase in the volume of savings entrusted to financial channels is also linked to the rapid growth in the number of high-net-worth individuals or HNWIs (people with more than a million dollars net in liquid assets, not counting their main home). According to estimates by defunct Merrill Lynch and Capgemini, this figure more than doubled between 1996 and 2006 (from 4.5 to 9.5 million), whereas the world's population grew three times more slowly over the same period (see Figure 1.2). Expressed in terms of world product, HNWIs' liquid assets rose from 56 to 77 per cent in the space of ten years. The rapid expansion of this privileged group reflects the rapid growth of the global economy, growing inequalities in income (with astronomical rates of pay for some company directors and executives) and the expansion of private rents derived from exports of raw materials, particularly oil.[41]

Pension funds and insurance companies, and to a lesser extent very wealthy individuals and banks (to be discussed below), now hold, on their balance sheet, volumes of savings which have to be available on more or less predictable dates to meet contractual obligations. Liquidity of the accumulated saving is therefore crucial. This creates a link with the other key institutions in the financialization process: the organized market and financial products. Rather than being *invested* in the classic

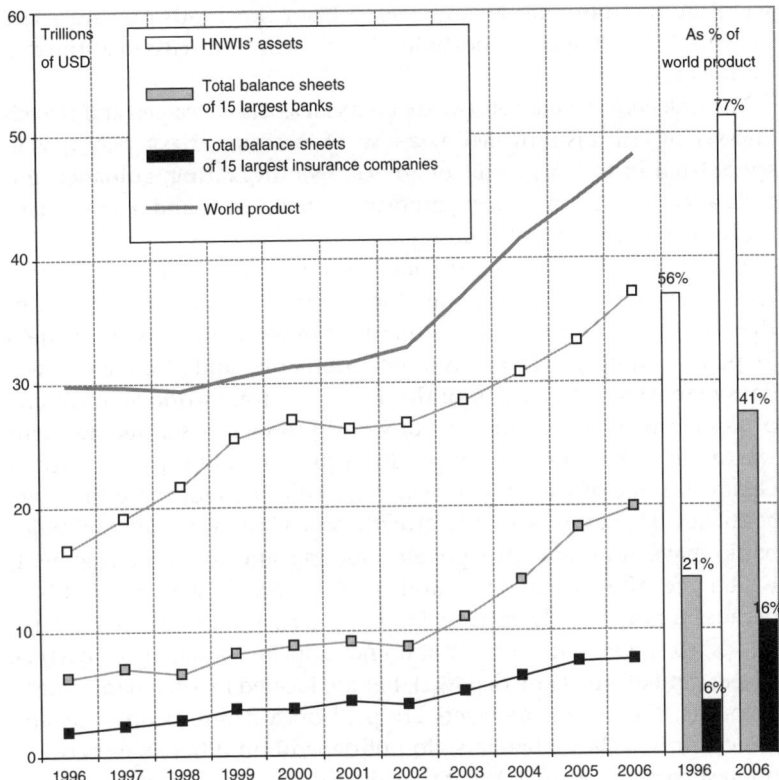

Figure 1.2 Expansion of 'savings silos'[42]
© Observatoire de la Finance, 2008 [www.obsfin.ch]
Primary data: Thomson Financial, World Bank and *World Wealth Report*

sense in order to increase productive capacity, savings are now *placed* on financial markets simply in order to make a return. The common use of the term 'financial investment' to describe the latter should not be allowed to obscure the fundamental difference between the two.

The consolidation of savings silos during the euphoric years and the fact that savings are now invested in the financial rather than the classic sense led to the emergence of a new kind of economic player. Such players were not entrepreneurs, for they did not build or produce anything, nor were they consumers, for they did not consume. Instead, they managed value over time, much as captains of ships weathered the (financial) storms of the raging oceans to bring their vessels (assets) and their cargoes (of value) safely into port. In response to this, a new scientific discipline began to develop from the 1950s onwards. The new discipline, known as portfolio theory, will be discussed at the end of this part.

The link between markets (where financial assets are valued and traded) and savings silos is provided by a host of intermediaries – players who specialized in various forms of advice, valuing, rating, guidance and assistance, or even in creating innovative investment and management tools such as investment funds.

One activity that deserves special mention here is asset management. Asset managers agree to manage their clients' liquidity to the best of their ability and skill. A large proportion of world savings, assets held by pension funds, HNWIs, insurance companies and so on, are nowadays managed by 'stewards' of this kind. The total worldwide volume of assets involved is a multiple of world product. Asset management was traditionally the preserve of Swiss private banks (particularly in Geneva), some of which had been engaged in this for more than two centuries. However, with the growth of savings silos, all the major banks have now got into private banking and asset management, which are often their safest and most profitable activities. This is because funds are only entrusted to managers, and thus do not change hands, so the amounts involved do not appear on managers' balance sheets (unlike, say, bank deposits), but are located in 'off balance sheet' accounts. Moreover, managers are paid on a commission basis and hence, unlike classic bankers, do not depend on differences between interest paid and earned. What they do is draw up financial investment strategies for their clients, perform the necessary transactions and monitor the entire process. They use their expertise to give appropriate advice, and in most cases also perform the transactions they have recommended or prescribed. Clients' trust in their asset managers' ethical integrity plays a key role in their relationship. Managers may find themselves torn between the need to defend their clients' interests and the lure of the commissions they earn on the transactions they prescribe. Ultimately, the only thing that can prevent such conflicts of interest is the profession's ethical integrity.

The euphoric years did not mean the end of banks' traditional activity of using customers' deposits to make loans. However, they were forced to adapt to the changes that were taking place, and this in turn made it easier for the changes to continue. Two aspects of this process should be mentioned here. First, 'classic' banks gradually adjusted their business models so as to earn a greater share of their income from client services (payment services, expertise, advice, asset management, etc.). Although the figures vary, commissions now account for around 50 per cent of major banks' income, compared with 25 per cent only twenty years ago. Second, major banks responded by going global. In 2006 the total balance sheets of the world's fifteen largest banks equalled 41 per cent of world product, compared with just 21 per cent in 1996. With their balance sheets increasing by a factor of 3.1 and world product growing by a factor of 1.6 (see Figure 1.2), the banks' growth in size has admittedly been slower than that of insurance companies, but the amounts involved are twice as great. International expansion, especially through acquisitions, has been a major part of this process. To take just one example, in 2004 – fifteen years after the fall of the Berlin Wall – more than 90 per cent of Polish banks' balance sheets was under foreign control. This goes to show the extent to which leading Western banks have penetrated countries where banking previously played a restricted role.

The lure of activities that generate commissions and the scarcity of 'free' household savings owing to the increase in 'forced savings' have not led banks to radically cut back their traditional deposit and lending activities. They have – at least so far – resisted the temptation to stop lending altogether, for two reasons. First, they want to keep a loyal client base for current operations, since those very clients generate a major share of the commissions they earn from asset management and payments. Second, they want to hold on to 'good deals' (succession and transmission of enterprises, loans in what are theoretically the safest areas, such as mortgages, and participation in carefully selected major projects). Slowly, however, they are beginning to disengage from the risks associated with lending. This is clearly reflected in the events of 2007–8: banks had deliberately granted loans to relatively insolvent borrowers, earned their commissions and then resold the risks to other financial players in the form of derivatives or structured products and instruments. In this way they limited the growth of their balance sheets, and the same time acquired a new client base and earned commissions.

There is a tendency for lending to move out of the traditional banking sector and be taken over by specialized financial players. There has thus been an increase in standardized loans by producers or suppliers of consumer durables (deferred-payment schemes for cars and electrical appliances, consumer loans in department stores, etc.) and, more recently, by estate agents. Instead of approaching banks, enterprises now increasingly seek finance from other enterprises with which they have technical links. In some cases a major corporation will even help finance the development of its strategic suppliers. Finally, major projects are increasingly financed by capital markets, through bond issues.

All the financial transactions performed by pension funds are designed to strengthen their long-term relationships with the clients who contribute to them. One might therefore have expected pensions institutions to take over traditional banks' role as lenders for long-term projects. Although banks may face sudden demands for liquidity at any time, pension funds know exactly when their commitments will fall due and what additional sums will be paid in. Yet, for reasons of liquidity and transparency, they prefer in their majority to stick to liquid instruments and market transactions rather than enter credit relationships and classic investment. Taking advantage of the opportunities for quick entry and exit that market liquidity provides, they 'manage' risk and uncertainty just as other players do, always on the alert and ready to adjust their positions in response to the latest information. Mindful of the need to reassure clients, supervisors and the general public that they are managing things properly, pension funds constantly seek to match 'market performance' (the 'benchmarking' mantra). If they fail to do so for any length of time, their directors may incur individual or institutional penalties. Thus, rather than make markets more stable, pension funds may in fact make them more jumpy (as was the case during the 1987 crisis). They bear their share of responsibility for the 'dot-com bubble' of 1999–2000. However, the largest of them, such as California's civil service pension fund CalPERS and France's *Fonds de Réserve pour les Retraites*, are well aware of their individual influence and the aura that surrounds them. They are therefore alert to the risk of triggering uncontrollable movements among other operators. Their very size makes pension funds both masters and prisoners of the markets.

Custodians of the market temple

Besides financial mega-players, increasingly refined financial investment strategies have generated demand for instruments, vehicles and services that can make intermediary operations more efficient. Among these are investment funds – joint-stock companies that own nothing but portfolios of financial assets. Investors who buy shares of funds which are themselves financial assets thus become the owners of a fraction of a basket of assets. As far as the investors are concerned, the funds are both investment vehicles like any other financial asset, and institutions or enterprises that manage portfolios. These miniature replicas of the financial market (or market segments) can be combined and split up at will. Their profiles are determined when they are launched, with reference to a particular sector of the economy, type of risk or method of management. They are then built around an algorithm that creates an automatic link between the profile and the mathematized world of investment. These investment vehicles are sources of income for their directors. The prices at which shares of the funds are sold to financial investors therefore include the directors' remuneration, in the form of commissions which may or may not be readily identifiable as such.[43] While some funds make constant use of financial markets either to adjust the composition of their portfolios or to advertise their performance by being quoted, others, such as private equity funds or hedge funds, prefer to remain discreet. Investment funds are intermediation vehicles, in the sense that they can indirectly enable otherwise unauthorized financial assets or management strategies to be quoted on organized markets. Risks linked to US subprime mortgages thus ended up in small investors' portfolios when quoted funds took positions in specific not listed and poorly rated instruments and other less transparent funds.

Besides pension and investment funds, financialization has boosted demand for and supply of other financial or quasi-financial services, especially ones that provide the information and analyses investors need in order to reach decisions. Traders, market operators, investment banks that handle initial public offerings (IPOs), mergers and acquisitions, analysts and auditors, rating agencies and, of course, technology suppliers and managers are thus all service providers whose living depends on the volume and prices of market transactions. This wide range of skills encourages and facilitates the transactions instigated by asset managers, investment funds, pension funds and private investors. Such services are rewarded either by direct or indirect volume-based commissions, or by fees, or in some cases by retrocession. Some of these activities (such as analyses), though not directly profitable, are nevertheless an essential part of client service, and this raises the question of how they should be organized in relation to other services. The important thing is to remain viable and, ideally at least, avoid 'churning', i.e. 'rotating' clients' portfolios simply to generate commissions.[44]

Today's financial markets are inconceivable without the underlying relationships on which the transactions depend, or without the broad range of specialized players and intermediaries with an economic interest in ensuring that the markets function smoothly. As we have seen, markets are no longer mere abstractions, but have become more or less uniform sets of procedures, professional codes of practice, laws, infrastructures and standards, with often conflicting interests and hidden rewards. Markets are not only one of the pillars of public trust in the monetary-financial regime (which is why players all agree that markets should be sustained and defended), but also the scene of unobtrusive but fierce battles to capture the largest possible share of the vast income they generate. In practice, like the payment systems discussed earlier, financial markets are sets of links and procedures that enable transactions to be performed and services to be provided. Each operator pursues his or her own profit-maximizing strategy, which is aimed at the ultimate client or the competitor. As in payment systems, transactions vary greatly in price, precision, speed or settlement period. The exact nuances and differences are known only to professionals, who use the first hand knowledge – and in some cases misuse it – for their own benefit.[45]

Operators are well aware that markets are ultimately far less stable than they are cracked up to be, that they can be distorted in a matter of seconds by means of appropriate strategies, that their valuations are by no means as objective as the public are led to believe and that company accounting is likewise less 'objective' than might be thought. As the bearers of public trust, these mega-intermediaries imply in their press releases and public comments that they are on a par with the high priests and priestesses of Greek and Roman antiquity. Protected – and to some extent trapped – by their august role, and cynical because they know what is really going on behind the scenes, they may become unscrupulous and abuse public trust for their own ends. As 'custodians of the temple', only they are permitted to enter the holy-of-holies for their secret consultations with invisible market forces. It is increasingly hard to tell where reality ends and myth begins.[46]

The spread of 'over-the-counter' financial transactions (ones that take place outside organized markets) shows that financialization can just as easily operate in the informal shadows. A good example is the foreign exchange 'market', which is not actually a market, but a stratified network of players linked to global information platforms. The various strata differ in their 'admission fees', in the time it takes for information to become available and in transaction costs. Yet, to keep up the appearance of scientific rigour, financial operators still speak in terms of a theoretically perfect organized market.

Public deficits and how they are financed

Governments' contribution to the spread of finance should not be underestimated. During the euphoric years, the OECD countries ran large public deficits. This is still the case today, with frequent breaches of the stability pact rules in the euro zone and a deficit of quite dizzying proportions in the United States. At the start of the 1980s there was a major change in the way in which deficits were financed, inflation was declared Public Enemy No. 1. This change in attitude took place just as conservative governments which were close to business – and particularly financial – circles came to power on both sides of the Atlantic, under Margaret Thatcher and Ronald Reagan.

Inflation and finance are indeed arch-enemies, for inflation erodes the monetary standard on which finance depends. It distorts and undermines the whole basis for inter-temporal calculation. In times of inflation, liquidity holders tend to get rid of purely financial assets, especially bonds, and take positions in more stable, tangible assets not to exclude 'real' investments. During the 1980s the growth in bond markets was encouraged by the development of orthodox monetarist

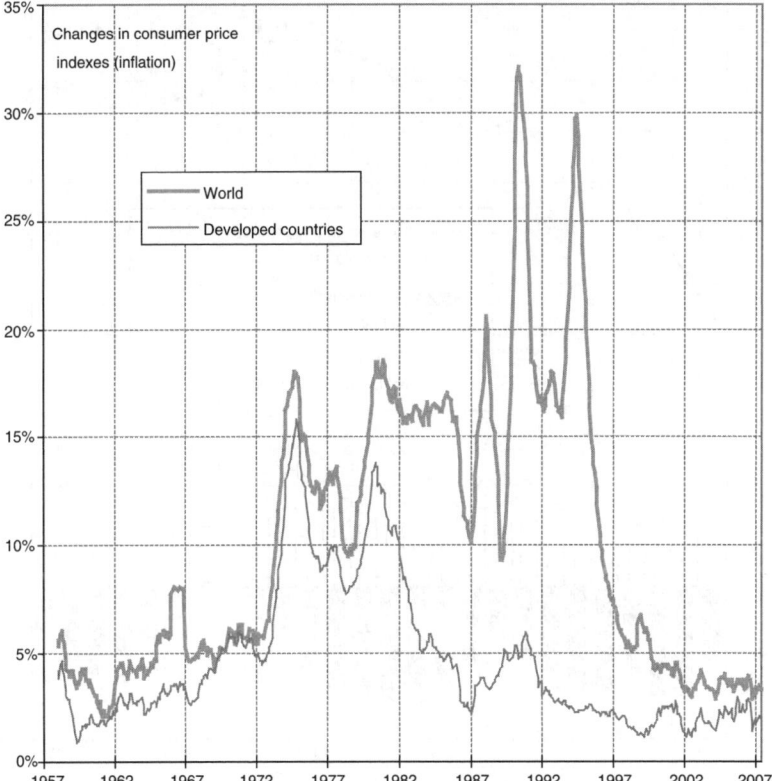

Figure 1.3 Half a century of inflation
© Observatoire de la Finance, 2008 [www.obsfin.ch]
Primary data: Thomson Financial

views about how the OECD countries should manage their national debt. The need to protect the monetary standard against inflation seemed until recently as self-evident to most people. Most central banks used to see it as one of their main tasks, almost as dogma that no longer required rational justification. However, things change quickly, and in mid-2008, central banks are torn between their dogmatic and anti-inflationary stands and the requirements of preserving the financial system by easing liquidity constraints in some market segments.

With the Maastricht criteria and then the stability pact rules on which the euro is based, the last twenty years have seen monetarism triumph over Keynesianism. Financing of public deficits by more or less overt monetization, i.e. by creating money (with attendant risks of inflation),

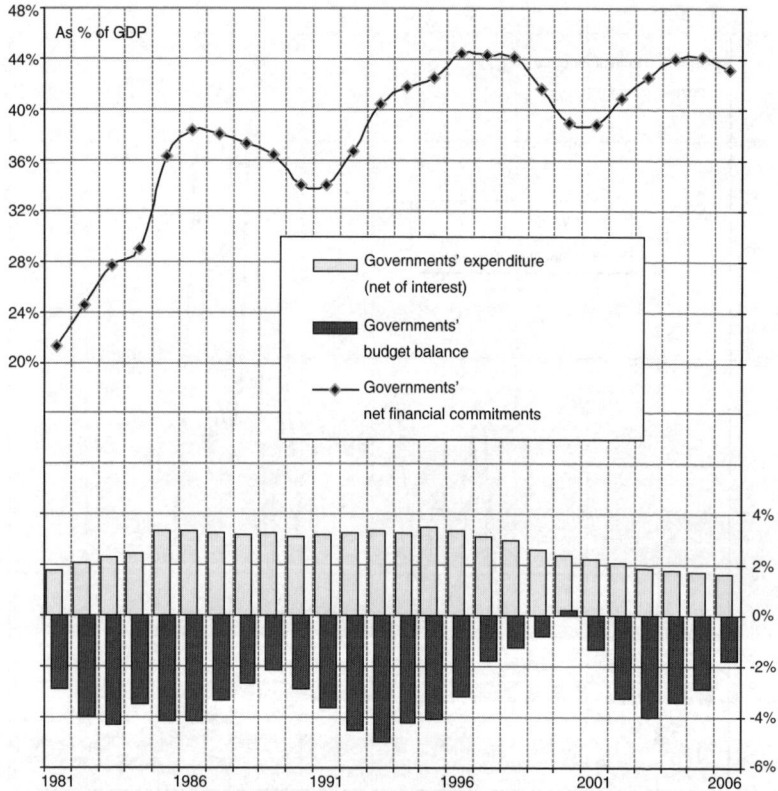

Figure 1.4 Public debt and interest burdens in the OECD countries
© Observatoire de la Finance, 2008 [www.obsfin.ch]
Primary data: OECD

has been replaced by financing through debt. This change of attitude is due to an ideological consensus that maintaining the value of borrowed capital matters more than the financial burden of servicing and paying back debt. Increased reliance on debt has naturally led Western governments to make greater use of financial markets. OECD countries' net public debt nowadays accounts for some 45 per cent of their GDP, and total outstanding government bonds are equivalent to global GDP (see Figure 2.1 below). This change in the way deficits are financed has led governments to use a large proportion of their current receipts to pay their creditors (see Figure 1.4). The result is a net transfer from taxpayers to creditors, and particularly to savings silos (temporary stores of uninvested liquidity). There has been relatively little analysis of the amount of wealth transferred in this way.

It is important to mention here that some governments' borrowing policies have been accompanied by major tax breaks. Examples include tax-free bond issues on euromarkets, which have attracted undeclared savings (ironically, the same governments are trying hard to combat tax evasion). Although this has enabled borrowing governments to contain the costs of their debt, it is also one of the factors that helped bring down the Bretton Woods system.

1.3
The Financial World View

The previous two sections have described (a) the historical background to financialization, and (b) the players and ways of behaving that initiated the process. It is striking how these two largely independent developments have converged. Although much depends on how things are presented, there is something disturbing about the newly emerging pattern. Is it pure coincidence, a plot, a historical necessity or something else altogether?

Financialization first emerged in free societies that respect human rights, democracy and free markets. The idea of a conspiracy (which has been put forward by some Marxist thinkers), or indeed of some external force acting on finance, must therefore be dismissed. Finance has developed not only because it does not collide head-on with the fundamental principles of free society, but also because it provides responses – though perhaps only partial ones – to society's needs, desires and even fears. In other words, financialization – at least some of it, if not all of it – is something society really wanted.

Like all free-market economic activities, finance has developed out of the interplay between supply of services and solvent demand for them. Close interaction between opportunities (supply) and needs or wishes (demand) has gradually led them to permeate one another, creating a consensus on the social role of finance. This has led to the emergence of specialized practices, institutions and enterprises, and has come to influence society's cultural and ethical values. Financialization has progressed from microeconomic decisions to macroeconomic realities, and is now one of society's main organizing principles.

The social and institutional changes that paved the way for financialization and helped it spread were the sum total of countless microeconomic decisions. These were taken in specific circumstances by players with specific motives and ways of thinking based on bounded rationality. Few of these decisions had more than a marginal impact on the whole, yet together they led to the changes that are the subject of this book. The new overall pattern resulting from these individual decisions emerged stage by stage and was clearly not apparent to the people who made them, yet they led to the gradual spread of practices, instruments and techniques that were originally confined to the realm of finance. If people who behave in a given way can see that it gets results, its influence on society will increase. This has been pointed out by authors such as Douglass North among economists and Michel Crozier and René Girard among sociologists.[47] Financialization was able to transform the institutional structures of the West because the technical and political potential of the euphoric years converged and interacted with the *Zeitgeist*. It is now time to look at this process more closely. What was the way of thinking, the rationality behind it? What were its mechanisms and motives? And what were its underlying aspirations and values?

The efficiency ethos

Philosophically speaking, the rationalist revolution that began with the Enlightenment and may now be coming to an end undoubtedly 'emancipated' man in his pursuit of technical efficiency, for it deposed God and made man – whether the lone individual or society – the ultimate master of his own fate. This put the question of who man was in a completely new light. 'Human nature' was interpreted in may different ways. To liberals it meant individual utilitarianism tempered by free markets, whereas to socialists it meant the good of society as perceived by clear-sighted leaders. These two philosophies clashed, sometimes bloodily, throughout the twentieth century. Yet, despite their irreducible political differences, these two schools of thought share the assumption that man – the individual or society – can rationally choose his goals and efficiently choose the means of attaining them. This is the core of political rationalism, which sees technical efficiency as a way to attain non-technical goals.

The same rationalist revolution, fuelled by a succession of scientific discoveries over the previous centuries (particularly the Copernican and Newtonian revolutions), produced a rich harvest of technical breakthroughs that led to the industrial revolution and, more generally, to social and institutional changes that apply to this day. Jacques Ellul believed that the 'technological system' he identified in the middle of the Thirty Golden Years was the culmination of these centuries of change. The technological system, he said, had gradually imposed its logic on contemporary society. According to Ellul's brilliant and still very relevant analysis, this logic – equivalent to the notion of the 'organizing principle' used in this report – had two main features. First, in its pursuit of progress, Technology was driven by an unceasing quest for new means that were the most efficient at any given moment, a quest whose sole *raison d'être* was absolute technical efficiency, and which was an intrinsic part of human nature. Second, the technological system therefore developed in response to existing opportunities for growth, rather than specific goals.[48] Thus, unlike the political rationalism referred to above, the pursuit of technical efficiency was a potentially autonomous state of mind – or force, as Ellul called it – that did not require external goals. According to this theory, which emphasized the recursive nature of the pursuit of efficiency, the only relevant motive was performance.

The rationalist revolution and the rise of technology in the eighteenth and nineteenth centuries coincided with the end of political and religious control over the economy. Although technical and economic efficiency were not the same thing, both were based on a quantified, predictable approach to reality. Economic efficiency could be achieved through accounting, and the development of engineering gave technical efficiency a means of expression and enabled it to gain society's trust.[49] As Ellul said, the pursuit of technical efficiency could be a motive in itself; but the motivation was stronger when technical and economic efficiency were pursued together. The result was the 'efficiency ethos'.[50]

The efficiency ethos was most clearly reflected in the mentality that accompanied the rise of the middle class, or bourgeoisie. Sombart's clear-sighted analysis contrasted the middle-class mentality – which focused on economic efficiency and balanced accounts (budgetary constraints, as economists would later say) – with that of the aristocracy, which was based on the obligations of rank and took it for granted that the accounts would be balanced eventually.[51] The middle-class notion of rational, measurable economic interests left little room for unbridled, uncontrollable desires or passions which, by definition, could not be quantified.[52] Unlike technical efficiency, which was objective and absolute, economic efficiency operated in relation to a 'subject' – an individual, an enterprise or a society – that sought to maximize results (gains or profits). Thus, in middle-class society, economic efficiency was the ultimate criterion for deciding which of the many technological solutions to adopt.[53]

The efficiency ethos is thus one of the pillars of economics, which Lionel Robbins neatly summed up in 1932 as a science that studied ways of satisfying as many needs as possible with limited resources. Sombart identified prudence, calculation, tidiness and thrift as elements of the middle-class mentality that spread in the wake of urbanization and the industrial revolution. Capital gradually became an economic player in its own right, distinct from whoever might own it. Max Weber's *General Economic History*[54] provided an excellent analysis of capital accounting which marked the emergence of capital not only as an autonomous factor of production but also as an economic 'subject' (as embodied in the notion of the enterprise as a 'legal person'). As capital became established from the mid-nineteenth century onwards as an autonomous subject with rights and obligations of its own, economic efficiency acquired an unchallengeable 'objective' basis. The days when the aristocratic ethos could dismiss the emerging efficiency ethos with contempt – when ownership still depended on social status and the vicissitudes of royal and noble power – were over.

Now that capital was autonomous and entitled to remuneration, ownership of wealth and property ceased to be a mere accessory of social rank and became an independent source of income. Nascent capitalism thus offered the wealthy a hitherto unknown opportunity to live off income from remunerated capital, rather than income derived from rank or status. This made the economy even more independent of political control. The capitalist, now freed of all allegiance, gradually became a model for the working classes, a future prospect that brightened their daily lives and held out hopes of better fortune as an entrepreneur.[55] Although 'pure' capitalists – who lived entirely off the income from their capital – were a tiny minority, the idea appealed to the imagination, and was to form the theoretical basis for capitalization-based pension schemes and the Thatcherian 'property owning democracy'.

Capitalism is thus simply a new version of the 'efficiency ethos', based on a combination of technical and economic efficiency with the financial efficiency of capital – an autonomous, calculable factor of production. In order for this financial version of the efficiency ethos to trigger the financialization process, remuneration of capital – application of the efficiency ethos to capital – needed a moral justification and a social group capable of putting it into practice. This did not take long.

Remuneration of capital did not become established as a key part of the Western economy and Western society until a moral justification was found for it and the gates of Heaven were opened – if only grudgingly – to financiers. Jacques Le Goff has plausibly suggested that purgatory was 'invented' in the early Middle Ages specifically to give

Christian financiers some chance of getting into Heaven.[56] However, the first real moral justification for 'making money out of money' was provided by Calvin who, in a letter to Sachin in 1545, distinguished between loans made for investment purposes (in which case interest was justified) and ones made to people in distress (in which case it was not). Over the centuries this distinction became more widely accepted, and with the publication of Pope Benedict XIV's encyclical *Vix Pervenit* in 1745 the Catholic Church – always more cautious in this regard – began to recommend that each case be judged on its merits.[57] This coincided with the rise of the middle class during the industrial revolution. Although Sombart and Weber disagreed about which led to which, the two were quite clearly connected.

Sombart identified two stages in the development of capitalism: the stage at which the amount of remuneration sought depended on what opportunities were available for the owner to make use of it (nascent capitalism) and the stage at which maximum remuneration was sought for its own sake, without regard to wealth or specific needs (mature capitalism). With the advent of mature capitalism, the notion of efficiency changed. Previously measured in absolute terms (technical efficiency) or in relation to an external factor such as satisfaction of needs (economic efficiency), it was henceforth measured by a mathematical progression. With the introduction of financial efficiency as a factor in its own right, the efficiency ethos now held out the prospect of infinite accumulation of wealth. It was this that enabled finance to develop as a perfect means of maximizing the remuneration of capital.

The efficiency ethos (particularly its financial version) has been spread through present-day society not only by formal education – technological and management colleges – but also by informal education, for the notion of productivity and return now dominate every aspect of people's lives. This is even true of political decisions, in which efficiency is now usually the main criterion.

Risk and return: a neat paradigm

As capital came to be seen as an autonomous factor of production and a legal, economic and moral entity, the notion of risk, and the way financial efficiency could cope with it, came to the fore. Risk meant the possibility of a reduction or even loss of capital that was exposed to economic uncertainty. It was thus the negative counterpart of return on capital. Risk was known to economic players well before the technique of calculating probabilities and the study of distributions enabled it to be quantified.[58] Mediaeval Italian merchants were only too aware of the risks to which their goods were exposed on voyages to and from distant parts of the world. Techniques for covering and pooling risk have always been part of finance.[59]

It was only gradually that finance emerged as a separate concept. The 1950s and 1960s were a watershed that would profoundly influence the *Zeitgeist*. It was the work of Harry Markowitz that laid the foundations of modern portfolio theory. This created a unique link between the two key mechanisms of the efficiency ethos: risk and return. Henceforth the theory and practice of finance would revolve around these closely connected mechanisms. This is how Markowitz himself described what was new about modern portfolio theory in the lecture he gave when awarded the 1990 Nobel Prize in Economics (along with two others): 'First, it is concerned with investors rather than manufacturing firms or consumers. Second, it is concerned with economic agents who act under uncertainty. Third, it is a theory which can be used to direct practice, at least by large (usually institutional) investors with sufficient computer and database resources.'[60]

In identifying 'financial investors' – holders of temporarily idle liquid savings – as specific players on the economic stage, Markowitz not only justified their existence but also gave them a rationality and tools of their own. Their main aim was not to channel resources into manufacturing, but to use financial assets to increase their immediate value while containing the risk to which they were exposed. In defining portfolio theory, Markowitz opened up hitherto unsuspected prospects for economics without abandoning its rationalistic paradigm. Thus the rational basis for 'homo oeconomicus' remained unchanged. 'Homo financiarius', the product of nascent portfolio theory, simply applied the same rationality to risk and return.[61]

Modern portfolio theory is one of a series of conceptual breakthroughs that began with the Newtonian revolution and ended with the 'mathematization' of reality, the cornerstone of technological civilization.[62] Alexandre Koyré's analysis of the impact of the Newtonian revolution applies equally to the portfolio theory revolution: '[T]here is something Newton must be held responsible for – or rather, not just Newton, but modern science in general – namely the division of our world into two. [... Science] did this by replacing our world of qualities and sensory perceptions, the world in which we live, love and die, with a different world – a world of quantity, of reified geometry, a world in which there is room for all things, but not for man. Thus the world of science – the "real" world – became distant and completely separate from the world of life, which science was unable to explain, even with the help of a solvent explanation that would turn it into a "subjective" phenomenon. In reality, the two worlds are always – and increasingly – linked by praxis. Yet there is a theoretical gulf between them. Two worlds, which means two truths – or no truth at all. This is the tragedy of the modern mind, which has "solved the riddle of the universe" only to replace it with another one – the riddle of itself.'[63]

The mathematization of the world that was set in train by Newton broke up the 'totality' into atoms. The same revolution, extended to the economy, led to the emergence of financial assets – protean molecules made up of atoms of reality bonded together by a set of constraints, rights and obligations. Just as the mathematization of reality provided tools for the analysis and hence the gradual implementation of technical efficiency, the mathematization of economic reality via portfolio theory provided tools for the implementation of financial efficiency. In both cases, the Newtonian revolution created specialized areas in which the necessary mental processes could take place before being transposed to reality with all their imperfections. This was probably what Koyré had in mind when he spoke of 'the division of our world into two.'

As recalled earlier, efficiency and economic calculus rationalized the behaviour of entrepreneurs in their pursuit of profit. Financial rationality provided a basis for the behaviour of speculators, who juggled positions within the financial area without ever leaving it and without ever coming into contact with reality. This is not to say that finance did not affect reality – quite the contrary! – but it did so only indirectly. Modern finance therefore involved the development of mentalities and skills that could operate within a mathematized area that was remote but not cut off from tangible reality.[64] Shuttling back and forth, finance linked the two worlds so brilliantly identified by Koyré: the mathematized world of theory and the world of tangible reality.

This newly emergent financial 'area' was instantly occupied not only by financial operators, but also by 'scientists' who attempted to explain its underlying laws and rationality. The 'science' of modern finance was born in the early 1950s. Unlike its elder sister corporate finance, 'modern' or 'market' finance focused on the markets where financial assets were transacted. It attempted to make models for them, not only to understand how they worked but also – and perhaps above all – to help players behave more efficiently. The financial area lent itself to mathematization – the ultimate 'proof' that it was objective and serious – and so the relevant practical knowledge could be certified as scientific.[65]

If the purpose of economics – according to the now generally accepted definition – was to satisfy as many needs as possible with limited resources, the purpose of finance was to maximize the value of capital at a given level of risk. By the late 1990s, wrapped in its aura of scientific integrity, finance even felt entitled to dictate whole ways of behaving to the human race, claiming they would propel it to unprecedented levels of happiness.[66]

Operating rationally in mathematized cyberspace, modern finance became self-contained. All that operators had to do was manipulate the various elements in that space by buying them, selling them or bringing them together. The trader now famous for bringing Société Générale to the verge of ruin, Jérôme Kerviel, repeated almost verbatim the words uttered by the man who brought down Barings, Nick Leeson: 'In cyberspace you don't feel you're dealing with real money!' Operators could even create new financial objects by taking pieces of reality that had previously had no counterpart in the financial area and turning them into assets. Reducing complex reality to its purely financial dimensions – risk and return – made comparison, arbitrage and optimization much simpler. These two dimensions could be used to describe and assign parameters to any financial asset, i.e. any piece of reality that was brought within the financial area. Operators could thus assemble 'portfolios' to suit their own needs – sets of asset 'molecules', each with their own levels of risk and prospects of return.

In order for finance to grow to its present dimensions, not only did the pieces of reality that were turned into assets have to be mathematized, but they also had to be capable of being traded on markets. The autonomy of financial cyberspace thus depended on the expansion of financial markets, which in a sense were its counterpart in the tangible world. Without the transactions, and the market place where it occurs, that links the two worlds, finance could never have become even partly independent of the economy.

The emergence of capital as a financial asset in its own right encouraged the development of an almost infinite number of financial 'objects'. These owed their existence to the mere fact that they could be mathematized and were underpinned by a legally coherent set of rights, duties or agreements. They were derivatives of an underlying reality. Practically any piece of reality could thus be subjected to the theory – and practice – of finance. This is what happened to foreign currency when the system of fixed exchange rates broke down, and the same has since happened to raw materials, conditional contracts, synthetics and so on. Tomorrow it may be the turn of the climate, 'health capital', 'human capital', 'skill capital', 'intellectual capital' or 'social capital'. The underlying reality is always the same: an autonomous store of wealth in search of 'remuneration', which must be protected against risk, preserved and if possible increased. At that point, labour can all too easily be treated as just another means of making capital yield a return.

During the euphoric years, Western economies saw a marked shift towards services, mainly owing to the increase in jobs involving what Robert Reich called 'manipulation of symbols'. These jobs were created by profound changes in the economy and society brought about by growth in administrative, planning and research activities (in turn made possible by greater technological capacity to process, store and transmit information). The emergence of a separate area in which financial symbols were manipulated was just part of a more general development: the emergence of conceptual instruments that could control the tangible world. Validated and justified by a supposedly scientific paradigm, finance was an ideal area in which to apply the efficiency ethos. Here, at the boundary between the 'two worlds' – the worlds of mathematized finance and financial practice – the rationality of 'homo financiarius' attracted a growing throng of eager players.

Risk – fear of risk – a risk-free future

The main claim of modern finance was that it could control risk. According to the leading expert on the subject, Peter Bernstein, the notion of risk and the wish to control it typified this period and distinguished it from all earlier ones. Finance set out from two interrelated assumptions: (i) risk could be quantified, and (ii) disasters could be compensated for by money. Both of these were bold assumptions.[67] Risk could be properly quantified only if all the possible outcomes had been identified *and* assigned probabilities. Failing this, there was no reliable way to measure risk, let alone cover it. Finance could not provide a complete answer to this problem, but it could help to manage it by means of dispersion, diversification or insurance. As for the second assumption – that disasters could be compensated for by money – it was only partly true, for it was based on the idea that loss could always be measured in monetary terms. As the World Trade Centre attacks reminded us, no amount of money could compensate for loss of life. Koyré's 'two worlds' overlapped only in theory too. The idea of compensation more or less works if the object exposed to risk is fungible 'capital' expressed purely in figures, with no tangible content. The same could not be said if the figures had a clearly designated equivalent – a house, a factory, a school, or indeed a human life. The 'equivalent' in the financial area is purely arithmetical.

The spread throughout society of the idea that finance offers protection against risk had a profound impact on people's attitudes. A proactive response (coping with uncertainty to the best of your ability and responsibility) seemed to have made way for a more passive one ('covering your back' by taking out insurance). Rather than take specific steps to reduce risk, people now sought insurance cover. Risk cover through insurance and compensation probably had three effects: (i) secure in the knowledge that they were covered by insurance, some players no longer felt responsible for reducing their risk taking attitude; (ii) the illusion spread that all risks were insurable, and hence that there could be such a thing as a 'risk-free society'; and (iii) family and social risk-pooling mechanisms were dismantled in favour of financial insurance or management products, which in turn led to more individualized risk-cover strategies. Informal prevention and solidarity seem much less attractive now that people were being told risk could be controlled arithmetically.

The development of financial innovation in recent decades led to the creation of models for new risks and corresponding methods of cover or diversification. This interplay of supply and demand, fuelled by the nervousness of sated, ageing societies, brought great wealth to suppliers of financial cover. The new methods of risk cover were in fact transaction strategies – i.e. services – that needed constant updating, for risk assessments were changing by the minute. From the point of view of suppliers of such services or financial products, risk was by definition a perishable commodity and the market for it would never be saturated. It is surely no exaggeration to say that risk – or rather risk cover – was one of the best-selling products of the past quarter-century. Financial operators grew rich on it and made it their stock in trade. However, the limits of risk management were revealed when, as in mid-2007, markets seized up, liquidity evaporated and the true face of risk – or rather uncertainty – became pandemic, in other words impossible to diversify and so avoid.

From interest to greed: unbridled passion

The efficiency ethos was the cornerstone of the world view on which financialization was based. It held out new prospects to mankind, in terms of both technical performance and economic living standards. It focused entirely on the ratio of resources used to results achieved. Maximization of results with constant resources thus became an unchallenged goal. In the pursuit of economic or financial efficiency, the goal was stated purely in terms of how much money would be earned. In other words, it was a purely quantitative goal, with no direct link to the tangible world. This raised three issues.

First, such a world view was highly materialistic. The goal was stated in abstract, quantitative accounting terms, in a mathematized area that left no room for either man or society. If left uncontrolled, such a rationality or world view inevitably led to fanatical selfishness, in which other people were treated as mere resources or instruments in the pursuit of quantitative goals. Greed and the ruthless pursuit of gain could then easily become primary motivations that overshadowed all others.[68]

Second, the efficiency ethos reduced human relationships to a mechanical equilibrium of exchange. This made everyone a potential trading partner, and in that sense everyone was equal or indeed equivalent, interchangeable and ultimately quite anonymous. Greed made people see trading partners as potential suckers, as mere instruments in the pursuit of their own goals. A society where a pure efficiency ethos prevailed would leave no room for sentiment, sympathy or solidarity, not even for empathy. The most efficient attitude would be a predatory one.[69]

Third, in macrosocial terms, the efficiency-based world view very much depended on markets' claim to resolve conflicts. Markets were the scene of confrontations between selfish players. They resolved conflicts by assuming that all the players shared the same view of interest. As long as greed was curbed by reason – and hence moderation – and remained an interest rather than a passion, it helped markets to function smoothly.

In the days before the Invisible Hand, the social fabric had been sufficiently dense for greed to remain curbed by reason.[70] Now, as the social fabric was dislocated by the spread of the efficiency ethos, greed is unleashed. As current behaviour made clear, greed is now no longer an interest, but a passion. Uncontrolled by reason and impervious to all other considerations, it threatens to undermine the very structures whose cornerstone it had once been – markets.[71]

This excessive greed is now a threat to world finance. After observing the situation for many years, America's leading financier judged the situation sufficiently serious to issue a warning about what he called 'infectious greed'. In his speech, he offered a diagnosis: 'It is not that humans have become any more greedy than in generations past. It is that the avenues to express greed had grown so enormously.' Commentators were free to speculate on what he meant. Two things were clear: technical resources had given greed unprecedented leverage, and passions and desires had been rehabilitated by the contemporary moral discourse. This was particularly worrying since the market had claimed it would curb them, on the assumption that interest was superior to passion.[72]

The world view based on the efficiency ethos left no room for the idea of the common good, of each person's contribution to the harmony of the community. In the event of market failure, government could at most be called upon to compensate or regulate. This took place in the name of the public interest, where it was government's responsibility to defend, rather than the common good, to which all members of society contributed of their own volition from a sense of solidarity, or simply gratitude for having the good fortune to be part of a community.[73] As this sense of the common good was lost, the market, like the rest of society, became a battlefield where all the players are out to maximize immediate efficiency – remuneration as spoils of war – and then swiftly transfer it to the private sphere in order to build a fortress of lonely individual happiness. Taken to the extreme, the efficiency ethos threatened the very idea of the common good, for it created an unbridgeable gap between the sphere of acquisition, whereas efficiency was at its chilliest, and the sphere of use, where every form of generosity was possible.[74]

The previous pages have described the political, technological and philosophical context in which financialization could take place. They have also discussed the main players and their way of thinking. We are now witnessing the emergence of a new pattern, as though a new organizing principle is starting to govern life around the globe. The second part of this book will look more closely at how the new pattern works. The basic question – which will be examined in Part III – is ultimately very simple. To what extent are the changes now taking place conducive to the common good or, on the contrary, a threat to it – and, if the latter, what room for manoeuvre, means of action and responsibilities does each and every one of us have?

Notes

1   See, in particular, Jonathan Lear, *Aristotle: the Desire to Understand*, Cambridge, Cambridge University Press, 1988, 352 pp., and a forgotten masterpiece of precision that we owe to a Jesuit physicist: Théodore de Régnon, *La métaphysique des causes*, Paris, Victor Retaux, 1906, 663 pp.
    Methodological interpretations and commentaries on 'multimodal causality' are nowadays few and far between. The reason for this is the dominance – especially in the 'hard' sciences and hence, by extension, in economics – of

positivistic research methods based entirely on mechanical causality, which corresponds to Aristotle's 'efficient cause'. These methods set out to identify the cause, i.e. the act or phenomenon that immediately produces the effect in question. Only a systemic approach is capable of offering any resistance to this positivistic dominance, for it explicitly focuses on complexity, which by definition cannot be reduced to mechanical causality. Thus, in a sense, System's Theory may be seen as an extension of Aristotle's multimodal causality.

2. Multimodal causality can be used to organize disparate observations. See, for example, Paul H. Dembinski, 'Towards a Multimodal Causation Framework of Entrepreneurship', in *Estudios de Economía Aplicada*, Vol. 24, 2006, pp. 339–58.
3. Fernand Braudel, *Ecrits sur l'histoire*, Paris, Flammarion, 1969, 315 pp.
4. Paul H. Dembinksi, *The Logic of the Planned Economy: the Seeds of the Collapse*, op. cit.
5. Denis Piveteau and Jean-Baptiste de Foucauld, *Une société en quête de sens*, Paris, Odile Jacob, 1995, 300 pp.
6. Miroslav Novak, *Du printemps de Prague au printemps de Moscou: les formes de l'opposition en Union soviétique et en Tchécoslovaquie depuis 1968*, Geneva, Georg Editeur, 1990, 470 pp.; Miklos Molnar, *La démocratie se lève à l'Est: société civile et communisme en Europe de l'Est*, Paris, Presses Universitaires de France, 1990, 360 pp.
7. Bernard Lecomte, *La vérité l'emportera toujours sur le mensonge*, Paris, Editions J.-Cl. Lattès, 1990, 370 pp.; George Weigel, *Witness to Hope: The Biography of Pope John Paul II*, New York, Cliff Street Books, 1999, 1040 pp.; Michael Sherwin, 'Une anthropologie dissidente dans une théologie johannique: La vérité et la liberté dans la pensée de Jean Paul II', in *Car c'est de l'homme qu'il s'agit: défis anthropologiques et enseignement social chrétien*, edited by Paul H. Dembinski, Nicolas Buttet and Ernesto Rossi di Montelera, Paris, Desclée de Brouwer, 2007, pp. 37–56.
8. Raymond Aron, *Dix-huit leçons sur la société industrielle*, Paris, Flammarion, 1986, 378 pp.; John K. Galbraith, *The New Industrial State*, London, Pelican Books, 1967, 288 pp.
9. Dany-Robert Dufour, *Le Divin Marché: La révolution culturelle libérale*, Paris, Denoël, 2007, 342 pp.
10. Francis Fukuyama, 'The End of History?', in *The National Interest*, summer 1989, and *The End of History and the Last Man*, London, Penguin Books, 1992, 328 pp. See also the book by two members of the McKinsey Global Institute, Bryan Lowell and Diana Farrell, *Market Unbound: unleashing global capitalism*, New York, John Wiley & Sons, 1996, 268 pp.
11. Of course, the doctrine of the market-based economy has been strongly criticized, particularly by the multifarious anti-globalization movement. Most of this criticism is an extension of Marxist dogma and is tendentious rather than persuasive. However, there are several works that point to the radically new socioeconomic context of the euphoric years. Among them are the Lisbon Group's *Limits to competition*, Cambridge, MIT Press, 1996, 189 pp., Philippe Thureau-Dangin's *La concurrence et la mort*, Paris, Editions Syros, 1995, 215 pp. and Bernard Perret, op. cit. See also the article in *Finance & the Common Good/Bien Commun*, No. 15, summer 2003, entitled 'Globalization in crossfire'.

12 See the special issue of *Finance & the Common Good/Bien Commun*, No. 22, summer 2005, '*Homo oeconomicus*. Le mal-compris et le mal-aimé', and Michael Jensen and William Meckling, 'The Nature of Man', in *Bankamerica*, Vol. 7, No. 2, summer 1994, pp. 4–19.
13 The ideas referred to here took shape slowly. The circle that sprang up in the USA around Ayn Rand is symbolic of this; see Ayn Rand, *The Virtue of Selfishness*, London, Signet, 1964, 172 pp. and *Capitalism: the Unknown Ideal*, London, Signet, 1967, 348 pp. In the second of these books, the contributions by Alan Greenspan are of particular interest in view of his later career as head of the US Federal Reserve. See also No. 23 of the journal *Finance & the Common Good/Bien Commun*, winter 2005–6, 'The Enterprise: Matter and Form(s)'; Raquel Lázaro, *La sociedad comercial en Adam Smith: Método, moral, religión*, Pamplona, Ediciones Universidad de Navarra (EUNSA), 2002, 355 pp.; Christian Laval, *L'homme économique*, Paris, Gallimard, 2007, 396 pp.
14 Jean-Noël Giraud, *Le commerce des promesses*, Paris, Seuil, 2001, 370 pp.
15 Jean-Marie Thiveaud, 'La gestation séculaire et l'Etat dépositaire dans l'Europe des Lumières', in *Caisse des Dépôts et Consignations – 175 ans*, a special issue of *Revue d'Economie Financière*, Paris, 1999, pp. 9–31.
16 A phrase used by Robert Reich in *The Work of Nations: Preparing Ourselves for 21st-Century Capitalism*, New York, Random House, 1991, 340 pp.
17 Harlan Cleveland, *Birth of a New World*, Hoboken (NJ), Jossey-Bass, 1993, 292 pp.
18 Paul H. Dembinski, *L'endettement international*, Paris, Presses Universitaires de France (*Que sais-je?* series), 1989, 128 pp.
19 Paul Einzig, *The Euro-dollar System*, Basingstoke, Macmillan, 1977, 132 pp. Today's regulatory package known as 'Basle II' is designed to close the last of the legal gaps that allowed euromarkets to emerge in the first place. In this connection, see issue No. 21 of the journal *Finance & the Common Good/ Bien Commun*, spring 2005, 'From Bretton Woods to Basel II'.
20 This dilemma is not new, as witnessed in the clash in early nineteenth-century Britain between proponents of the 'banking principle' and the 'currency principle' (see Thomas Guggenheim, *Preclassical monetary theories*, London, Pinter Publishers, 1989, 199 pp.).
21 This extremely technical agreement may be seen as the starting point for a new system of international financial governance. In this connection, see issue No. 21 of the journal *Finance & the Common Good/Bien Commun* (*op. cit.*); the editorial deals with this document which in many ways has laid the foundations for a new Bretton Woods system.
22 Jacques Ellul, *op. cit.*
23 Richard O'Brien, *Global Financial Integration: The End of Geography*, New York, Council on Foreign Relations, 1992, 120 pp.; Charles Goldfinger, *La géofinance*, Paris, Seuil, 1986, 422 pp.; Frances Cairncross, *The Death of Distance*, Boston, Harvard Business School Press, 1997, 302 pp.
24 Georg Simmel, *The Philosophy of Money*, London, Routledge and Kegan Paul, 1978, 512 pp., Thomas Crump, *The Phenomenon of Money*, London, Routledge and Kegan Paul, 1981, 366 pp., and Jacques Bichot, *Huit siècles de monétarisation*, Paris, Economica, 1984, 238 pp. See also *Finance & the Common Good/Bien Commun*, No. 4, summer 2000, entitled 'The Break-up of Money', and Paul H. Dembinski and Christophe Perritaz, 'Towards the break-up of

money: when reality, driven by information technology, overtakes Simmel's vision', in *Foresight*, Vol. 2, No. 5, October 2000.

25 See *Finance & the Common Good/Bien Commun*, winter 2001–2, 'Will the Euro shape Europe?'.

26 In the lowest compartment of such a system are immigrant workers, as witness the high transaction costs charged to immigrants who send money home to their families. See *Sending Money Home? A Survey of Remittance Products and Services in the United Kingdom*, Profile Business Intelligence Ltd., 2005, 42 pp.

27 *Access to Financial Services: Strategies towards Equitable Provision*, Final study (5th International Conference on Financial Services, Gothenburg, 22–23 September 2000), Hamburg, Institut für Finanzdienstleistungen, 2001, 220 pp.

28 Paul H. Dembinski (leading contributor), *Economic and Financial Globalization: What the Numbers Say*, New York and Geneva, United Nations, 2003, 160 pp.

29 The book *Financial markets: mission impossible (op. cit.)* was one of the first to point out that stock exchange indexes could reflect an inflationary boom.

30 See Tommaso Padoa-Schioppa, *Regulating Finance, Balancing Freedom and Risk*, Oxford, Oxford University Press, 2004, 147 pp.

31 Paul H. Dembinski and Patrick Vauthey, 'La bourse dans la transition: l'expérience de Varsovie', in *Revue d'études comparatives Est-Ouest*, Vol. 25, No. 1, 1994, pp. 59–79.

32 *Enron and World Finance: a Case Study in Ethics*, edited by Paul H. Dembinski, Jean-Michel Bonvin, Andrew Cornford and Carole Lager, London, Palgrave, 2005, 320 pp. See also *Finance & the Common Good/Bien Commun*, No. 18–19, spring/summer 2004, 'Enron and the World of Finance'.

33 Such assets may nevertheless end up in small investors' portfolios, for example as parts of investment funds they have joined.

34 Some leading global banks are now considering setting up large 'in-house markets' for their own clients and operations. These global operators are now big enough for such arrangements to be economically justified.

35 Hyman Minsky, 'The financial-instability hypothesis: capitalist processes and the behaviour of the economy', in *Financial crises*, Charles P. Kindleberger and Jean-Pierre Laffargue (eds), Cambridge, Cambridge University Press, 1982, pp. 13–39; Charles P. Kindleberger, *Manias, Panics and Crashes*, London, Macmillan, 1989, 288 pp.; John K. Galbraith, *A Short History of Financial Euphoria*, New York, Viking Penguin, 1993, 113 pp.

36 Robert W. Parenteau, 'The Late 1990s' US Bubble: Financialization in the Extreme', in Gerald A. Epstein, *op. cit.*, pp. 111–48. This article shows how, since the 1987 crisis (which happened to coincide with the start of the Greenspan era), protecting financial markets has gradually become the US Federal Reserve's main concern – even at the expense of what used to be its sacred cow, control of inflation. Nine years later, in December 1996, Greenspan spoke in a similar vein of the 'irrational exuberance' of stock-market prices, triggering a temporary minor correction which earned him the wrath of leading operators. See also Tommaso Padoa-Schioppa, *op. cit.*, and the review of his book in *Finance & the Common Good/Bien Commun*, No. 21, *op. cit.*, pp. 115–18.

37 However sophisticated procedures may be, trust ultimately depends on human beings and human values. In other words, trust in institutions and mechanisms must be based on trust between people. Alan Greenspan's famous

speech of 15 July 2002 on 'infectious greed' is particularly relevant here (see chapter 1.2). See also the alarming book by Claude Bébéar, *op. cit.*, and John Plender, *op. cit.*

38 *Institutional Investors in the New Financial Landscape*, Paris, OECD Publications, 1998, 488 pp.; Philip E. Davis, *Pension Funds, Retirement-Income Security and Capital Markets: An International Perspective*, Oxford, Clarendon Press, 1997, 337 pp.

39 Tito Boeri, Arij Lans Bovenberg, Benoît Coeuré and Andrew Roberts, *Dealing with the New Giants*, Geneva Reports on the World Economy, Geneva, International Centre for Monetary and Banking Studies, 2006, 140 pp. See also *Ageing and pension system reforms: implications for financial markets and economic policies*, Bank for International Settlements, drawn up by a group of experts led by I. Visco, Basle, September 2005, and Gordon Clark, *Pension Fund Capitalism*, Oxford, Oxford University Press, 2000, 342 pp.

40 'World insurance in 2005', in *Sigma* (a periodical published by the reinsurance company SwissRe), No. 5, 2006.

41 Capgemini and Merrill Lynch, *World Wealth Report 2006* (one of a series published each year since 1996).

42 All the data (particularly GDP) are given in nominal terms, i.e. without any correction for inflation. Readers from non-English-speaking countries, in particular, should note that the term 'trillion' means a million million (10^{12}).

43 See Harold Parrish, 'Thoughts on the Path Forwards for Financial Services Regulation', *Finance & the Common Good/Bien Commun*, No. 4, summer 2000. See also Kevin R. James, *The Price of Retail Investing in the UK*, London, Financial Services Authority, Occasional Paper Series No. 6, February 2000.

44 Luc Thévenoz and Rashid Bahar (eds), *Conflicts of Interest: Corporate Governance & Financial Markets*, Leiden, Kluwer Law International, 2007, 416 pp.

45 Andrew Crockett, Trevor Harris, Frederic Mishkin and Eugene White, *Conflicts of Interest in the Financial Services Industry: What Should We Do About Them?*, Geneva/London, Centre International d'Etudes Monétaires et Bancaires and Centre for Economic Policy Research, 2003, 119 pp.; see the review in *Finance & the Common Good/Bien Commun*, No. 17, winter 2003–2004, pp. 76–7.

46 Arthur Levitt (with Paula Dwyer), *Take on the Street: What Wall Street and Corporate America don't want you to know. What you can do to fight back*, New York, Pantheon Books, 2002, 338 pp.; see the review by Catherine Sauviat in *Finance & the Common Good/Bien Commun*, *op. cit.*, pp. 65–6.

47 Douglass North, *Institutions, Institutional Change and Economic Performance*, Cambridge, Cambridge University Press, 1990, 159 pp.; Michel Crozier and Erhard Friedberg, *L'acteur et le système*, Paris, Seuil, 1977, 436 pp; René Girard, *Je vois Satan tomber comme l'éclair*, Paris, Librairie Générale Française, 2001, 254 pp. In another context, see also Jacques Bichot, 'La personne humaine aux prises avec les structures de péché', in Paul H. Dembinski, Nicolas Buttet and Ernesto Rossi di Montelera, *op. cit.*

48 Jacques Ellul, *op. cit.*, pp. 37–8 and 263.

49 Theodore Porter, *Trust in Numbers: The Pursuit of Objectivity in Science and Public Life*, Princeton, Princeton University Press, 1996, 324 pp.

50 Jacques Le Mouël, *Critique de l'efficacité*, Paris, Seuil, 1991, 184 pp.

51 Werner Sombart, *The Quintessence of Capitalism*, London, Unwin, 1915; republished New York, Fertig, 1967 (originally published in German as *Der Bourgeois*, Munich and Leipzig, Duncker and Humblot, 1913, 540 pp.).
52 Albert Hirschman, *The Passions and the Interests*, Princeton, Princeton University Press, 1997, 180 pp; Augustin Gonzalez Enciso, *Valores burgueses y valores aristocraticos en el capitalismo moderno: una reflexion historica*, Cuadernos Empresa y Humanismo, Pamplona, Instituto Empresa y Humanismo – Universitad de Navarra, Vol. 78, 2000, 45 pp.
53 However, other criteria can be envisaged. During the Second World War and the Cold War (when Ellul was writing), one key criterion was military efficiency. The fact that Ellul took little account of military goals may explain why he viewed the pursuit of technical efficiency as an autonomous force.
54 Max Weber, *General Economic History*, New York, Greenberg, 1927, 425 pp.
55 A prospect brilliantly described in Emile Zola's novel *Money*. In her book *Entrepreneurs, entreprises: Histoire d'une idée* (Paris, Presses Universitaires de France, 1982, 262 pp.), Hélène Vérin has convincingly shown that it was entrepreneurs who truly revolutionized society.
56 Jacques Le Goff, *La naissance du Purgatoire*, Paris, Gallimard, 1981, 500 pp. and 'The Usurer and Purgatory', in *The Dawn of Modern Banking*, Centre for Medieval and Renaissance Studies, University of California, New Haven & London, Yale University Press, 1979, pp. 25–52.
57 See Jean-Claude Lavigne OP, 'Antonin des Conseils, un théologien de l'usure au XVème siècle' and Edouard Dommen, 'Calvin et le prêt à intérêt', in *Finance & the Common Good/Bien Commun*, No. 16, autumn 2003, 'Interest Rates and Moral: Religious Perspectives'.
58 Peter L. Bernstein, *Against the Gods: the remarkable story of risk*, New York, John Wiley and Sons, 1996, 382 pp. See also Christian Walter and Eric Brian, *Critique de la valeur fondamentale*, Paris, Springer, 2007, 200 pp.
59 Jean Favier, *De l'or et des épices: naissance de l'homme d'affaires au Moyen Age*, Paris, Fayard, 1995, 380 pp. See also Jean Halpérin, 'La prohibition de l'usure et la naissance de l'assurance', in *Finance & the Common Good/Bien Commun*, No. 16, op. cit.
60 Harry Markowitz, 'Foundations of Portfolio Theory', in *Nobel Lectures, Economics 1981–1990*, Karl-Göran Mäler (ed.), Singapore, World Scientific Publishing Co., 1992, p. 279.
61 Cf. *Finance & the Common Good/Bien Commun*, No. 20, op. cit. See also Paul H. Dembinski, 'Le piège de l'économisme: quand l'arithmétique remplace l'éthique', in Beat Sitter-Liver and Pio Caroni (eds), *Der Mensch – ein Egoist ?*, Fribourg, Universitätsverlag Freiburg, 1998, pp. 227–45, and Etienne Perrot, 'L'homo financiarius dans son environnement culturel', in *Finance & the Common Good/Bien Commun*, No. 30, I/2008. See also Michaël Gonin, *The Social Disembedding of Business Theory and Practice*, Lausanne, University Lausanne, HEC, 2008, 127 pp.
62 Giorgio Israel, *La mathématisation du réel*, Paris, Seuil, 1996, 350 pp.
63 Alexandre Koyré, 'Sens et portée de la synthèse newtonienne', in *Etudes Newtoniennes*, Paris, Gallimard, 1968, pp. 27–43.
64 See Ernesto Rossi di Montelera, Ernesto, 'Epargne : entre l'exigence de libéralité et la quête de sécurité', in *Finance & the Common Good/Bien Commun*, No. 4, op. cit.

65 See the box on LTCM.
66 Hélène Rainelli-Le Montagner, *Nature et fonctions de la théorie financière*, Paris, Presses Universitaires de France, 2003, 225 pp.
67 Ulrich Beck, *Risikogesellschaft: Auf dem Weg in eine andere Moderne*, Frankfurt am Main, Suhrkamp Verlag, 1986, 391 pp.
68 Alasdair MacIntyre's book *After Virtue* (Notre Dame, University of Notre Dame Press, 1984, pp. 22–35) explains with reference to the prevailing emotivism (lack of rational justification for objective morality) why human relationships that are manipulatory cannot be distinguished from ones that are not.
69 Michel Villette and Catherine Vuillermot, *Portrait de l'homme d'affaires en prédateur*, Paris, La Découverte, 2007, 294 pp.
70 Raquel Lázaro, *op. cit.*; Paul H. Dembinski, 'Le piège de l'économisme: quand l'arithmétique remplace l'éthique', *op. cit.*
71 Viviane Forrester, *The Economic Horror*, Oxford, Blackwell, 1999, 156 pp. (originally published in French as *L'horreur économique*, Paris, Fayard, 1996, 186 pp.); Marion Gräfin Dönhoff, *Zivilisiert den Kapitalismus: Grenzen der Freiheit*, Stuttgart, Deutsche Verlagsanstalt, 1997, 222 pp.; Claude Bébéar, *op. cit.*
72 Philip Augar, *The Death of Gentlemanly Capitalism*, London, Penguin Books, 2001, 416 pp.; Charles Handy, *The Empty Raincoat*, New York, Random House, 1995, 288 pp.; Frank Partnoy, *Infectious greed: how deceit and risk corrupted the financial markets*, London, Profile Books, 2003, 474 pp.
73 David Hollenbach, *The Common Good and Christian Ethics*, New Studies in Christian Ethics, Vol. 22, Cambridge, Cambridge University Press, 2002, 270 pp.; Etienne Perrot, *Le Chrétien et l'argent*, Paris, Assas Editions, 1994, 122 pp.
74 This accounts for the current paradox of extreme efficiency at a time of unprecedented philanthropy.

Part II
A New Pattern

The first part of this report dealt with the motives behind financialization, its main players and the historical and institutional context in which it first emerged. The second part will attempt to identify the main features of the new pattern created by the organizing principle of finance.

It will look in turn at (i) the main components of finance (financial relationships and financial transactions); (ii) the tendency of present-day financial systems to perform more and more transactions; (iii) the quoted enterprises that are the main objects of these transactions; (iv) consumers as basic financial assets; (v) the financialization of individuals; and (vi) various other aspects of the financialization process. These six sections will provide the report's main diagnosis.

2.1
Financing Relationships and Financial Transactions

Financing relationships

Financial activity is based on a relationship between two supposedly autonomous parties, one of whom has temporarily idle liquidity and the other a plan to make use of it. Aristotle condemned what he called 'chrematistics', i.e. self-enrichment by hoarding wealth, especially species money. This, he said, was particularly damaging because it withdrew means of payment from circulation. The central argument in similar strictures down the centuries, particularly in the New Testament parable of the talents, was that accumulation of money (as a specific form of liquid wealth) reduced liquidity, which in turn could have an adverse impact on prosperity, growth and prices. In the seventeenth century Quesnay showed that the purpose of money was to irrigate the economic fabric, like blood in the human body. Without it, the economic circuit was disrupted and the creation of wealth would suffer. People were thus encouraged to make idle monetary resources available for both economic and moral reasons. Of the many kinds of financing, two deserve special attention: credit (with debt as its counterpart) and participation in investment projects.

Credit, and the debt that is indissociably linked to it, is probably the oldest and commonest form of financing.[1] Credit extends over time and consists of three distinct moments: it begins when the sum (or thing) lent is transferred from the creditor to the debtor, it ends when the sum or thing is paid back, and in the intervening period the debtor uses the loan and remunerates it, while the creditor is remunerated or waits and does without what he has lent. The two parties have asymmetrical roles: the creditor waits passively, while the debtor works actively to earn the resources that will enable him to pay back the loan. Credit thus enables the debtor to spend money he does not yet have. This inverted timeframe is useful in times of emergency (shortages, war, etc.) or when carrying out promising plans (investments, conquests, etc.). Although credit is both economically and morally useful because resources that would otherwise be idle are brought into circulation, it raises two problems – the problem of trust, and the problem of remuneration.

Credit depends on trust. This may be based on various things: guarantees, which may be material (security), personal (guarantors) or social (legal penalties, punishments for bad debtors or social pressure, as in microcredit operations), trust in the debtor as an individual (his word, reputation or honour) or – less usually – confidence in the debtor's plans. Trust has been expressed in different ways at different times and in different cultures, but credit relationships have always depended on it.

The problem of how credit is remunerated is far more complex. According to the Greek philosophers, money was unable to multiply – only living creatures could do that – and hence it could not produce more money. It was therefore contrary to the natural order that creditors – as passive lenders – should be paid back a larger sum than they had lent. This view was adopted, with slight variations, by all three monotheistic religions. In their various ways, they prohibited or strictly limited the charging of interest on loans. For centuries the Catholic Church totally outlawed the practice, arguing that money was not a factor of production but simply a means of payment. This attitude persisted until 1745, when the encyclical *Vix Pervenit* acknowledged that interest was justified in very specific circumstances. The same caution still prevailed in the 1983 Code of Canon Law, which tolerated interest-bearing loans without formally authorizing them. The question of principle thus remained.[2]

The Koran prohibits interest-bearing loans, which are thus ruled out in the Islamic world. Scholars have justified this on the grounds that the risks are asymmetrically distributed, to the debtor's detriment.[3] Judaism makes a distinction between relationships between Jews, in which interest-bearing loans are strictly circumscribed, and those with Gentiles, in which they are allowed.[4]

The Reformation, particularly the Calvinist version of it, made its attitude to interest-bearing loans clear back in the mid-sixteenth century. In his famous letter to Claude de Sachin – which some say laid the foundations of capitalism – Calvin introduced two new considerations. The first was that the purchasing power of the sum might be eroded while it was on loan. Calvin felt it was then morally justified for the creditor to receive nominal compensation. The second concerned the purpose of the loan. Here Calvin distinguished between loans made to help someone out by financing his vital needs, and loans made to finance investment. In the case of loans made to help someone out, it was still strictly prohibited to charge interest, for helping one's neighbour was a moral duty; but in the case of loans made to finance investment, Calvin authorized interest on the grounds that the lender had to wait and run a risk, and was therefore morally entitled to part of the debtor's gain from the investment.[5] It is important to remember here that investment projects take place over a length of time and are only meaningful if there is a prospect that they will make money. Although interest on loans made to help out one's neighbour has to come out of the neighbour's own pocket, interest on investment loans can – hopefully – be paid out of newly earned wealth, under conditions agreed in advance.

Calvin's analysis, which removed the moral objection to interest-bearing loans as such, paved the way for the development of the economic concepts of investment, financial calculation and credit-based finance. This encouraged the growth of financial intermediaries, such as banks, which engaged in the large-scale conversion of savings into credit (especially investment loans). In the nineteenth century, this change – which was not only economic, technical and institutional, but also moral – led to the rise (above all, as Weber's famous thesis indicated, in Protestant countries) of industrial capital financed by bank loans.

Credit-based finance is a medium-term asymmetrical relationship which enables the borrower to establish a value-creating momentum that will be maintained after the loan is paid back. Almost all investment projects are based on the prospect of long-term profit. However, credit-based finance places a heavier economic burden on a project than finance based on equity capital. The project has to generate sufficient funds to service the debt (interest and capital), allow physical capital to be replaced when it ceases to be productive, and finally yield a profit for its initiator. If the investment project can bear this threefold burden (debt servicing, replacement of physical capital and profit), it will be financially independent. If, on the other hand, it does not generate enough funds to replace the physical capital when the time comes, further credit will be needed. Credit-based finance thus entails a risk that the borrower will remain dependent on the lender – a situation many creditors are only too happy to exploit.

Apart from loans, the second way of financing projects is to get someone else to put money into them. This involves a partnership in which – very basically – some partners provide the funds and others carry out the project. All the partners are responsible for the project, they all take risks and they all live in hope that the project will succeed and earn them money. While credit-based finance is based on a contract between just two individuals, this type of shared finance is more complicated. In the nineteenth century, in response to the need to give it a legal form, a new entity came into being – the joint-stock company.[6] Since the risks were distributed symmetrically among the partners – usually in proportion to their respective input – there were no moral objections to this form of funding. Even more clearly than credit-based finance, it was designed to create and multiply wealth, and by definition could only be used for projects designed to create new wealth.

The great advantage of the joint-stock company is its ability to bring together a theoretically unlimited number of providers of capital, and hence to finance extremely large projects. It acts as a screen through which purely financial input is converted into shares in the project and the company. Unlike credit relationships, whose duration is predetermined by the payment date, modern joint-stock companies – except for certain closed investment funds such as venture-capital, private-equity or hedge funds – have no predetermined timeframe. They are therefore nearly always set up and financed with a view to the long term. The spread of joint-stock companies during the nineteenth century showed just how well they catered to the specific needs of industrialization.

The two kinds of financial relationship described above can be compared on the basis of three criteria: (i) duration, (ii) trust, and (iii) remuneration and distribution of risk. They both last a certain length of time, and hence entail considerable uncertainty as to the future. The length of a credit relationship is determined by a contract between two partners, and does not depend on the length of the project being financed. This imposes an external duration on the project. The loan may have to be repaid before the project generates enough funds to do so. With shared finance, things are different. The point at which the project is abandoned or the shareholders reimbursed depends entirely on its internal duration – on how soon it makes a profit. In the former case, financial duration determines economic duration; in the latter, the reverse is true. With trust, things are similar. In a credit relationship, trust usually depends on something external to the project (security, guarantors, legal institutions); only seldom does the creditor have enough confidence in the actual project to provide a loan. In the case of shared finance, trust depends entirely on the quality of the project and the partners' ability to carry it out. Like duration, trust is external to the project in the case of credit-based finance, and internal to it in the case of shared finance. The same applies to remuneration and distribution of risk. In the case of credit-based finance, both remuneration and risk are essentially external to the project, whereas in the case of shared financing they are entirely internal to it, for they depend on its success.

The previous discussion is based on textbook cases, but financial reality is more complicated. Shared finance and credit may be used jointly in two different situations. An individual may used borrowed money to help finance a project, or a joint stock company may (as often happens) use credit to increase its financial capability. In such situations, the risks, duration and sources of trust peculiar to each type of relationship become closely interwoven and interact dynamically.

From financing relationships to financial transactions

When partners establish a financial relationship, they implicitly declare – assuming they are rational – that they each believe their mutual undertakings to be balanced. This means they have received satisfactory answers to three questions that are inherent in all financial relationships: (i) whether payments made at different times will still be equivalent; (ii) what will be done if something unforeseen happens during the relationship; and (iii) how the initial terms of the relationship will be revised or adapted as time passes and things change.

Finance uses interest rates to compare the value of payments made at different times. For those due to be paid on a future date, the present value of the payment will be reduced by an amount equivalent to the interest they would have had to pay in order to borrow the same sum. The justification for this is that the further off the payment date is, the longer the lender will have to wait and do without the sum lent. The borrower, on the other hand, will be willing to pay more, for the further off the payment date is, the longer he will be able to make use of the sum before having to pay it back.

Dealing with the unforeseen is the essence of financial relationships, for the partners are by definition exposed to risks and uncertainty. Unforeseen events may concern the partners themselves, the purchasing power of the means of payment used in the contract, the general context, etc. All these risks call for specific types of protection which the partners will specify in the initial contract. In some cases, the terms of the relationship may even be changed halfway.

A series of instruments may be included in financial relationships to take account of the partners' specific choices:

- Interest rates: in practice, their use to offset risk merges with their use as 'compensation' for having to wait for payment. In theory, premiums or 'spread' are added on to the basic ('risk-free') rate, according to how risky the debtor is. Credit, lending and borrowing relationships are governed by interest rates. The level of interest rates or the way they are calculated is usually specified by the partners when the relationship is established. As mentioned earlier, interest rates are also the most morally controversial financial instrument.
- Shares in profits: unlike interest rates, which impose an asymmetrical obligation on one of the partners, shares in profits puts the partners on an equal footing with regard to risk. This is a principle that is specified *ex ante*, when the relationship is established, and continues to apply until the project ends. If things go wrong, the partners may lose their entire investment; but if things go well, they may in theory make infinite gains.
- Options: these are instruments or clauses that explicitly allow one of the partners to make unilateral adjustments either at predetermined points in the relationship or if predetermined events occur. An option is a clause in the initial contract whereby a special financial 'object' is grafted onto an existing relationship. This is why options are described as derivatives.
- Insurance: this is usually a financial relationship in its own right. It entails the payment of a premium that entitles the insured person to a predetermined compensatory amount if the adverse event covered by the insurance occurs.

Financial relationships – whatever form they take – are partnerships set up to achieve a more or less shared goal. The spread of such relationships has resulted in *ad hoc* legal arrangements which have helped them spread even further. They are thus one of the main vehicles of financialization. Financial relationships as described above are relationships between identifiable partners who know each other. All relationships last a given length of time and, in appropriate cases, this allows relations between the partners to be readjusted. There is one major proviso – the partners must agree. The famous master/slave paradox illustrates just how unstable a relationship between interdependent partners can be. The master may be the master, but his existence depends on that of the slave, so his power is not unlimited. Much the same applies to financial relationships, particularly credit relationships, as long as the partners remain dependent on one another. However, modern finance has managed to protect certain financial relationships against the risks of the master/slave paradox by allowing partners to give up their places in existing relationships to others. The possibility of quitting a financial relationship unilaterally by selling rights and obligations to a third party is an asymmetrical method of risk management that has been written into numerous financial contracts. Such a clause allows a transaction to take place while the relationship is still going on. It allows one of the partners to step out, his duties and obligations being taken over by a third party. In this sense it is an option granted to one party of the relation. The quitting partner and his replacement can then take account of any relevant new information that has become available since the relationship began, and decide on the terms of their trade. During the transaction, the other partner remains passive – and captive. Such replacement is only possible if the relationship assumes the form of a tradable 'object'.

The conversion of financial relationships into tradable objects – financial liquid assets – and the increasing number of transactions involving them are the basis of the financialization process. Before examining how this process has transformed world finance, we therefore need to look at financial transactions, which, by making partners interchangeable, have enabled the process to take full effect.

Financial transactions

Unlike trade in goods or services, financial transactions concern rights, commitments or promises relating to partners in a financial relationship. They enable one of the current partners in a financial relationship to get out of it, and allow others to enter relationships they did not initiate. Rights, duties, commitments or promises relating to financial relationships form a very special set of economic goods known as 'securities' or 'financial assets'. These tradable assets differ from other economic assets in three ways:

- Unlike goods and services, financial 'objects' cannot be used directly and hence have no actual 'value in use'. Their value is entirely monetary. It depends on their resale value, or the cash flow they generate, or both. They are recorded expressions of rights or obligations. As such they are part of their holder's wealth or assets and are recorded on the asset side of balance sheets.

- Financial 'objects' usually include one or more future commitments, promises or intentions, whereas other economic transactions mainly involve goods and services that are immediately available. In fact, the very use of money means that all trade involves a promise, for money itself is a promise of purchasing power that the seller will be able to exercise later on. However, the purchasing power of money is a 'social' promise, whereas financial 'objects' are personal, private ones.
- Financial 'objects' depend on sustained regulatory systems which put their seal on partners' intentions and promises and maintain a legal record of them for as long as the 'objects' exist. This is why financial transactions have spread in countries whose legal systems are very stable and where the rule of law prevails.

Securities or financial assets are the formal expression of underlying financial relationships in which the partners undertake to make payments or provide services at different points in time (the present, the future and in some cases the past). Unlike classic trade transactions, which are entered into and concluded in an instant, relationships that give rise to financial 'objects' are also, as we have seen, lasting relationships between the partners. The period that elapses between the beginning and the end of the relationship is marked by predetermined rights and duties that are laid down in the 'object' or 'security'.

Many financial assets allow the financing partner to transfer his rights and obligations to a third party at any time without consulting the financed partner. This means that assets can change hands without affecting the content of the underlying relationship. To take just one example, a enterprise or a government which issues a bond undertakes to fulfil its obligations towards whoever happens to hold the bond when it falls due. Similarly, shares in an enterprise can change hands without the other shareholders' agreement (unless the shareholders make a pact to prevent this). A clear distinction must therefore be made between financial relationships and financial transactions. First, all financial transactions presuppose the prior existence of a relationship, whereas the reverse is not true – some relationships cannot be transferred. Second, a given relationship can in theory be involved in an infinite number of successive transactions. Third, transactions usually involve the financing partner, be it the creditor, the provider of funds or the shareholder – the financed partner remains constant, and in some cases even passive. In other words, the partners in financial relationships do not all have the same opportunity to get out of them by performing a transaction. Fourth, a given financial relationship can in theory be split up into an infinite number of tradable objects. A whole range of tradable derivative instruments has thus been developed from a basically limited number of financial relationships. In recent decades, financial innovation has focused on the development of transactions rather than relationships. Finally, transactions make the financing partner anonymous, whereas the financed partner remains fully identifiable until the relationship is over.

2.2
The Spread of Transactions

Modern finance, as described in the previous part of this report, is based on the possibility of transactions. It assumes that asset managers can instantly buy or sell securities on more or less organized, liquid markets. The financial version of the efficiency ethos can only take full effect if there are numerous transactions. Financialization has spread through the economy and society by fundamentally altering the relationship between financial relationships and financial transactions. This change has affected not only the relative numbers of each, but also the underlying goals. Until the euphoric years, transactions were the exception rather than the rule – partners in relationships were expected to remain faithful. Transactions were essentially the by-product of relationships, whereas today – once again – the reverse is true.[7] Increasingly, financial relationships are established and projects launched purely with a view to a transaction. This is precisely what has led to the subprime crisis of 2007–8 and was dubbed the 'originate and distribute'. This shift towards transactions at the expense of relationships will be discussed below in terms of (i) how it has transformed financial systems, and (ii) statistical orders of magnitude.

The institutional process

Financial relationships recorded in financial assets that change hands during transactions are the raw material of modern finance. This raises the question of how such relationships, which by definition are interpersonal, link up to form a visible, measurable financial sector. Financial relationships provide a link over time between idle liquidity and demand for it (either for immediate use or for medium- and long-term production projects). They can thus be established by private individuals and families as well as by enterprises and public bodies. Each of these players goes in his life or operations through successive periods of excess and insufficient liquidity. Any community is made up of people with temporarily idle liquidity and people who temporarily lack it.

The primary economic and social function of financial systems is to establish relationships and perform transactions that bring the various players' situations into harmony while making optimum use of the available monetary resources. With varying degrees of efficiency, all financial systems thus channel idle savings towards the most pressing needs – including investment needs – and promise not only to maintain the savings but to increase them through economic growth.

It is now generally accepted that all financial systems perform the following resource-allocating functions: they provide payment services, they allocate savings and finance investment projects and, at the same time, they manage, value, consolidate and negotiate risks.

Though the situation varies from country to country, financial systems are nowadays essentially rooted in one of two main logics. The two logics inspiring financial systems use different methods and institutions to perform the general functions mentioned above. The basic distinction is between 'bank-based economies' and 'financial-market economies'. As this terminology suggests, the difference concerns the role finance plays in the economy as a whole, rather than simply financial techniques. Financial systems in bank-based economies focus on establishing and maintaining financial relationships, whereas in financial-market economies they focus on transactions, which bring liquidity to existing relations and which are their cornerstone. Both systems will be briefly discussed in the following paragraphs. Over the last thirty years, the financial-market model has expanded and in consequence become the universal model, nationally as well as globally.[8] As the following pages will show, this is not just a technical change. The relative positions of financial relationships and financial transactions have been inverted, profoundly altering the role of finance in the economy and society.[9]

For simplicity's sake, this brief analysis will disregard private financial relationships, sometimes also known as 'informal finance' (relationships that do not involve professional intermediaries but are established between parties on the basis of trust).[10] Until the recent expansion of financial intermediation, most financial relationships where internal as they did not involve specialized institutions. In bank-based economies, most financial functions are performed by banks, which are therefore partners in all financial relationships and most transactions. They collect excess liquidity and savings, grant loans to governments or enterprises and redistribute part of the income thus generated to savers. When loans are granted or savings deposited, banks assess the risks and set terms and interest rates accordingly. Such relationships are not based on 'objects' or securities – they are an integral part of the bank, which keeps a close eye on the relationship and intervenes whenever something unforeseen occurs. Banks are remunerated by the difference between the interest they receive from debtors and the interest they pay to savers. Bank-based economies thus leave little or no room for substitution of parties though financial transactions, but they do allow contracts to be renegotiated in the course of relationships.

In bank-based economies, risks are covered by carefully managing their financial relationships, payment dates and balance sheets (assets and liabilities). Banks do this by establishing and terminating corresponding credit and deposit relationships. Banks' remuneration ultimately depends on their ability to contain the risks inherent in their relationships and on differences between interest rates. Although a pure debt or bank-based economy has never existed, some countries have come closer to it than others. This is particularly true of 'continental' – or, to borrow a term coined by Michel Albert, 'Rhenish' – economies such as Germany, Switzerland, France, Italy, Spain and in some respects Japan.[11] The financial euphoria described earlier in this report has left a deep mark on the financial systems of this countries. The volume of transactions has greatly expanded, and relationships, which used to be established between identifiable partners, now tend to be anonymous and standardized.

In financial-market economies, financial relationships, as inscribed in securities or stocks, are the raw material for transactions involving and allowing for replacement of partners. When relationships are transient, the identity of the financing partner can change and hence no longer matters. When transactions take place, contract law ensures that sellers' rights and commitments are transferred to purchasers in their entirety. Relationships thus become completely impersonal, anonymous and mechanical, and are punctuated by transactions. The financed partner is no longer dealing with a single financing partner but with an anonymous mass of 'nomads', any of whom may be willing to enter into (or quit) a relationship with him. In financial-market economies, transactions thus tend to predominate over relationships. New financing (share emission or IPOs) accounts for a mere 3–5 per cent of stock-market trading in OECD countries. The bulk of stock-market activity thus involves substitution of parties in existing relationships.[12]

Although a pure financial-market economy has never existed, this way of organizing finance is part of the Anglo-Saxon tradition. In both the United States and the United Kingdom, savings and lending banks have always existed, yet both government and enterprises (even medium-sized ones) have traditionally preferred to obtain their financial resources from markets. Financial markets are thus a key part of these countries' economies, and in some respects of their societies. To paraphrase Marx, anonymous transactions on financial markets are the heart of a heartless world.

Over the last twenty years worldwide, financial systems have focused strongly on transactions at the expense of relationships. At national level, systems that have traditionally been based on relationships (bank-based economies) now leave more room for transactions. This has happened in countries such as Japan, France, Italy, Germany and Switzerland, where organized markets developed significantly in the 1980s and 1990s (see Figures 2.3 and 2.4). According to the International Finance Corporation (IFC), the number of developing countries with organized markets rose from about twenty in the early 1980s to over a hundred by the end of the twentieth century. At global level, a system of financial linkages has developed, based on global mega-markets and the local networks of major international banks, which perform traditional banking tasks at regional or local level and act as intermediaries between the local and global levels. All this reflects the growing predominance of transactions over relationships and the rapid financialization of the present-day economy.

The global financial system that is now emerging can – purely for purposes of analysis – be divided into two levels. Excess liquidity and savings at local level are 'repackaged' by mega-players and channelled towards global financial markets. Leading players – governments, major enterprises and retail banks – obtain their monetary resources from this financial 'wholesale market' (based on a network of organized markets and a high volume of over-the-counter transactions), and it is here, too, that shares in the world's economic giants are traded. This global market interacts constantly with the local level via globalized banks. At local level, institutions that have emerged from native traditions and practices act as 'retailers'. They collect savings and channel them to the global level, which they approach for additional finance. They also offer local investment products with specific risk/return profiles which may appeal to global investors. Only a quarter century ago the relative performance of the two types of financial system was the subject of vigorous debate. Today – at least for the time being – this is no longer the case, though the theoretical question remains.

Financial markets as sounding boards

Organized markets, which were discussed in Part I, are both the emblem and the linchpin of financial-market economies. In their shadow, however, are countless pseudo-markets which are far less transparent, and where most over-the-counter transactions take place. Organized markets (which are transparent and can be 'read' from the outside) not only put savings in touch with investment projects, but also represent a kind of collective intelligence known as 'market sentiment'. Such markets, if sufficiently transparent, determine the prices of financial assets and assess the associated risks.

The theoretical claim of financial-market economies to be superior to bank-based economies is based on the assumption that markets process information efficiently. As they determine prices, they supposedly pool all the available macroeconomic and microeconomic information and use it to produce a perfect instant picture of the risks and potentialities of the various financial relationships (shares or bonds) and the economy as a whole. Portfolio holders can then use this constantly updated information to adjust the composition of their portfolios by performing such transactions as they deem appropriate. These transactions generate new information that serves as a basis for subsequent portfolio adjustments. Things are different in bank-based economies. There is no market to 'synthesize' the circulating information, which is therefore more disparate, and often private or confidential. Lacking the escape route that transactions provide, parties in relationships use the available information to induce their partners to change their behaviour (where necessary), and banks use it to choose new relationships they are about to establish. Bank-based economies thus process information through completely different channels. The question of how efficiently they do so cannot be answered by standard economic methods, which are biased toward market efficiency as they analyse price changes. However, this does not mean they do so inefficiently.

The two types of financial system assess and manage risk in very different ways. In bank-based economies, partners keep a close eye on their relationships in case they need to intervene or renegotiate. In financial-market economies, the knee-jerk response to doubts or unforeseen events is to quit the relationship by selling the security. Increased risk initially leads to a fall in price, so anyone who decides to sell will incur a loss. The underlying player will then attempt to respond to the fall in 'his' price by changing his behaviour to 'reassure' the market. In bank-based economies, the process is quite different. While perceiving an increase of the level of risk, banks approach their partners and encourage them to change their behaviour. If things continue to deteriorate, the banks may have to take unilateral provisions, and if necessary write off one of the amounts concerned. In financial-market economies, risks are thus reflected by a fall in prices as soon as they are perceived, i.e. before they actually materialize; conversely, new potentialities are instantly reflected by a rise in prices. In bank-based economies, risks are covered gradually, in three stages: immediate action to encourage the partner to change behaviour, making provisions if the situation gets worse, and write off only if the risk actually materializes. The same applies to new potentialities: unlike financial-market economy, bank-based economies do not acknowledge improvements in results until they actually materialize.

Financial-market economies are thus far more dependent on perception, anticipation and changing states of mind than debt economies, which rely more on facts. By definition, the former are much more volatile and nervous (not to say neurotic), and more susceptible to herd behaviour or even panic.[13] Financial markets respond instantly to new information, which they magnify and disseminate, whereas in bank-based economies the processes are slower and more discreet. There is a fundamental clash of views on the pros and cons of the two systems. There are some (now a small minority) who consider bank-based economies more robust – less exposed to financial crises – because they manage risk discreetly and smoothly, without over-dramatizing things. However, the prevailing opinion nowadays is that the theoretical advantages of bank-based economies are outweighed by those of financial markets, which publicly identify, condemn and penalize risk as soon as it appears, and so prevent minor problems from degenerating into crises. The success of the debt-economy approach depends on the skill and integrity of the captains of finance and industry, on their ability to solve problems before they really arise. The success of the financial-market approach depends on its ability to withstand rumours, shifts of opinion and other types of mass behaviour that have no foundation in economic fact, and to maintain sufficient liquidity to keep markets operating and prevent panic in times of trouble. The events of August 2007 and October 2008 revealed just how fragile this mechanism is.

Accounting standards are the means whereby market price changes are reflected in savings. How fast this happens will depend on how these standards are formulated. The current trend is towards transparency that favours the almost immediate 'mark to market', which means that every change in market value immediately affects every account. By imposing market value as the basis for accounting, the new standards bind all financial players tightly to a heart whose every beat is instantly felt by the whole economy.[14] Regulators, concerned that financial statements should be as transparent and reliable as possible, have recently begun to focus on market value as the basis for accounting standards. In doing so, they have simply taken it for granted that markets are inherently truthful – a questionable assumption. This also explains their suspicion of financial players who may have more recent information and attempt to take advantage of it at the expense of others who have less access to it. Accordingly, the penalties for 'insider trading' are severe. Despite all these good intentions, the fact that market signals are transmitted almost instantly to even the remotest players makes the whole system more 'nervous', among other things because it eliminates the delays which previously allowed rumours and rash presumptions of risk to be dispelled before they did any damage. This subservience of accounting to market value is part and parcel of the financialization process. However, the need for transparency surely also extends to financial assets that are not quoted on organized markets and whose prices are therefore based on unvalidated estimates or assessments. In the period leading up to mid-2007, for lack of a properly working suitable market, the value of securities based on subprime mortgages was estimated rather than validated; it was discovered through a full-fledged market process. This raises a number of questions. What is the 'quality' of accounting information generated in this way? How 'truthful' is it? And how easily can it be used by unscrupulous operators to camouflage risks?

In the absence of a suitable market, unquoted securities or contracts are valued by rating agencies after supposedly careful scrutiny. The crisis of 2007–8 has raised serious doubts about the impartiality and competence and role of such agencies, which are by no means omniscient.[15]

Finance as intermediary

The fact that the world's finance systems are now based on the financial-market model rather than the bank-based economy model, and hence focus on transactions rather than the underlying relationships, creates four problems: (i) focus on the resale price above all else; (ii) a broader notion of risk; (iii) inversion of the relative positions of relationships and transactions; and (iv) disintermediation, and a growing tendency on the part of financiers to simply put potential partners in touch with each other.

By focusing on market value, i.e. resale value during transactions, rather than the cash flow generated by the underlying relationships, financialization makes financial assets holders extremely sensitive to market valuations. In their concern to increase the value of their holdings at all costs, they will tend to see things in the short term rather than the more uncertain medium or long term. They will be more sensitive to fashion and rumours, and at the first sign of trouble they are likely to sell or buy in the hope of making a quick profit. Furthermore, as their positions and reputations grow, some (or their asset managers) may be tempted to make appropriate rumours that will encourage other market players to buy or sell, and so shift prices in the direction they want. They may even be tempted to exert direct or indirect influence on society as a whole to make it behave as the markets would wish. Here again, the wish to perform short- or medium-term transactions may prevail over any concern for the long-term viability of the underlying relationships.[16]

When savers are only concerned about resale value, they will tend to take account of all factors that are likely to influence the value of their securities, including those not directly related to them. This broadens the notion of risk to include the behaviour of other market players. The school of thought known as 'behavioural finance' attempts to forecast the value of securities in the light of other players' behaviour. The emphasis is no longer on their 'true' value based on economic fundamentals, but on how their value is perceived and assessed by markets. The focus has thus shifted towards market psychology and away from economic content.[17]

The emphasis on resale value as perceived by the market (fuelled by the greed that is encouraged by the efficiency ethos) at the expense of underlying relationships may lead to relationships being established simply in order to turn them into tradable assets. In this connection the Bank for International Settlements (BIS) alerted on the potential pervasive consequence of the 'originate and distribute strategies' (O&D) in its 2007 annual report. Intermediaries who were hungry for profit and commissions had allegedly lured the most vulnerable segments of American society onto the mortgage market simply in order to repackage and to resell the loans over the counter to other financial institutions. The discovery in mid-2007 that these mortgage relationships were largely insolvent rocked the financial world. This case clearly illustrates how financialization has inverted the relative positions of relationships and transactions. In financial-market economies, transactions supposedly serve the underlying relationships by making them flexible and sustainable. In practice, however, they may end up exploiting them. All that then matters is resale value. With appropriate information and ratings, a number of precautions and a euphoric atmosphere such as the one that prevailed during the dot-com boom, the value of a security may become independent of the underlying relationship. During one such euphoric period, securities based on unrealistic projects were bought and sold for astronomic prices. If the link between relationships and transactions were to be permanently reversed as it happens in O&D strategies, the theoretical superiority of financial markets' logic over the debt-based one would be called into question.

The emphasis on transactions rather than relationships has encouraged some operators to create untransparent 'products' that are meant only for savers and earn their originators large commissions. They were created to be sold rather than held. Such practices increased distrust among professionals. In mid-2007, leading international banks stopped lending to one another, and hence trusting one another. Raising distress may lead the bank to cut back their traditional credit related banking activities even further, and to confine themselves to putting potential buyers in touch with originators of securities. This trend, known as disintermediation, creates a risk – condemned by the BIS as early as 2006 – securities whose risk/return profiles cannot be assessed are introduced by unscrupulous intermediaries into small investors' portfolios. Risks may thus spread beyond the circle of those who are in a position to understand and control them.

Relationships and transactions: statistical orders of magnitude

As financial systems have expanded, financial transactions have come to predominate over financial relationships. It is therefore not surprising to find that transactions are a key element in modern financial statistics and thinking. Before reviewing the main financial statistics, it is important to recall the conceptual and technical problems involved:

- The first problem is how to distinguish financial transactions from the underlying relationships. This is because most financial statistics focus on the tip of the financial iceberg, namely organized markets.
- The second problem is how to link up partial observations into a consolidated overall view. There is still no single, generally accepted methodology for interpreting finance activities on a macro level as a whole. There are approximate ways of recording flows of funds, but none of these is fully satisfactory or internationally accepted (although the intergovernmental efforts that have led to the establishment of the Financial Stability Forum are a step in the right direction). All this goes to show just how conceptually challenging an overall interpretation of present-day finance really is.

- The third problem is how to avoid double counting and omissions. In the absence of a single methodology, partial statistics may be gathered for institutional, fiscal, supervisory or regulatory purposes. Those gathered for purposes of market supervision focus on transactions, whereas those gathered for purposes of bank supervision focus on financial relationships (via banks' balance sheets).

However, despite these difficulties and reservations, individual observations can, if carefully handled, provide a statistical picture of the tip of today's financial iceberg.

The staggering expansion in financial transactions and relationships over the past quarter-century is shown below in a series of figures.

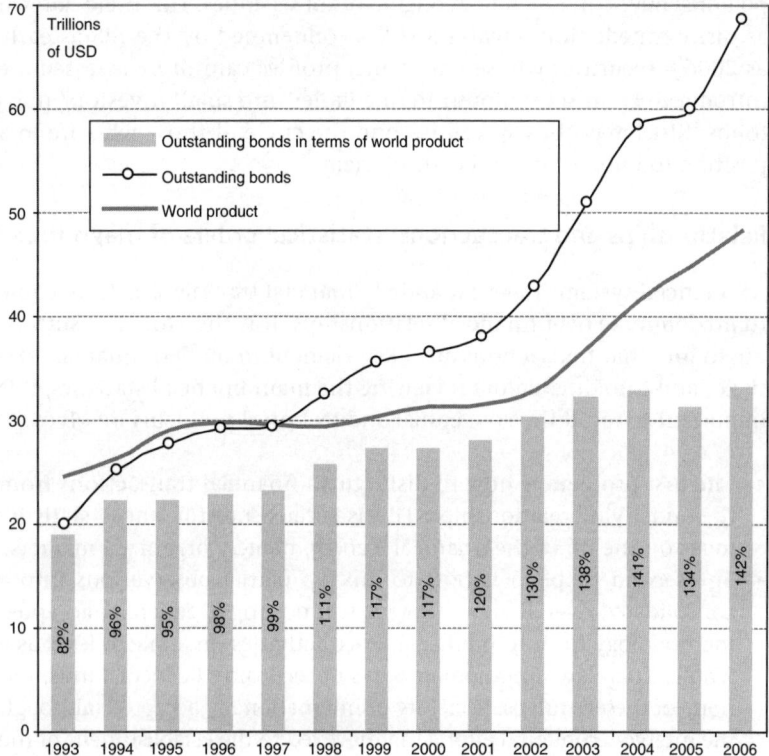

Figure 2.1 Outstanding bonds and world product
© Observatoire de la Finance, 2008 [www.obsfin.ch]
Primary data: International Finance Corporation

As regards financial relationships, readers are referred back to Part I, which discussed the mega-players (see Figure 1.2). Banks' total balance sheets are estimated as equivalent to about half of world product, those of private insurance companies to about a quarter of it, and the assets of the leading pension funds again to about half of it. To this must be added relationships arising from outstanding bonds (see Figure 2.1), now equivalent to almost one and a half times world product. As for financial relationships linked to joint-stock companies, only those quoted on stock markets can be assessed. Rather than total world stock-market capitalization, which is about equivalent to world product, Figure 2.2 shows the averages by region. Ten years ago this was equivalent to just over half of world product. Today, the value of all the

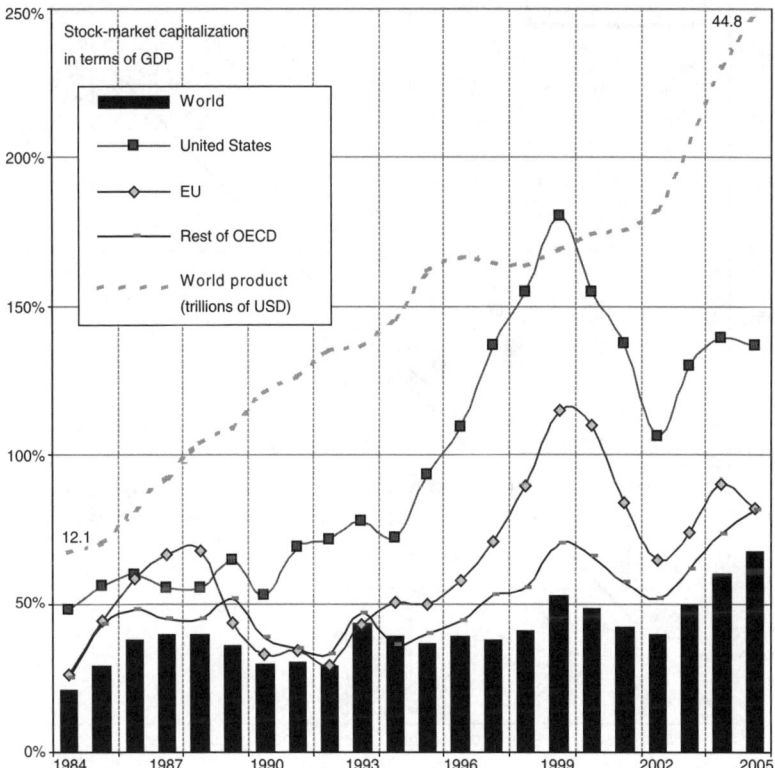

Figure 2.2 Average stock-market capitalization by country and world product
© Observatoire de la Finance, 2008 [www.obsfin.ch]
Primary data: International Finance Corporation

financial relationships in the world can thus be very approximately estimated at about four times world product. Ten years ago, it was about twice the then level of world product. In ten years, the volume of financial relationships may thus have doubled in relative terms compared with world product.

As regards the volume of transactions, Figures 2.3 and 2.4 speak for themselves. They show the changes in capitalization and the value of transactions both expressed in terms of GDP for the world's twenty-five leading stock markets. The x-axis shows the capitalization of each stock market in terms of that country's GDP, while the y-axis does the same for the value of transactions. The plot for each market between 1995

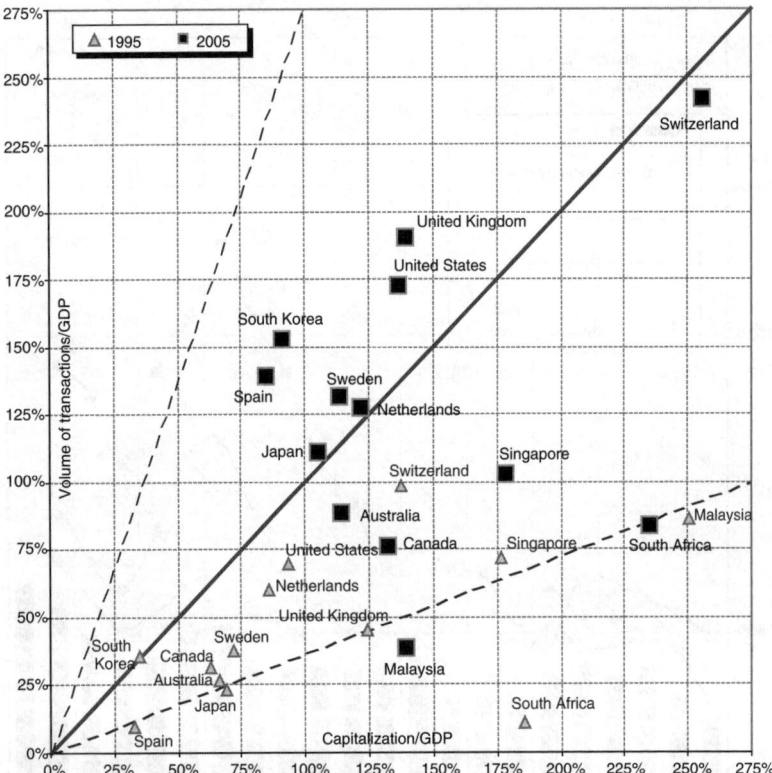

Figure 2.3 Stock-market growth in terms of capitalization and transactions between 1995 and 2005 (fast-moving countries)
© Observatoire de la Finance, 2008 [www.obsfin.ch]
Primary data: International Finance Corporation

and 2005 shows how fast capitalization and the value of transactions have expanded. Figure 2.3 provides an overall view, on a scale from 0 to 275 per cent. Figure 2.4 zooms in on the 0 to 100 per cent quadrant of Figure 2.3 and only includes the countries whose plots fit inside it.

The diagonal line of the two figures mark a theoretical expansion path in which the ratio of capitalization to transactions remains exactly one. This means that each security on such a market changes hands once a year on average. All the markets whose development lies on a straight line passing through the origin maintained a stable ratio of capitalization to transactions as they developed. This was more or less true

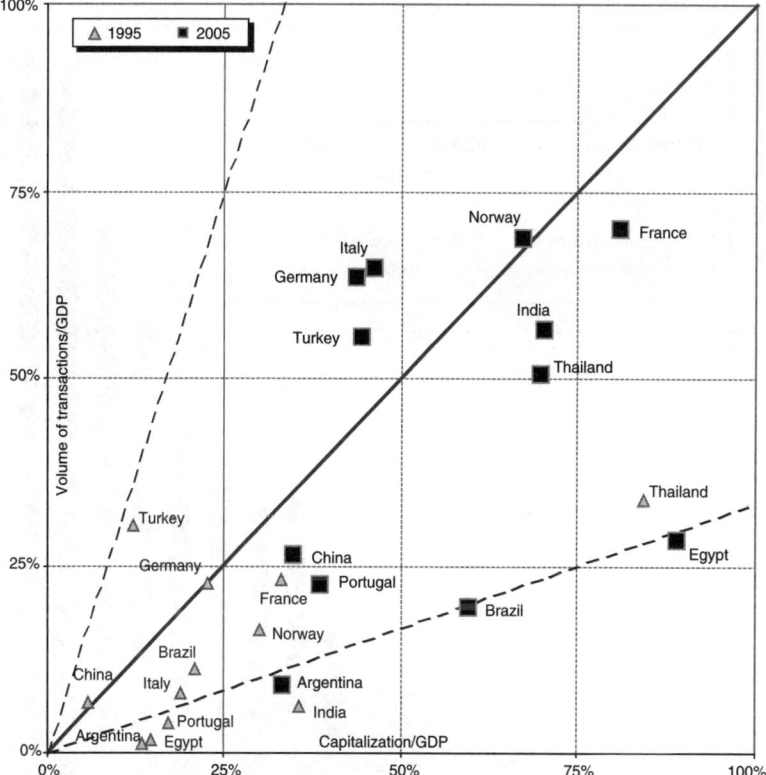

Figure 2.4 Stock-market growth in terms of capitalization and transactions between 1995 and 2005 (slow-moving countries)
© Observatoire de la Finance, 2008 [www.obsfin.ch]
Primary data: International Finance Corporation

of countries such as Canada and Switzerland as shown in Figure 2.3 and France, China, Argentina and Egypt in Figure 2.4. Two countries, Malaysia and Thailand, were unusual: their stock markets contracted in GDP terms in the wake of the Asian crisis (in terms of both capitalization and transactions in the case of Malaysia, and in terms of capitalization only in the case of Thailand). South Korea, another country affected by the Asian crisis, increased in terms of both capitalization and transactions.

The changes in leading world markets such as London, New York or Tokyo should be emphasized: their rise was almost vertical, which means that the volume of transactions expanded far faster than capitalization. In London and Tokyo the volume of transactions increased

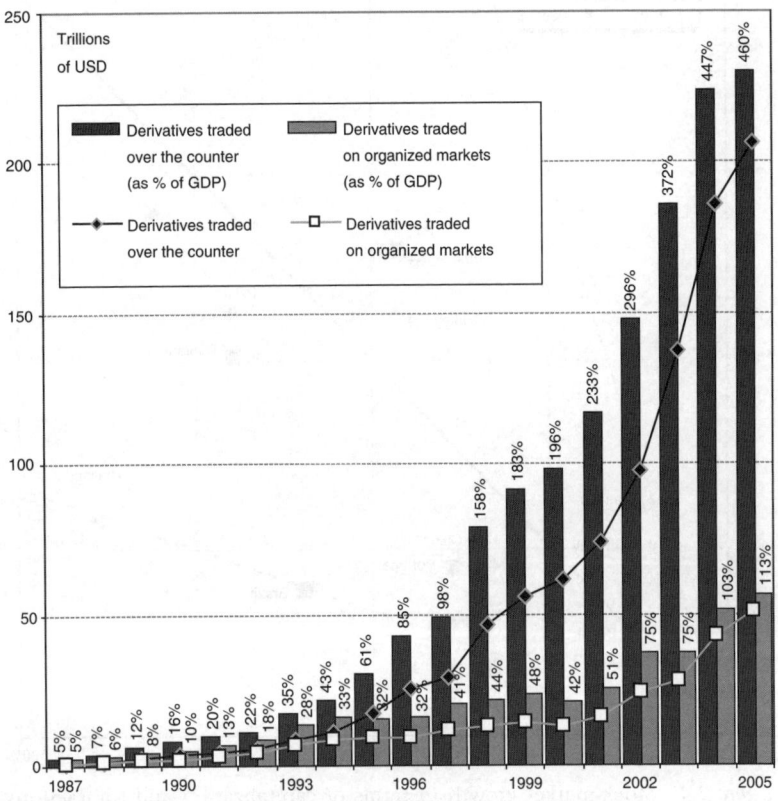

Figure 2.5 Annual volume of transactions in derivatives
© Observatoire de la Finance, 2008 [www.obsfin.ch]
Primary data: Bank for International Settlements

fourfold in GDP terms. Of the smaller markets, Spain and South Africa also saw an explosive increase in transactions. If transactions are increasing faster than capitalization, this means that the rate of rotation of securities is increasing – for example, they are changing hands four times a year, rather than once a year as would have been the case if their trajectory had been diagonal.

Following this brief analysis of stock markets, we may conclude that the value of stock-market transactions is today more or less equivalent to world product, compared with about one-third of it in 1995. To these stock-market transactions must be added those involving bonds, which – in the absence of estimates – will be assumed to equal the amounts outstanding. The other two figures (2.5 and 2.6) show the

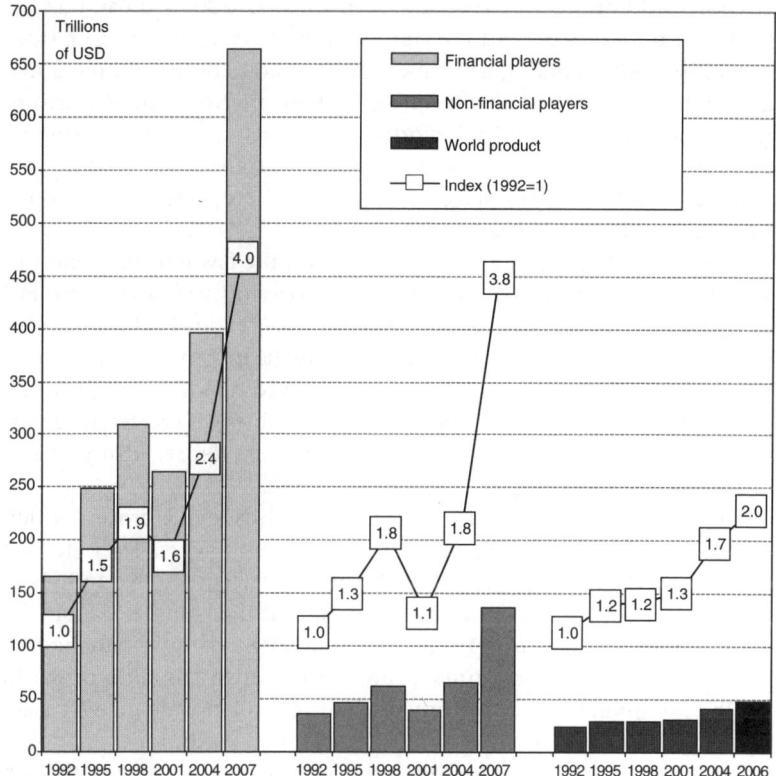

Figure 2.6 Annual volume of foreign-exchange transactions
© Observatoire de la Finance, 2008 [www.obsfin.ch]
Primary data: Bank for International Settlements

development of transactions in private assets: derivatives – in notional, i.e. underlying value (Figure 2.5) – and foreign-exchange transactions (Figure 2.6). Transactions in derivatives rose from the equivalent of world product to six times that, while foreign-exchange transactions rose from nine to eighteen times world product. In the case of derivatives, most of this increase involved over-the-counter transactions, whereas in the case of foreign exchange it involved transactions between financial players.

To recapitulate, in 1995 the volume of financial transactions was two and a half times world product not including foreign-exchange transactions, and eleven and a half times including them. By 2005 these figures had risen to seven and twenty-five times respectively. If these orders of magnitude are compared with those concerning relationships – twice world product in 1995 and four times in 2005 – it can be seen that over ten years the ratio of transactions to relationships rose from one to two not including foreign-exchange transactions, and remained at five including them. This means that there are two dollars' worth of transactions for every dollar's worth of relationships in the course of a year. Put very simply, in every relationship a transaction leading to a change of partners takes place twice a year, whereas ten years ago this happened only once a year.

The orders of magnitude indicated here for the last ten years point to a profound change in economic thinking. Leaving aside the turmoil of foreign-exchange transactions, in 1995 one unit of added value (recorded as annual world product) was created by relationships worth twice as much. On average, those relationships changed hands just once in the course of the year. In 2005, the same added value was created by a network of relationships that was relatively twice as dense, with partners changing twice a year.

These statistics only cover the most recent decade of a process which undoubtedly began at the start of the euphoric years. They do not allow the process to be traced back with any accuracy. Nonetheless, some as yet fragmentary estimates suggest that the volume of financial transactions in the early 1970s was equivalent to less than half of world product. If these estimates are correct, then the ratio of world product to financial transactions (including foreign-exchange transactions) has increased by a factor of fifty! In other words, for every dollar of added value that is created today, twenty-five dollars are traded on financial markets, compared with just fifty cents thirty-five years ago! In other words the 'financial intensity' of world product increased significantly in the last decades.

Most financial transactions involve economic mega-players and financial markets in developed countries. In absolute terms, the expansion of finance in emerging countries has been insignificant. The value of global transactions (not including foreign exchange) is today equivalent to about twenty times the OECD countries' GDP.

Despite several crises that have rocked world finance over the last three decades, the general tendency of the system's transactional capacity to expand has not essentially altered. From the debt crisis of the 1980s, the Asian and Russian crises and the repeated crises in Latin America to the collapse of players such as LTCM or Enron, the response has always been to create new opportunities for transactions and new types of assets.

Financial intermediaries have become veritable mega-players in the world economy because of the volume of resources they are able to mobilize, their global presence and the range of services and skills they can provide. However, the figures suggest that their role as 'relationship builders' may have become somewhat subordinated to the more profitable role of 'transaction operators'.

The recent explosive growth in the volume of financial transactions suggests that the 'risk management, assessment and distribution' function of the global financial system is getting too large.

Finance and the rest of the economy

A distinction is commonly drawn by non-economists between 'finance' and 'the real economy'. Convenient though this distinction may be, it has no empirical basis, for two interrelated reasons. First, finance is an economic activity like any other – it generates added value and thus contributes to national product. Indeed, in most countries it is one of the most productive sectors of the economy in terms of added value per employee. Second, finance and the real economy are closely linked. Financial events (changes in rates or asset prices) influence the behaviour of players in the 'real' sphere (households, enterprises or government), whereas the reverse is not always true. Paradoxically, despite its crucial importance to the economy, this interdependence between the two spheres is scarcely appreciated by economic researchers and has never been fully explained. This very uncertainty about how finance and the real economy are linked explains central banks' hesitation about how best to deal with financial upheavals, particularly in 2008.[18] In the absence of accurate studies, opinions differ: some see finance as a form of tyranny, while others see it as the mirror of the real economy. In its 2007 annual report, the Bank for International Settlements stated in unusually clear terms that economics was not an exact science, and that responses to the question of how finance and the economy were linked were determined by historical circumstance and political choice.[19] The alternative set out in the title of the present report points to one of the most important socioeconomic dilemmas now facing society. Do we want finance to be servant or deceiver? Do we want to set goals for finance, or let finance set them for us? Do we want finance to serve the real economy, or take complete control of it?

Before examining this issue in Part III, we need to look more closely at the hypothesis that financialization is an emerging organizing principle that is deemed to make our socioeconomic system more coherent and efficient. Such process would by no means remain confined to the financial sphere, but would extend its influence to the real economy and from there to the daily lives of each and every one of us. Thus, although authors such as Maurice Allais have compared financial markets to casinos, the close, and unstable, links between finance and the real economy mean that this analogy has its limits.[20]

Despite differing definitions of the financial sector, finance's contribution to national product in the leading OECD countries has been estimated at around 5–10 per cent, with countries such as Luxembourg, Switzerland and the United Kingdom at the upper end of this range or even above it.[21] In most countries this figure has increased – by two or three percentage points – over the past decade. The added value generated by the financial sector consists of the salaries and other rewards that it pays to labour, its remuneration of equity capital and the interest it pays. In macroeconomic terms, this added value is a cost – an operating cost – that financial services charge to the economy and society as a whole. In return, the economy and society delegate to the financial sector responsibility for ensuring fluid payments, for collecting savings and channelling them towards investment projects by establishing the necessary relationships, and for managing the risks that threaten accumulated savings by performing appropriate transactions.[22] The upheavals caused by financialization have clearly increased this macroeconomic cost. This raises two questions.

The first concerns the contribution that finance makes to economic growth. Two arguments have been advanced, particularly in development literature, to justify the growth of finance in terms of its contribution to national product: 'financial deepening' and increased economic efficiency. Despite numerous attempts to confirm either of these hypotheses with the help of quantitative data, the results remain inconclusive, and a recent article concluded that the jury was still out on the subject. The main problem is one of causality: is the expansion of finance the cause of growth, or merely one of its effects?[23]

The second question follows on from the first. If finance – especially in its present form, financial markets – is a luxury that wealthy, sated societies indulge in to ensure their material survival (or convince themselves they are doing so), what is the maximum price they could afford to pay for such a service? According to statistics provided by the Swiss Bankers Association, banking in the strict sense of the term (deposits and loans) accounts for about a third of the total value added by the sector. This means that other two-thirds come from asset management;[24] however, since this is a Swiss speciality, the share assigned to it may be somewhat exaggerated. Assuming that *half* of financial added value in OECD countries comes from transactions and management of accumulated savings, the annual cost of this service can be put at 2–3 per cent of those countries' GDP. Set against the volume of savings mentioned in Part I, which is close to the level of their annual GDP, the cost would be around 2 per cent a year. In order for savers to consider this expenditure worth their while, the additional assets value generated by financial markets needs to be a multiple of the cost of the service. Given that pension funds are assumed to need a net annual rate of return of about 4 per cent to remain demographically viable, we must conclude that financial-market economies are only viable if transactions are able to generate more than 6 per cent of gross returns on portfolios, year after year.[25]

A continuing increase in stock-market prices and financial return is only conceivable if two theoretical conditions are met. First, there must a constant influx of liquidity that keeps prices rising. However favourable the economic conditions, no such rise can last forever. Second, listed enterprises must attain productivity levels that will enable them to keep growing a good deal faster than the rest of the economy.

If nothing else, Figure 2.7 certainly provides food for thought. Focusing on the American economy, it compares four trends over a 42-year period. It uses the cumulative return method, which enables the return on one dollar (1964 = 1) invested at the start of the period to be measured at any given date in nominal terms. It is assumed here that any payments in the form of dividends, profits or remuneration on loans are immediately reinvested in the same instrument. The four trends compared here are:

- American GDP. It is assumed that one dollar is invested in a medium-sized, unquoted enterprise whose profits (which are immediately reinvested) grow at the same rate as the American economy.

- Ten-year US Treasury bonds: here again, the return on the bonds is cumulated to indicate their immediate reinvestment.
- The total return on stock-market investment, calculated on the basis of the Standard & Poor's 500 (S & P 500) index. The value of this investment is increased by reinvested dividends and rising stock-market prices.
- The 'internal' return of quoted enterprises (the same as those listed on the S & P 500), based on the growth in their profits (including dividends). Like a growth rate in the economy, the rate of growth in profits is cumulated to give an idea of what the enterprises' internal value would be if they were not quoted.

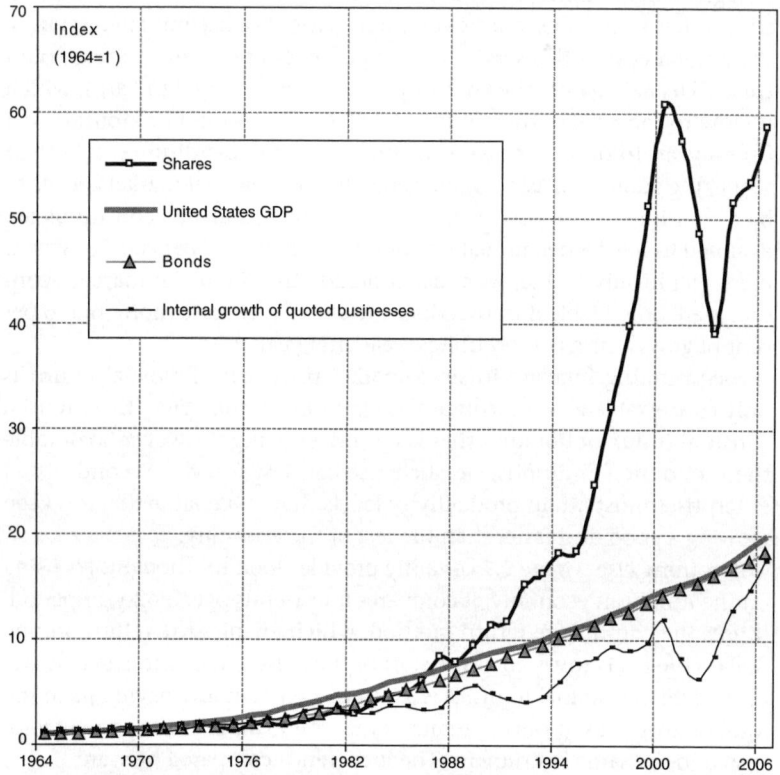

Figure 2.7 Economic and financial rates of return in the American economy
© Observatoire de la Finance, 2008 [www.obsfin.ch]
Primary data: Thomson Financial, and Professor Robert Shiller (http://www.irrationalexuberance.com)

Figure 2.7 reveals a huge difference between the 42-year cumulative returns on stock-market investments (a growth factor of 59) and the other three investment vehicles (a factor of around 20). This suggests that the rise of finance has driven quoted securities up to levels that bear no relation to the performance of the country's economy, or the performance of debt instruments, or the internal performance of the enterprise the securities represent.

The stock-market index is thus the vehicle with the most impressive results, which are unrelated to bonds or to enterprises representative of the US economy. There are two theoretical explanations for this, which have already been mentioned: (a) quoted enterprises are by far the best economic performers and 'pull' the rest of the economy along with

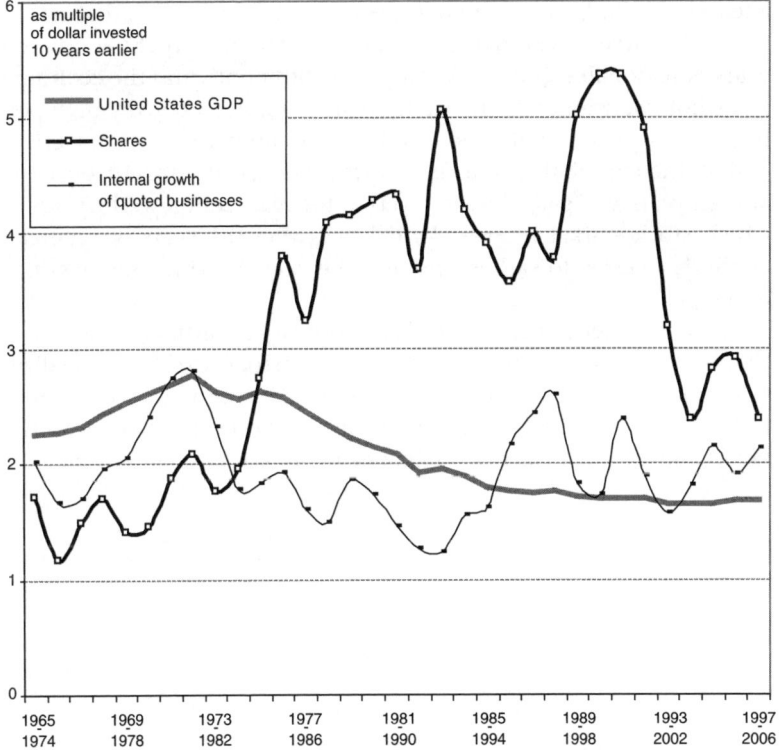

Figure 2.8 Ten-year rates of cumulative return (mobile average)
© Observatoire de la Finance, 2008 [www.obsfin.ch]
Primary data: Thomson Financial and Robert Shiller

them – all the more plausible because they are global enterprises and the sources of their performance extend well beyond the US economy; (b) these types of investment are assessed by different methods, particularly because the financialized 'form' of the listed enterprises' securities is remunerated by a consistent liquidity premium.

Some answers to these questions are provided by Figure 2.8, which compares two cumulative return curves relating to the same group of enterprises (the S & P 500). On the one hand there is the stock-market perspective (total return), and on the other the 'internal' (or real) perspective which only takes account of rates of growth in profits. Two things stand out clearly: the huge difference referred to above, and the fact that in terms of purely economic performance these particular enterprises are below the national average. This impression is confirmed by Figure 2.8, which compares cumulative returns, this time only over a ten-year period, using a mobile average and which shows that return on stock-market investments fluctuated greatly over that period. Ten years of reasonable growth as compared with bonds and the economy as a whole were followed by twenty years of unprecedentedly high performance – which collapsed like a soufflé after the dot-com crisis. Today, the cumulative returns on stock-market investment over the last ten years are again close to levels in the real economy. The years in which stock-market returns skyrocketed were the years of financial euphoria referred to earlier, and also the years in which savings silos developed.

As already mentioned, quoted enterprises – or rather the securities that represent them – are an essential counterpart to the financialization process. It is here that finance and the real economy become interlinked. Which enterprises are they, and how do they respond to the savers and asset managers who finance them or hold shares in them?

2.3
Very Large Corporations: The Vehicles of Financialization

How and why have quoted corporation adapted to the predominance of transactions over relationships? How have they responded to the advent of the nomadic anonymous shareholder? How has financialization affected them? We will start by looking at the economic and financial influence of the leading quoted corporation. This will be followed by a discussion of the main changes taking place within them. The next section will examine how this process has been communicated to the corporations' clients. This will make clear that financialization has now reached the point where it affects each and every one of us, as savers, consumers and workers who create added value.

Very large corporations (VLCs)

The shares of some 50,000 enterprises are quoted on world stock markets. However, in 2005 the top 2,000 financial and industrial enterprises in terms of stock-market value accounted for almost half of world capitalization, and the top 1,000 for a full 46 per cent of it. As Figures 2.10 to 2.12 below make clear, the equivalent figure on leading markets (US, Europe and Japan) is close to 80 per cent. Stock markets thus focus on a mere 2 per cent of quoted enterprises – a tiny proportion of the world's economic players.[26]

The lack of data on large corporations makes them hard to analyse economically. First, they are not covered by national statistics, for their activities extend across national borders. Second, the annual reports they produce for their shareholders and the authorities are drawn up from an accounting or financial perspective rather than an economic one. Finally, beyond accounting data, their reports are descriptive and hence impossible to sum up in statistical terms. However, although accounting data do not fully meet the needs of economic analysis, no other source can give even an approximate idea of how financialization is permeating these enterprises and subsequently reorganizing the economy and society. The following analyses are based on various accounting and financial databases, particularly Thomson Financial.[27]

The first illustration concerns the 800 largest non-financial enterprises' share of world product. According to estimates by the Observatoire de la Finance (see Figure 2.9), their share is about 11 per cent – equivalent to that of the world's 144 poorest countries. This contribution is made with the help of thirty million staff worldwide (an average of just over 35,000 per enterprise), whereas the active population

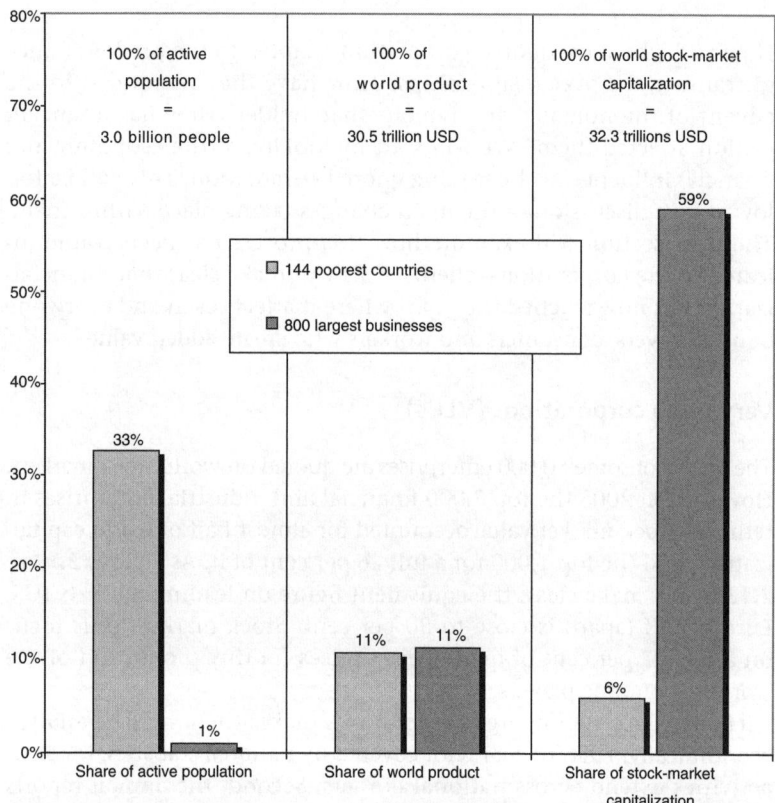

Figure 2.9 Very large corporations and the poorest countries: a comparison (2000) © Observatoire de la Finance, 2008 [www.obsfin.ch]
Primary data: Thomson Financial, Datastream Advance; World Bank, World Development Indicators; ILO, Economically Active Population 1950–2010

in the 144 poorest countries is more than one billion – almost thirty times as many people. This difference reveals the huge abyss in labour productivity between the powerhouses of the world economy and the developing countries. The difference in average productivity between these enterprises and the OECD countries is substantially less but still considerable, especially as a growing proportion of their staff are located outside the OECD zone. Figures 2.10 to 2.12 present equivalent data for each of the world's leading markets: Europe, the United States and Japan.

These very large corporation have also spearheaded globalization.[28] Over the past half-century they have developed a vast network of branches through which they constantly reorganize their value-generating activities as efficiently as possible. Rough estimates suggest that they may

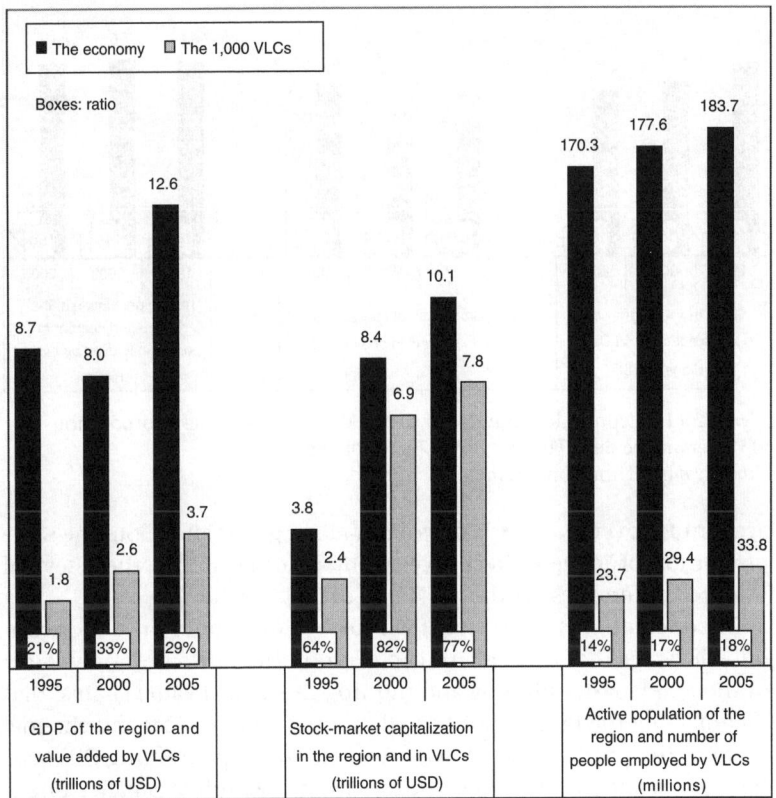

Figure 2.10 Economic influence of the 1,000 largest European corporations
© Observatoire de la Finance, 2008 [www.obsfin.ch]
Primary data: Thomson Financial

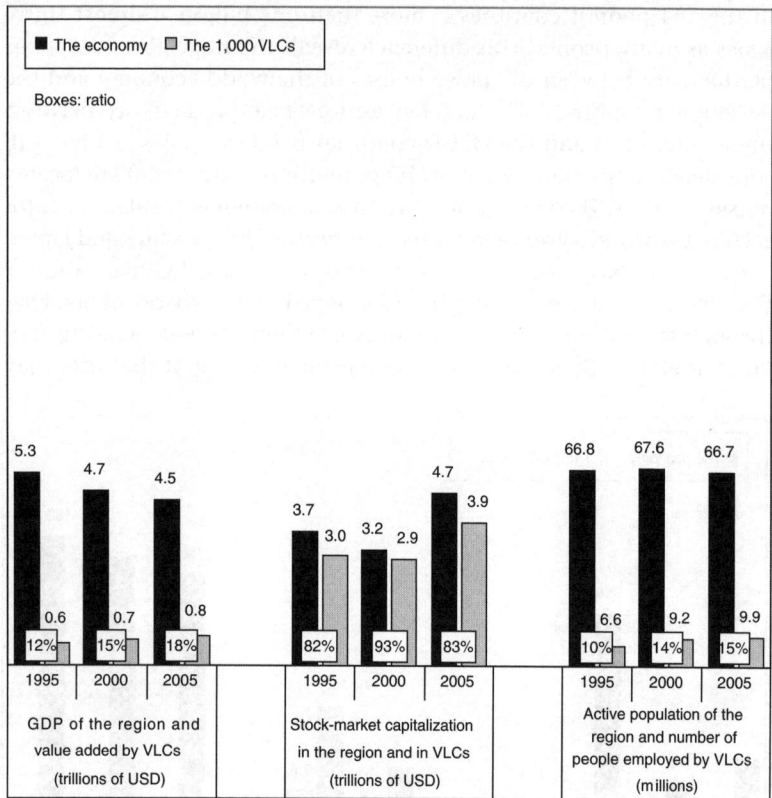

Figure 2.11 Economic influence of the 1,000 largest Japanese corporations
© Observatoire de la Finance, 2008 [www.obsfin.ch]
Primary data: Thomson Financial

account for over two-thirds of world trade in goods and about the same proportion of foreign direct investment. In other words, these several hundred enterprises are the backbone of globalization.

To conclude this rapid statistical survey, we should note the economic leverage that these giants can exert on the world economy. Most of them are masterminding and running the 'global value chains' that manufacture the most sophisticated products and services and channel them to their final users.[29] VLCs are not alone in performing this task; they are helped by countless other enterprises (often smaller ones), either as suppliers of components and services or as distributors. The turnover of non-financial VLCs gives an idea of their leverage upon suppliers, for besides the added value generated by the VLC, turnover

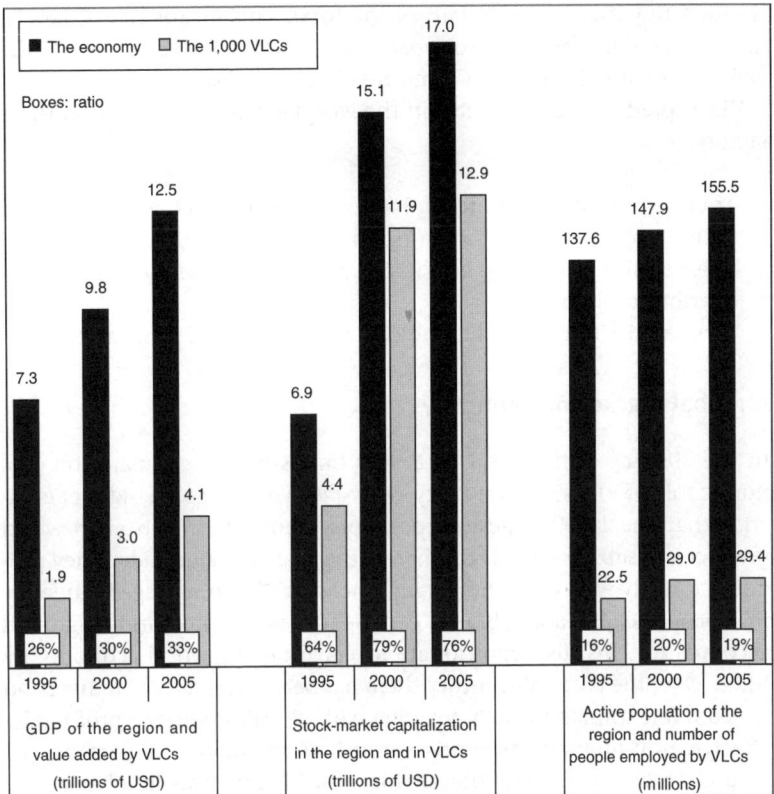

Figure 2.12 Economic influence of the 1,000 largest American corporations
© Observatoire de la Finance, 2008 [www.obsfin.ch]
Primary data: Thomson Financial

includes also that of its entire supply chain. Thus, in addition to the 11 per cent of world product that they generate directly, the 800 VLCs exert at least as great an indirect influence through their orders, which account for a further 15 per cent of world product. The corresponding figures on the leverage exerted by VLCs on their distribution can only be estimated. If the distribution margin is conservatively assumed to be one-third of the final price, the contribution that this part of the VLCs' value chain makes to global product can be estimated at an additional 15 per cent. To sum up, the 800 VLCs indirectly influence 30 per cent of world GDP and directly produce 10 per cent of it, which means that they have a strong influence on nearly half of world product. As it happens, the 1,000 largest corporations' share of world stock-market capitalization is much the same – nearly half of the total. This means that financial markets have an unparalleled capacity to influence whole sections of the global economy through VLCs and their value chains.

VLCs' predominant position in the world economy is based on three factors:

- Their privileged access to global financial markets, which enables them to obtain finance under optimum conditions;
- Their ability to develop and maintain control of global brands and distribution networks;
- Their ability to control technology and the pace of innovation.

A global marketing economy

In the absence of historical data, it is impossible to compare the economic role of VLCs now and fifty years ago. There is some indirect evidence that the 1,000 largest corporations' indirect influence on world product was substantially less, whereas the share of value added they produced directly was somewhat larger. The widely acknowledged tendency to subcontract as leading brands experienced rapid international growth accounts for this disproportionate leverage on the world economy by VLCs. Over the past half-century there has been a fundamental inversion in economic thinking which, together with globalization, has profoundly affected non-financial enterprises and had an indirect impact on the financial relationships and transactions in which they are involved.

From the late 1970s onwards, Western markets for consumer goods and equipment reached saturation point. This gradually forced a change of approach. Enterprises created by engineers specializing in production chains and fostering technical efficiency made way for enterprises led by salesmen specializing in marketing. Like American car manufacturers in the 1920s, Western industrial enterprises discovered in the 1970s that the real challenge was no longer to manufacture but to sell, and hence market their products. From then on they had not only to keep producing but above all to expand their ability to sell – which meant masterminding the markets for their goods. Today, manufacturing costs seldom account for more than a third of the final prices of goods – the rest goes into persuading and pleasing consumers, in other words marketing in the broad sense of the term.[30] This inversion of the relative positions of manufacturing and marketing was a lengthy process, but it had fundamental implications for both the management and the financing of enterprises.

Economic globalization broke down barriers between national markets by opening them up to international competition. Enterprises fought fierce battles to reach consumers, wooing them with slick advertising and customized products, and if necessary waging price wars. Globalization enabled the victors to expand globally out of all proportion to the local competitors, particularly with the help of financial markets. The result was a global concentration process which, surprisingly, has yet to be analysed in depth.

Enterprises' value: new forms of capital

The inversion in the positions of manufacturing and marketing was accompanied by a change of approach to the valuation of enterprises. In the wake of the Depression, their value was no longer assessed on the basis of the historical book value of their various assets, but of their future ability to generate cash flow. The 'discounted cash flow' method was unquestioningly adopted by professionals,[31] who henceforth focused on the components of enterprises that were most likely to generate future cash flow. Although 'capital asset valuation' gave an idea of enterprises' manufacturing capacity and revealed the efforts they had made in the past, it was not enough to reassure bankers, shareholders or financial markets about their ability to generate future income.[32] Financial partners want guarantees that enterprises could sell, rather than just produce (which now seems almost irrelevant). They therefore look for 'intangible assets' such as brands, intellectual property, distribution networks and innovations, all of which maintain or even increase enterprises' profitability and market influence. It was in the 1980s that this new approach to the valuation of VLCs became firmly established. Unlike capital assets, intangible assets seldom appears as such in accounting statements and therefore have to be identified and assessed by specialized analysts and agencies in the light of less structured information. The way in which enterprises communicate could now have a considerable influence on how they are perceived. At the time of the 'new economy' euphoria of 1990, enterprises' future potential seemed more important than their current state – until the over-positivistic evaluation became evident, and the dot-com bubble blasted.

Classic valuation methods could still be used for, say, buildings or production lines, but the same did not apply to some intangible assets. What was the value of a brand, a reputation for quality, a logo or a jealously guarded piece of know-how? And what value could be placed on innovative potential, spending on research and development, an advertising campaign, a partnership or a call or put options? All these items had two things in common: (i) enterprises had spent money on them, but, unlike traditional capital assets, they seldom appeared on balance sheets; and (ii) they could have a positive impact on enterprises' future sales and hence their ability to generate cash flow. Even though they were not recorded on balance sheets, they contributed in one way or another to enterprises' future prosperity and were sought after by financial analysts. This focus on intangible assets, critical in helping enterprises to sell their products in future, which partly explained the increasing gap between book value and stock-market capitalization. In case of merger and acquisition, this gap was captured in monetary terms as 'goodwill', which the buyer paid over and above the enterprise's accounting value and recorded on his balance sheet before it is amortized and written off.[33]

This new approach to valuation thus encouraged enterprises to emphasize, in their public communications, aspects of their activities that did not feature in their financial accounts. Indeed, from the 1980s onwards some enterprises indulged in what was known as 'creative accounting' by including items which had previously been excluded from their accounts because they were based on conjecture. Although these accounting tricks did not – in general – actually involve deceit, they made things that were merely possible look as if they were true. It took twenty years, after a series of financial scandals at the close of the century, for people to acknowledge just how specious and potentially damaging creative accounting was. The world was reminded of two classic problems associated with accounting: the link between financial accounts and economic 'reality', and – related to this – the true extent of the perimeter of the enterprise's assets.

The focus on assets and their subsequent valuation by financial markets gave a strong signal to listed enterprises. By attaching financial value to brands, logos and similar labels, financialization focused attention on consumer loyalty to particular product lines or brands. It was almost as though loyal consumers were turned into assets in themselves. In the take-over battle between Germany's Mannesmann and Britain's Vodafone, each of the German network's customers was 'valued' at DM 10,000. A similar tendency to financialize the future could be seen in attempts to attach value to innovations, patents or business models that were deemed revolutionary mainly because they involved use of the Internet. The dot-com boom was just one such episode. Enterprises were able to raise staggering amounts of funding for projects that had not yet earned them a cent. Pieces of intellectual property, copyrights, reproduction fees and so on were assigned financial value with the help of complicated calculations that were all too often based on no realistic assumptions. According to the International Monetary Fund, intangible assets now account for almost a third of enterprises' total capital stock proportion, which has been growing substantially since 1997.[34]

Shareholder value: the mantra of the new foremen

In their constant search for anything that would increase the value of quoted enterprises, investors were spurred on by the ease with which transactions could now be performed. They could 'get out' at just the right moment, pocketing the capital gains that were generated almost instantly by good news. Such capital gains were an attractive prospect to all concerned, for today's buyers saw themselves as tomorrow's sellers. When buying securities, they hoped the underlying assets or activities would soon be found to have some previously undisclosed feature which, once made public, would further push share prices. At that point the securities would be resold and the sellers would, in a now popular phrase, 'take the profit'.

This endless search for quantum leaps in stock-market valuation was reflected in the doctrine of 'shareholder value', which prescribed that management had a duty to fuel share price rises by constantly finding new 'seams' of value within the enterprise. To keep management focused on this goal, the doctrine recommended that their monetary interests be aligned with those of shareholders, and hence that they be paid in the form of stocks or stock options. Because it explicitly encouraged managers to attach financial value to more and more areas of their enterprises, it was a key element in the financialization process. Like foremen who were traditionally paid according to how well their team of workers performed, managers increasingly saw the defence of shareholders' interests as their sole task, and booming stock-market prices as their just reward.[35]

In pursuing shareholder value, VLCs ceased to be organic entities made up of coherent, stable elements, and instead became sets of loose assets which managers assembled and divided up again according to how the various combinations were assessed by the financial markets.[36] As in fashion shows, quoted securities were encouraged to show off one feature after the other. This endless catwalk parade took place under the shrewd gaze of financial analysts who were on the alert for any new information that might cause prices to change, for fluctuations – in either direction – fuelled the flow of transactions, and hence the analysts' and advisors' commissions.

Because of the doctrine of shareholder value, enterprises now bore only a passing resemblance to those that had flourished during the Thirty Golden Years and were analysed by Peter Drucker, Alfred Chandler and Edith Penrose.[37] What had enabled those enterprises to carry out long-term projects was their internal coherence. Their managers and staff had identified with their economic – as opposed to financial – success, and their shareholders were patient. According to William Lazonick and Mary O'Sullivan, such enterprises had taken a double battering. First, the notion of enterprises as organic entities had made way for an essentially financial one in which they were seen as portfolios of assets (branches, product lines, technologies, markets, intangible assets, etc.). Managers' sole task was to keep rearranging the contents of these portfolios, mainly through disposal and acquisitions. Second, managers were now forced to think in the short term. Ever mindful of stock-market prices, they were no longer inclined to let their enterprises' internal processes unfold naturally, especially when it came to growth. Goaded by impatient markets and the prospect of greater personal wealth, they now tended to rush things.[38]

Economic globalization has opened up new global markets. As they try to increase their earning power and financial value, today's VLCs are getting global too. For both strategic and financial reasons, the volume of mergers and acquisitions has skyrocketed in the last twenty years, together with debt financing of corporation allowing them to considerably leverage their capital base. Taking over competitors or complementary enterprises enables managers to kill two birds with one stone. First, it strengthens their enterprises' strategic position (at least in theory); second, it increases the stock-market value, which is good for both shareholders and managers' own portfolios (not to mention their egos). The wave of mergers has continued despite analyses showing that more than half of them do not have the hoped-for medium-term results. Even so, they usually lead to an immediate price rise, which is what managers want.[39] In some of the most globalized sectors the pursuit of 'critical' or 'optimum' size by main players is a matter of life or death. In a constantly shifting world, everyone is scrambling for positions before their competitors wake up. Since internal growth processes are felt to be too slow, most VLCs now grow mainly through acquisitions. Slow gestation of investment projects – which Edith Penrose described fifty years ago as 'natural' to the growth of enterprises – is now a distant memory. One of the most serious consequences of this externalization and financialization of growth is that corporations are now transient, unstable, elusive and ever-changing. VLCs are turning into depersonalized systems, anonymous processes (see below).

It was application of the financial efficiency ethos to enterprises that led to the doctrine of shareholder value. For decades, this simple idea was presented as the product of 'positive' science, and generations of managers were trained to believe in it implicitly. Obsessed by the notion of shareholder value – and dazzled by their own bonuses – these men and women used their extensive technical skills to reshape the economy and society. Business schools – the temples of managerial training – repeated the mantra that financial performance should be enterprises' overriding concern. VLCs and, through them, the whole of the economy and society were profoundly transformed by managers trained to maximize return on investment and shareholder value at all costs. Some astute observers now began to sound the alarm.[40] A forceful book by Henry Mintzberg, for decades one of the world gurus of management 'science', pointed out the disastrous implications of management techniques that focused entirely on financial performance. According to his diagnosis, which has since been echoed by other authors, obsession with financial efficiency not only weakened enterprises but also undermined the social fabric and public institutions, and eventually corrupted managers themselves.[41]

Now obsessed with shareholder value, managers sought to increase it in three related ways: by increasing return on capital (among other things by squeezing labour); by putting pressure on suppliers and subcontractors; and by exploiting customers.

ROE rules

Apart from shareholder value, another sign of quoted enterprises' preoccupation with finance was the growing importance of return on equity (ROE) as an indicator of how enterprises were performing. Until the 1970s, operational valuations of enterprises had mainly been based on their earning capacity, i.e. the extent to which each additional unit of turnover contributed to profits. This approach treated enterprises as income-generating machines, and focused on how income was divided among factors of production, with profit going to owners of equity capital. The focus was thus on the operational side of things, and enterprises' financial structure was a secondary concern. The classic profit-margin approach set out from the idea that capital invested in enterprises was there to stay and hence that the return on it was of marginal importance, since there was no alternative. Shareholders were seen as an organic, existential part of the underlying financial relationship.

The growing importance of ROE from the 1970s onwards reflected a radical change of approach to the operational valuation of enterprises. Enterprises had long used the 'internal rate of return' method to compare various investment or expansion projects and choose the one that would deliver higher returns. The application of this method to enterprises themselves was the result of a change in viewpoint – nomadic holders of liquidity were choosing between various *enterprises*, whereas entrepreneurs were merely choosing between various projects *within* their enterprises. This change coincided with the emergence of 'financial investors' who were neither entrepreneurs nor consumers. As the role of financial markets expanded and transactions became easier to perform, shareholders ceased to be 'captives' of particular enterprises and instead became 'nomads'. ROE served as their compass, an easy-to-use indicator that guided their choices by showing them which enterprises were using their equity capital – fungible monetary units – most efficiently. In the 1990s, it became implicitly accepted that it was natural – and therefore compulsory – for globally quoted enterprises to achieve a ROE of around 15 per cent per annum. Pensions funds' actuarial requirements were partly responsible for this.[42] Managers trained to maximize shareholder value therefore sought ways to satisfy these minimum financial requirements. They did so in three related ways.

First by judicious use of debt financing and classic leverage, enterprises sought to minimize their need for equity capital, so as to increase their ROE while maintaining profits at a constant level. However, this was a delicate exercise, for two reasons: they had to convince banks that their risks were limited, and the average return on the capital they used (including debt) had to be higher than the banks' rate of interest, for only then could their net surplus return on loans be used to increase their ROE. Over a long period, the share of equity capital in non-financial enterprises' balance sheets decreased substantially, showing that managers were able to use leverage in favour of shareholders.[43]

The second way to increase ROE was to do everything possible to make remuneration of capital a greater part of enterprises' added value. This key feature of the industrial revolution was discussed at length by Marx and his disciples, and it still exists today, justified by the need to maximize ROE. Apart from reorganization, discussed below, there were two other methods that enterprises could use: using threats of 'relocation' to squeeze wages, and substituting people with machines. There was a clear trend towards automation in all industries as robots became cheaper and more effective. Even though they cost several times the annual wages of the employees they replaced, robots had only one drawback as far as enterprises were concerned – finance, which was increasingly provided through leasing. And they had many advantages: they worked longer and in many cases better, they did not make wage claims, go on strike or take sick leave, and if necessary they could be replaced by more efficient or more suitable models. The prospect of being replaced by robots has exerted pressure on both working conditions and wages. As Figure 2.13 shows, remuneration of labour has been a declining part of VLCs' added value (especially in Europe), and remuneration of capital a rapidly expanding part of it.

The third way to increase ROE was to keep restructuring enterprises so as to get rid of all activities that immobilized equity capital without

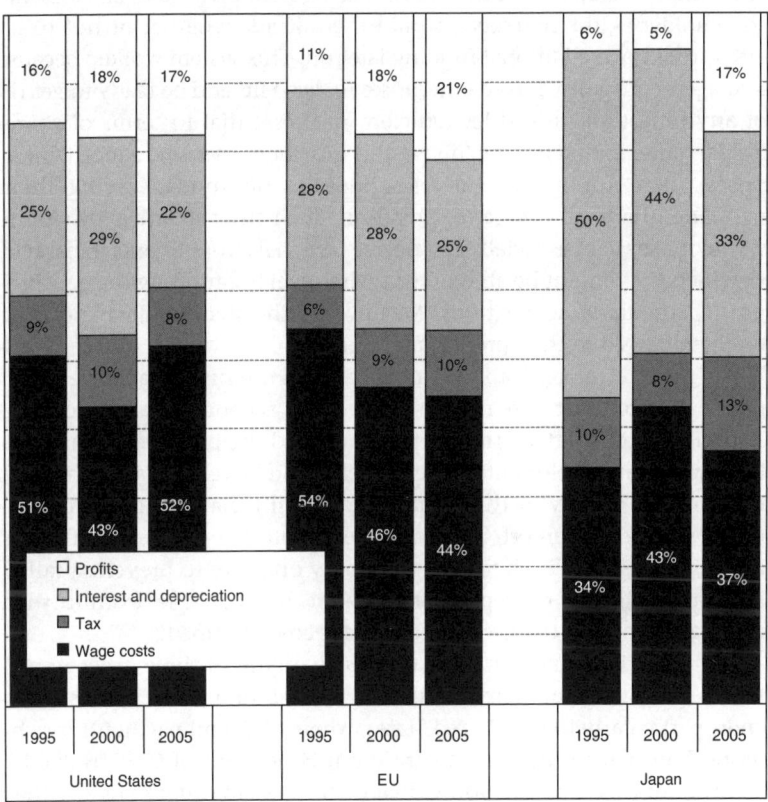

Figure 2.13 Distribution of added value in the largest quoted corporations
© Observatoire de la Finance, 2008 [www.obsfin.ch]
Primary data: Thomson Financial and Robert Shiller

yielding sufficient profit. This forced enterprises to slim down. As already mentioned, it even encouraged them – under the motto 'ROE rules' – to sell off or transfer activities on which their economic plans depended. It was this that set off the wave of 'outsourcing' which changed the faces of so many otherwise healthy-looking enterprises.[44] According to William Lazonick and Mary O'Sullivan, this double focus on shareholder value and ROE utterly changed the way that today's VLCs were managed. Not so long ago the rule had been 'retain and reinvest': shareholders had allowed enterprises to keep the profits they had generated so that management could allocate them to the survival and growth of the enterprise. The new rule was 'divest and distribute': enterprises were no longer lasting entities, and their sole task was to guarantee their shareholders maximum wealth, even if this meant risking their own survival. Nomadic shareholders – the markets – would then decide whether or not to let enterprises have additional funding later on. This system worked because managers constantly forced enterprises to 'keep fit' and be ready to get rid of anything that proved less efficient or inessential in terms of shareholder value and ROE. The 'divest and distribute' system reduced enterprises' room for manoeuvre by siphoning off funds, leaving them permanently on the verge of starvation. Such strict financial discipline would make them especially responsive to signals from financial markets, to which they might be able to turn when seeking funding for new projects, particularly acquisitions. Meanwhile, the shareholders and their foremen basked in their profits and bonuses.

The need to maximize ROE, together with the rush to acquire enterprises at prices that bore no relation to their accounting value, created a specific 'ratchet effect' that further increased the pressure of financialization. Prices paid for enterprises appeared on buyers' balance sheets as investments (partly in the form of 'goodwill') that would have to be progressively written off. This was an extra burden on their results and hence on their ROE. There was then only one way to prevent a fall in ROE, and that was to step up pressure on the 'machine' even further, using again one of the three methods already described.

The financial behaviour of VLCs was changing in three other important ways. First, they were distributing more and more generous dividends, particularly in the United States, where dividend payments rose by more than half in fifteen years, reaching 3 per cent of GNP in 2004.[45] Second, they were repurchasing their own shares in order to reduce their equity capital – all other things being equal – and so increase their ROE. This is what happened with the LTCM fund, as described in Part I. Finally, they were maintaining high levels of liquidity, to the point where they were becoming savers and hence net suppliers of finance for public bodies and households.[46] If this situation were to persist, it would mean an inversion of the classic financial relationship in which enterprises seek funding for their projects from savers or their trustees. Such an inversion would show just how seriously financial pressure has paralysed enterprises, making them rely on financial markets rather than their own industrial skills to boost their performance. In that case the role of VLCs would change – they would cease to be primarily investors that increased the productive capacity of the real economy, and instead, like financiers, would become managers of their nomadic shareholders' wealth.

If fear of how financial markets may respond were to prevent the medium-term immobilization of assets on which all major investment depends, this would be one of the most damaging and paradoxical effects of financialization. In the holy name of liquidity (a euphemism for hoarding and fear of the unknown), a process triggered by society's wish for lasting prosperity would succeed in stifling the very basis for growth – namely investment. It would undermine the very mechanism that led to the Thirty Golden Years: the ability to design and carry out long-term projects.

Procedures as a vehicle for efficiency

The financial pressure created by the new organizing principle and conveyed by the markets was felt throughout VLCs. It was symbolized by the fact that their headquarters all had giant screens showing real-time stock-market prices. Apart from the information these provided, they reminded staff that they were at the mercy of nomadic shareholders, symbolized by the markets. This crude display of the enterprise's *raison d'être* suggested that a graven image, like the golden calf in Genesis, had taken over the place which in other historical circumstances was reserved for political idols, and ultimately belonged to God.[47]

Symbolism apart, pressure for efficiency was spread through enterprises by a series of procedures. The latter, like the bureaucratic process described by Weber and later adapted to industrial production by Taylor, turned every process into a sequence of simple, standardized actions. This had at least three advantages: (i) it allowed quantitative reporting and hence monitoring, and made it easy to set standards and goals; (ii) it saved staff from having to do anything but keep to the procedures; and (iii) it was particularly suitable for hierarchical structures in which the function of each level was to perfect the procedures it imposed on lower levels and make them comply with those drawn up by higher levels.

Through these highly detailed procedures, backed up by an appropriate set of incentives, the financial efficiency ethos permeated the remotest corners of these generators of efficiency and shareholder value that VLCs had now become. As financialization became the predominant organizing principle, management techniques were updated and adapted for the task of maximizing financial efficiency within organizations.[48]

The pressure and uncertainties created by financialization had an immediate impact on wage relationships within VLCs. It was in the 1980s that the Fordist compromise was first challenged. Under the terms of this compromise, which was reached just after the Second World War, wage-earners made their energy available to enterprises within a strictly defined timeframe, and were paid decent wages and guaranteed secure jobs in return. Although not all countries adopted the compromise to the same extent, it formed the basis for industrial relations throughout the Thirty Golden Years. However, once the years of financial euphoria and the market-based economy began and unemployment increased, it began to be challenged. Wage-earners in all the OECD countries had to accept a serious reassessment of their rights, and the position of trade unions was weakened. In line of the explosion of the top managers' remuneration, a tendency spread out to link all remuneration to performance.[49] Pressure for financial efficiency was thus initially reflected in a change of attitude towards labour. It was no longer enough for wage-earners to make their time and energy available – if they were to be entitled to a decent wage (which by now was under constant pressure) they also had to *perform*.

Thoroughly proceduralized, blinded by their obsession with efficiency and in thrall to their nomadic shareholders, VLCs were looking less and less like normal enterprises. There were various reasons for this: behind their immense size and global spread lay extreme fragmentation, offset by their economic and financial coherence; their operating units could be bought and sold at short notice, and hence were very volatile; and internal relations had become impersonal. Some writers, such as Patrick de Varax, claim that VLCs have ceased to be players and instead become systems driven by their own impersonal logic.[50]

The notion of VLCs as depersonalized systems is supported by the fact that quoted VLCs transmit the pursuit of financial efficiency to the whole of their environment, and hence to the entire economic and social fabric. As we have seen, VLCs' economic and financial performance depends on their supply chains and their customers. The pressure to which they are subjected by financial markets is thus 'naturally' passed on to their partners – their suppliers, distributors and customers.

2.4
Financialization of the Economic Fabric

VLCs' subcontractors

In an age of global marketing, the ability to sell and to ensure cash flow became (as we have seen) more important than the ability to produce. Thus, under the motto 'divest and distribute', VLCs increasingly focused on customer relations. They therefore abandoned other activities – including manufacturing – and confined themselves to organizing logistical and other links with their partners, suppliers and subcontractors. These supply networks were built up like pyramids or concentric circles around the mega-enterprises which orchestrated the whole system. These owned the brands that 'signed' their products, and sold them through their distribution networks. They also controlled the design of their products and held the relevant intellectual property rights, and they made sure that fully integrated services were available when the products were sold.

The enterprises that formed the supply networks seldom had such high financial profiles. Many were small and medium-sized enterprises (SMEs) financed by family capital. They distributed few dividends, and mainly grew by self-financing. They were therefore mainly concerned with their operating results, were not prisoners of ROE and only indirectly felt the pressure of shareholder value. VLCs regularly used these SMEs and more generally not listed enterprises (which were so different from them) as counter-parties for outsourcing.

This growing tendency to farm out activities was part of VLCs' efforts to optimize their ROE, in particular by immobilizing as few assets as possible. Outsourcing therefore involved activities that were least 'valued' by stock markets and contributed little to ROE. Now that the ability to sell and appeal to consumers was the key to economic and financial success, the activities most often outsourced were manufacturing activities, in which large volumes of assets were immobilized and margins were low. Of course, in letting their products be manufactured by partners (often in other countries), VLCs were running two serious risks. The first risk was that subcontractors might acquire sufficient strategic knowledge and know-how to become competitors. The second was that they might acquire sufficient power to insist on their own prices or conditions.

VLCs that improved their financial performance by subcontracting their production lines were at the centre of a vast network that had to be managed with care. They could force their subcontractors to reduce their prices considerably by judicious use of the stick (competition) and the carrot (orders). VLCs – and through them financial markets – were thus able to take advantage of – or even 'hold up' – productivity gains that were none of their doing. This enabled them to improve their financial performance, and particularly their ROE.

Subcontracting their manufacturing activities has enabled VLCs to focus on their most profitable and strategic activities (their 'core business'), particularly in sales, while saving a good deal on equity capital. Industrial VLCs with very few tangible assets of their own – like 'fabless firms' – may well emerge. Their stock-market value would be entirely based on their ability to keep control of their markets, products and their countless subcontractors and suppliers. Enterprises that do nothing but generate added value may be the forerunners of tomorrow's VLCs. Their emergence reflects how financial pressure is being passed on to the rest of the economy.[51]

SMEs: private equity on the prowl

There was another aspect of the pressure VLCs brought to bear on SMEs: pressure to grow. VLCs had to cater to global markets, so they insisted that their most efficient partners either expand with them or else be 'dumped'. Some SMEs were thus forced to join the rat race of international enterprise. If they struggled to keep up, 'private equity funds' began to take an interest in them. These financial bodies specialized in takeovers, often using the debt they imposed on targeted enterprises to finance their operations. The enterprises were then 'restructured', usually by merging them, and resold on financial markets or to VLCs. With some exceptions, private equity funds were applying the logic of stock-market valuation on a smaller scale, giving VLCs what they needed to continuing reconfiguring their own assets.

Financial engineering was not a particularly new phenomenon in the SME sector, but the sums available to private equity funds now skyrocketed, pushing venture capital funds into the background. The spread of takeovers for purposes of short-term financial return – unlike classic mergers and takeovers – left SMEs at risk of being bought and sold against their will.[52]

A sales transaction which enabled one of the partners in a financial relationship to get out without asking the other partner might be seen by the quitting partner as freedom, but the partner who remained trapped in the relationship might well see it as betrayal. Partners in quoted enterprises – the first to be financialized – became used to the idea of their relationships being governed by fluctuating stock-market prices and the resulting waves of transactions. SMEs, on the other hand, still focused on operating performance (profits) rather than ROE, let alone capital gains. These traditional SMEs sought to generate enough added value to reward the combined efforts of two factors of production: labour and capital. They were places where labour and capital cooperated and confronted each other over how added value should be distributed. As long as capital and labour depended on each other for long-term cooperation, they remained faithful to each other. This compromise concerned not only the way in which added value was distributed among them, but also how it was generated, possibly including decisions to forgo production (or productivity) gains in order to protect labour conditions.

The possibility of quitting relationships – for instance by selling enterprises to private equity funds – gave owners (who were often shareholders and managers) a strategic advantage which was not available to other stakeholders. Financialization thus profoundly altered the way in which SMEs operated. Long-term cooperation based on forced but trusting loyalty was replaced by attempts to outsmart the other partner by getting out first. Short-term thinking prevailed, and the relationship between capital and labour, which by definition had been anchored in mutual trust because open-ended and hence constantly unbalanced, increasingly resembled a sequence of balanced, self-contained transactions.

By increasing opportunities for transactions, no-holds-barred financialization brought uncertainty even to unquoted enterprises. It threatened or promised – depending on one's point of view – to turn them into financial objects made up of potentially detachable assets which could if necessary be used to build up shareholder value. This undermined the whole idea of a network of SMEs as a local community with a basic minimum of internal solidarity. Some SME owners, aware of the risks that financialization could pose to their enterprises, preferred to stay on the sidelines and keep them within the family. Yet the temptation to 'cash out' and give up enterprises when the time came to pass them to the next generation, or when they were in trouble, was very great. Such operational difficulties confronted many SME owners with a painful dilemma – they could either sell their enterprises to gain the resources they needed in order to grow, or else let them sink slowly into oblivion.

The financialization of SMEs was boosted by two other factors: (i) banks were now more selective in the risks they took, and hence encouraged 'good' risks to grow; and (ii) leading banks, and regulations such as 'Basle II', were encouraging all banks to stop pooling risks and to base the terms they offered enterprises on actual risk levels. The riskier enterprises were perceived to be, the more interest they had to pay for credit. SMEs that could point to a strong position in the value chains of VLCs thus had a considerable advantage over those that could not. This new attitude penalizes young enterprises and those whose market position is weak, and pushes them into the arms of private equity funds, or else of VLCs, which are only too glad to gobble up such innovative green shoots.

2.5
Tying Customers to Enterprises

As we have seen, the value of quoted enterprises now depended on all its tangible and intangible assets, the most important of which was its ability to sell, i.e. its customers. Establishing and maintaining lasting relationships with customers, and getting this acknowledged by financial markets, was the main goal of many VLCs. Desperate for loyalty, enterprises unhesitatingly seduced, not to say stalked, customers in an attempt to capture them (or at least their wallets). This was a key aspect of financial value for VLCs which, particularly in developed countries, were faced with saturated markets. A detailed description of the various marketing and management techniques used by VLCs, which have been amply discussed elsewhere, is beyond the scope of this report. No more than a brief outline will be given here, to round off our review of the vehicles of financialization.

Planned obsolescence

A very effective way for manufacturers to deal with the problem of saturated markets is to limit their products' cycle life and field of application in order to keep up demand. Little has been written on the subject, for obvious reasons, but there can be no doubt that built-in obsolescence is a key aspect of product design. This is a delicate matter, for customers must not get the idea they are being taken for a ride. There have been frequent allegations that shaving foams are designed to make razor blades blunt, that mobile phones are designed to pack up after a certain number of calls, that shoelaces are designed to break every so often, and so on. Manufacturers of food, clothing, cars, household appliances and electronic goods seem to be masters of this subtle – though potentially embarrassing – skill. Materials, component design, and the limited availability and often prohibitive price of spare parts all help reduce the likelihood that products will be repaired rather than replaced, and make it hard for repair firms to do business in the first place. The resulting added value is pocketed by manufacturers and their networks. Designers work to make sure that products will become obsolete, and their replacement is calculated into sales forecasts as an integral part of the business model.

How else are we to explain the fact that London taxis remain in service for decades and drive millions of miles, whereas ordinary family cars fall apart within ten years, or that railway rolling stock keeps going for decades whereas gas cookers or dishwashers give up the ghost within a matter of years? The same applies to ordinary shoes or clothes, which are a good deal less hard-wearing, and indeed attractive, than certain professional garments.

Of the many ways to limit products' service life, there is one that deserves special mention. This is innovation (an otherwise positive-sounding term), or rather control of the pace of innovation, which is one more way to build in obsolescence. Most innovations concern secondary or aesthetic product features. They are seldom accidental, and are usually designed by VLCs to keep users on their toes and give them good reasons to keep buying or replacing goods. The pace of conspicuous innovation is particularly high in the field of electronics, where hardware capacity must constantly be increased to cope with software breakthroughs. As for clothing, sports equipment or furniture, fashion trends help reduce their service life even further. This once again goes to show how important sales have become to today's enterprises.

Massive advertising and publicity campaigns for new products help boost fashion trends. The dependence of the media on advertising has turned them into unprecedented amplifiers for such campaigns, which echo all around the globe. Fashion trends and product launches can now be planned with great precision. 'Killing' a product – the term used by the father of modern marketing, Philip Kotler – paves the way for its successor. Such advertising campaigns are backed up by attractive part-exchange or instalment-plan strategies. Customers are caught in a cleverly woven net and – unless they are careful – are easily tempted to jump onto the bandwagon of planned obsolescence. The products they buy wear out faster and faster, and at the same time, paradoxically, are becoming more and more essential. Financialization feeds on this twofold process of acceleration and habituation, thus swelling the stock-market value of quoted enterprises. Acceleration must be maintained, or recession will ensue. Quoted enterprises must constantly increase their turnover, which is why they are so sensitive to the consumer climate. In the wake of the 11 September tragedy, politicians of every stripe appealed first and foremost to consumers, urging them not to give in to terrorism but to 'do their patriotic duty' by continuing to consume!

To boost consumption even further, marketing experts of all kinds have attempted, with the help of psychological theories, to 'free' consumption from the control of the consumer's will or reason. Professional marketing literature is so full of psychological references that one could be forgiven for thinking it was a branch of applied psychology. For some years now attention has been focused on the highly promising fields of 'neuro-marketing' and 'neuro-finance'. These two disciplines are trying to develop sales techniques that can by-pass potential consumer defences such as willpower or tedium. The aim is to tie sales to automatic psychological or technical responses (as with smoking). At the same time, advertising agencies' constant efforts to give terms such as 'temptation', 'pleasure' and 'sin' a more positive connotation are symptomatic of sellers' attempts to twist language and appeal to consumers' passions, reflexes and instincts.[53] Another way to broaden the spectrum of needs, and hence sales, is to make products more and more specialized. By using various regulations or restrictions to reduce the field of application of a given tool or instrument, manufacturers are paving the way for additional sales. As goods become more specialized and less broadly applicable, users become more dependent and have less control over what they purchase.

Control of innovation, marketing, communication and distribution channels is nowadays more important than control of production, which is why VLCs' critical know-how and a large proportion of their spending are concentrated in these areas. Such 'breakthroughs' are once again reflected in increases in the enterprises' stock-market value, and in the bonuses and other premiums earned by top managers in their capacity as loyal foremen. What is the reason for these rewards? An increase in stock-market value achieved by turning consumers into slaves. Without being – or even wanting to be – aware of it, consumers are thus becoming enterprises' most precious intangible assets.

'Personalized' customer relations

If consumers and customers are to be successfully tied to enterprises, their slightest whims must be anticipated. Computers have given enterprises the technical means to monitor customers and hence get to know them personally, whereas in the past they inevitably remained anonymous. Traditionally, customers were approached by salesmen – not by the enterprise as such – who knew them personally. Nowadays, computers allow customer information to be stored, analysed and dissected at much higher levels of aggregation. Salesmen, the key component of traditional commercial systems, have made way for computer terminals. VLCs are well aware of the selling power they can acquire by establishing personal relationships with each individual customer. This explains why supposedly personalized loyalty schemes have become so widespread. In this way enterprises, rather than individual sales staff, can bind customers to them by establishing direct, 'personalized' relationships with them. This also enables enterprises to discover what each customer is likely to want, especially products they do not yet buy, and to adjust their product range accordingly so as make a higher return. In fact, the opportunity to sell additional products to a captive clientele has been one of the main stated reasons for banks and insurance companies to merge. The technique is known as cross-selling. Yet personalized marketing is only seemingly so – in reality, it is based on the use of giant databases ('data mining'), and is an increasingly effective way for suppliers to keep their customers without having to do them any special favours.

This development is asymmetrical, for customers still see enterprises as abstract entities, as mere logos in their mind's eye; enterprises, on the other hand, know their customers individually and can feed their databases with details of their behaviour. This information makes it easier for them to reach all and every one of their customers and hence increase the financial 'return' on their customer relationships. Suffice to say that from the enterprises' perspective such approach is often called 'yield management'. These seemingly individualized relationships disguise the fact that consumer behaviour is increasingly herd behaviour.[54] This asymmetry brings us to the delicate issue of privacy, which is nowadays increasingly regulated.

Personalized relationships between sellers and buyers are incompatible with the theoretical notion of the market, in which there are numerous, anonymous buyers and sellers who, by a mysterious process of confrontation and cooperation, generate a single 'market price' that applies to all transactions. With personalized marketing relationships there is no longer a single price; instead, there are countless different prices, depending on individual customers and their potential. Price ceases to be an objective, public factor and instead becomes a subjective, private one. This fragmentation of the market into countless private transactions enables sellers to exploit certain customers' potential. In the long term, however, there is a risk that it will bring the whole notion of the market – the cornerstone of modern economics – into disrepute, and challenge the only justification the markets have for their existence.

Dissolving products into services

This increasing focus on individual customers is part of – and in turn boosts – the overall tendency of today's economy to become more service-oriented. There are many different aspects of this, but the main one is the replacement of products by services as tradable objects.

Enterprises' attempts to bind customers to them have naturally led them to prefer stable relationships, with their regular flows of services and payments, to separate transactions which are spread over time and are ultimately uncertain. This pursuit of predictability has led enterprises in all sectors either to replace products with services or to surround them with a range of services without which they cannot be used (a good example being mobile phones).

All this is simply the logical outcome of the planned obsolescence discussed earlier. What difference does it make whether we buy a washing machine with a planned service life or purchase a laundry service for the same period? The trend towards more and more services at the expense of products reflects managers' and marketeers' wish to limit customers' independence and so predict future sales with ever greater accuracy. This will enable them to maximize stock-market value and manage their network of subcontractors and suppliers as efficiently as possible. The aim is not so much to serve customers as to reduce their freedom of manoeuvre.

In present-day society a good deal of energy is put into selling products with services attached. Enterprises are at constant pains to detect and exploit opportunities, to find customers and tame them, and to do deals – especially now that time has almost ceased to be socially organized and anything can be done at any time. Thus, at any given time, each and every one of us may be a seller or the object of demand. Specialized warehouses and distribution centres have lost their monopoly, partly because services have expanded so rapidly and partly because the Internet is so widely accessible. The seller that lurks within each of us, eager to make a profit out of his know-how, worms his way into social relationships which he then tends to exploit. Like Tupperware, enterprises have come to realize that private relationships – based as they are on trust and friendship – offer great sales potential.[55]

The expansion of services at the expense of products has made the typical seller's attitude commonplace. Private relationships have been invaded by exploitative attitudes that are incompatible with friendship and loyalty. This tendency towards greed has triggered defence mechanisms, including greater distrust within private relationships and the expansion of a grey area of 'relationships' that are neither private in the normal sense of the word nor truly professional. Fear of exploitation reduces trust and makes true friendship less likely. Exploitation also undermines existing relationships, for it encourages abuse of trust. Such behaviour is based on the same attitude as the pursuit of capital gains: relationships are unilaterally sacrificed by one partner as and when he sees fit, confronting the other with a *fait accompli*.

The pursuit for new opportunities for gain and the fear of sudden abandonment ultimately damage personal relationships, and can isolate and exclude those who are not, or have ceased to be, valuable or useful. Loneliness, exclusion and isolation have become more common as 'warm' relationships based on selfless friendship have been replaced by cold, professionalized 'care' services.

The alienation of the anaesthetized consumer

The change spearheaded by financialization has profoundly altered the entire economy. It has affected not only enterprises, as we have seen, but also the role and position of consumers – in other words, the place of human beings in the emerging economic system.

As products become more fragile and short-lived, and are ultimately dissolved into services, the relationship between humans being and things is fundamentally changed. The things people use are more and more specialized – and hence efficient – but also more and more brittle and dependent on extra services. Greater efficiency is counterbalanced by users' loss of independence in relation to manufacturers, for they always need services which must be paid for separately. One particularly grotesque example was the 'terminator' gene. A seed was genetically engineered to accept a gene that produced bumper harvests but left crops sterile. Farmers were forced to keep buying new seed, guaranteeing the producer a constant cash flow. Mounting protest led Monsanto to stop marketing the seed in 1999. Nevertheless, this remains the basic attitude of agro-business, as well as suppliers of music or films: the aim is to stop consumers continuing to use products that are supposed to become obsolete.

Left unchecked, such trends will eventually alienate consumers from their physical environment. They will become tenants on their own land and will have to pay for everything they do. All lasting relationships, all contacts and all direct control over things will depend on transactions, on specialized services that must be paid for. The economic and financial component of the 'technical membrane' described by Ellul, which isolates people from their immediate environment, is becoming more and more influential. Property relationships will be distorted as the notion of value in use is 'absorbed' by appropriate services. Any positive externalities which users could enjoy free of charge will cease to exist, because they will be internalized in service prices. At the same time, this trend will also increase enterprises' financial value, for consumers will be trapped in a vicious circle of payment, and sales will be guaranteed. Paradoxically, these increasingly alienated consumers will also be co-owners – particularly through pension funds – of these enterprises whose financial value is growing. So will this consumer prison be a gilded prison? Has the alienation diagnosed by Marx now come to affect not only how man relates to his instrument of labour, but also how he relates to his own life?

The previous paragraph is an important interim conclusion. It shows how the lure of capital gains through transactions is profoundly altering the workings and structure of the entire economy.

2.6
Other Aspects of Financialization

The age of anticipation: banks and their customers

Any loan that does not finance investment provides a link between the time when a good bought on credit is enjoyed and the time when it is paid for. The counterpart is the user's obligation to pay the interest. The untimely need or wish that leads buyers to incur debt has three major advantages for sellers/creditors: they are able to sell goods, to maintain cash flow while the loan is outstanding, and sometimes to earn a substantial commission. Sale on credit, and consumer credit in general, are all part of this 'consume now, pay later' mentality.

The spread of credit cards, department-store accounts with overdraft facilities and rental or leasing facilities provided by suppliers of consumer durables such as cars or homes are in keeping with the pattern of accelerating sales, which also help increase enterprises' value. However, from debtors' point of view, the lure of immediate enjoyment is counterbalanced by a long-term commitment which threatens their future by forcing them to generate additional cash flow in order to meet their obligations.

Banks and other financial institutions are using all their skills, resources and know-how to increase the part played by both large- and small-scale credit in people's daily lives, for their own stock-market value depends on their ability to generate cash flow in return for credit. One man's commitment is another man's source of value, and one man's curtailed freedom is part of a bank's financial assets and becomes another man's source of profit. The huge expansion of credit in Western countries has been helped by the development of information technology, which enables banks to manage risks more efficiently, reduces the cost of processing customer files and makes these more accurate.

Computers are not afraid to look ridiculous, and feel no compunction about sending out reminders for outstanding debts of no more than a few cents or payments that are only a few days late. As each reminder is accompanied by a bill for 'charges', the amounts owed steadily increase.

The sales techniques used, as well as people's loss of independence in an environment to which they only have access via specialized services, lead to growing frustration. At the same time, people seek compensation in the form of immediate enjoyment. Credit suppliers are often there to 'help' them assuage this passion, which is really a symptom of fragility, or even anxiety.

By allocating a substantial share of people's incomes to payments arising from long-term contracts (services, subscriptions, loans etc.), suppliers of products and services ensure sales and so reduce their own risks arising from fluctuating performance, while increasing their efficiency. By spreading the link between the moment of enjoyment and the moment of payment over time, they achieve two things. They make consumers less sensitive to cost (price), which is diffused over time, and they get them into the habit of using particular services or products, which is the best guarantee of continuity. In macroeconomic terms, the fact that an increasing share of people's income is allocated to 'forced' payments – such as the forced savings referred to in Part I – limits their room for manoeuvre. It thus reduces their ability to respond to unforeseen events, for it turns them into permanent debtors by financializing, through credit, the 'precautionary cash balances' (as Keynes called them) that guarantee their autonomy. The resulting fear of unforeseen events induces households to take out extra insurance, and so increases the total amount allocated to insurance, including social insurance.

Analysis of income cycles over an entire lifetime shows that between the two periods of people's lives when they need resources over and above their current incomes (childhood and retirement) there is a period in which they may earn more than they need. This naturally leads banks to offer their customers services appropriate to the various periods: credit while they are being educated and starting their professional and family lives, repayment of that credit and accumulation of assets while they are adults, and consumption of those assets when they reach old age. Each stage involves a service, and hence a commission. Thus tied to banks for life, customers effectively become assets whose profitability can be predicted fairly accurately, mainly through the law of large numbers.[56] The expansion of credit is entirely in keeping with the trend towards more and more services. Now even an empty wallet no longer prevents consumers from spending money. They are free to get deep into debt, thanks to the credit lines sellers have thoughtfully opened for them – a danger to which the youngest and weakest members of society are particularly exposed.

The fragmentation of products' lives cycle by service has its financial counterpart in the fragmentation of payments into yearly and monthly instalments. The immense advantage of these two parallel developments is that users/payers will never become owners, and will always remain customers. This change in the position of consumers may encourage the emergence of new mega-owners capable of setting up mechanisms whereby they can rent out the whole world for a fee. Together with VLCs, pension funds could well become such new-style players.[57]

Humanity in the grip of financialization

Financialization is affecting Western man's daily life in a number of ways. The most striking example is the subprime crisis in the United States, which has led to large numbers of family homes being repossessed. Without even reaching the critical stage, writes Randy Martin, 'the redefinition of the family home as an object of speculation and credits, together with the infusion of its interior design with financial tastes, displaces domestic life in a number of ways. When home stood for a sturdy separation of private life from public affairs, a good deal of violence could be swept under the carpet of patriarchal authority so as to retain the ordered tranquillity. When family too is transparent, run like a corporate boardroom with full disclosure, authority lies in the market place that bisects the domestic economy into a holy writ of allowances and unpaid chores' – with all the attendant educational problems, one might add.[58]

Financialization is changing the very notion of what human beings are. In a recent divorce case, the court held that one spouse's medical degree was a joint 'investment' and hence that the other spouse was entitled to an income from it. This is an extreme view of human beings as nothing more than portfolios of assets. Their job is then to use these 'intangible assets' consisting of technical or professional knowledge, contacts or networks of customers. This theoretical view fundamentally alters the meaning of labour relationships and of remuneration, which can then be interpreted in terms of return on investment and writing-off of earlier investment – a special kind of ROE.[59]

Like financial capital, which – in between two transactions – temporarily assumes the 'form' of a enterprise, human beings viewed as 'portfolios of assets' are temporarily tied to an environment – a enterprise – which must enable them to make a return out of their assets, increase their value and acquire new ones. Seen in these terms, their working lives become a sequence of jobs – similar to transactions on financial markets – in which the value of their 'portfolio' is supposed to increase just as their remuneration should be doing.

This view of labour, and of work in general, is very far removed from the classic view, for it blurs the distinction between labour and capital by turning people into portfolios of private intangible assets seeking to maximize their ROE. The same is true of labour relationships – jobs – which are simply reduced to two opposing ROEs: that of the employee's portfolio of assets, and that of the financial capital invested in the enterprise.

The traditional notion of cooperation between the two factors of production is accompanied by the notion of confrontation in order to appropriate the profits from the activity. What makes this confrontation particularly harsh is that it is multi-dimensional, and that it is easy to break the link (through resignation or dismissal). The partners – the enterprise and the employee – thus live in constant fear that the relationship may be unilaterally broken off by the other partner. Such an atmosphere encourages the proliferation of strategic games throughout the enterprise, including measures to protect shareholders' sacrosanct interests. Having no certain prospects of long-term coexistence, each partner in the tangle of interpersonal relationships that make up all enterprises starts looking for the best time to 'opt out', sometimes sacrificing loyalties in the process, and to maximize his 'capital gains' by taking the opportunity to appropriate new knowledge, new ideas, segments of clientele, etc. Once enough people are aware of it, this sword of Damocles becomes real, and triggers appropriate behaviour. The result is a spiral of distrust which may eventually paralyse the enterprise and erode its value, or even destroy it altogether.

Enterprises use a whole range of techniques, legal instruments and computer aids to minimize their dependence on their leading staff. This serves two purposes. One, which is defensive, is to prevent the employee from gaining access to strategic information; the other, which is more aggressive, is to ensure that the enterprise gains access to what the employee knows. Obviously, staff are wise to this and act in precisely the opposite manner. Distrust and suspicion become entrenched, and working relationships become forced and sterile.

The financialization of working relationships means that all jobs tend to be seen in terms of 'career prospects', i.e. future – and by definition transient – stages of a person's working life. This speeds up the rate of staff turnover both within enterprises and between them. Modern methods of assessing and remunerating employees all have one thing in common, namely a drastic reduction in seniority privileges, accumulated benefits and so on. In the name of flexibility, every single aspect of remuneration can be called into question. The benefits of 'personal development' are increasingly being deducted from employees' pay. There is a growing tendency to make a distinction between the 'capital gains' aspect of jobs – personal development and creation of new assets such as know-how, information and contacts – and their remuneration in hard cash.

The 'portfolio' model only really works for the small number of skilled people who can move between countries and professions. Nevertheless, this view of work as a sequence of purchases of specific assets, and remuneration of those assets, is spreading, and in particular serves as a model for young people who are undergoing training. Rather than a creative, enriching activity, work is increasingly seen as a means of making and accumulating money. This is true of wage-earners, students and even the self-employed, and indeed the creation of enterprises, which are often set up for the express purpose of reselling them.

Finance: a metaphysical response

A recent essay by Christian Arnsperger makes a clear diagnosis: 'Economic rationality seems of little help when seeking meaning in our lives, unless we see meaning solely in terms of economic success and the tensions it creates […] The things we do in the name of economic rationality may in fact mask the anxiety we feel when faced with the finiteness of our existence […] The major obstacles that now prevent us from "healing" society are not technical ones. They are existential obstacles created by the difficulty we have in accepting our finiteness.'[60] Arnsperger identifies two forms of anxiety associated with 'finiteness': anxiety associated with the finiteness of time, which is inherent in human mortality; and anxiety arising from limits imposed by others. This diagnosis highlights the link between the anthropological view of man and the promises held out by finance.

Modern finance, rooted in the efficiency ethos promoted by the market mechanism, copes with each of these types of anxiety in its own way. It does so by offering technical solutions that eliminate the sources of the anxiety. It thus presents 'capital' as a virtual, timeless object with a supposedly inalienable right to remuneration. The 'actuarial utopia' is full of promises, such as 'perpetual income'. Markets, backed by financialization, liberate the pursuit of gain both morally – turning 'private vices' such as greed into 'public virtues' – and technically, for the prospect of infinite growth makes limits seem pointless. The rationality and neatness of financial models makes them all the more appealing.

If modern finance seems to offer both eternity and infinity, they are virtual – i.e. they are accessible to human beings only through intellectual sleight-of-hand. In other words, finance's response to their existential anxiety may temporarily distract their attention but ultimately leaves them more exposed to it than ever. The reason why finance seems so appealing and is able to permeate every aspect of private and social life is that today's world is particularly ill-equipped to cope with existential anxiety. This in turn encourages the denial mechanisms that financialization keeps in place. The question of goals and finiteness is obscured by the luxury of the material and intellectual resources that are mobilized. All finance can offer is the promise of (purchasing) power in an intangible future.

2.7
Implications of the New Pattern

The method of analysis used in the previous pages is based on Aristotle's multi-modal causality with input from Braudel, which allows different timeframes to be taken into account. Part I of this report described the soil in which financialization first took root – the Thirty Golden Years and the period of economic liberalization – and looked at the phenomenon of 'savings silos', players specially designed and equipped to collect and manage savings. Finally, it showed that the eager pursuit of financial gain, rationalized by the modern science of finance, can be seen as an extension of the efficiency ethos that has underpinned Western civilization for almost two centuries. As for the actual financialization process, the subject of Part II, it is maintained by the tendency in all areas of the economy and society to replace relationships with transactions. The gradual replacement of a network of relationships with a dazzling display of transactions has fuelled the spread of financialization and enabled it to permeate every area of the economy and society. This process has not been automatic or peaceful; on the contrary, it has often involved one partner in a relationship being exploited by the one who is leaving it.

Throughout Part II, the various vehicles of financial thinking have been identified and analysed in the light of the report's central hypothesis that financialization has profoundly transformed the system. This analysis has shown how financial thinking is spreading throughout society. It originates in people's wish to make a return out of their savings and so ensure their medium-term security, it spreads via transactions on financial markets, it imposes itself on VLCs and, via them, on the whole of the economy and society, and finally it extends to one of man's most human aspects – his metaphysical anxiety. At the end of this analysis, which has inevitably remained superficial in places, the hypothesis that financialization is set to become the main organizing principle in Western society seems increasingly plausible. A new, coherent pattern of behaviour and social institutions appears to be emerging in response to it. After summing up our diagnosis in the next few paragraphs, we must finally turn to the future and consider the implications of the new pattern for the economy, for society and for civilization as we know it.

Notes

1 Jacques Bichot, *Huit siècles de monétarisation*, Paris, Economica, 1984, 238 pp.; Jean-Marie Thiveaud, 'Fait financier et instrument monétaire entre souveraineté et légitimité: l'institution financière des sociétés archaïques', in Michel Aglietta and André Orléan, *La monnaie souveraine*, Paris, Odile Jacob, 1998, pp. 85–126; 'De la foi publique', in *La construction sociale de la confiance*, Philippe Bernoux and Jean-Michel Servet, Paris, Monchrestien, 1997, pp. 45–72.
2 Jean-Claude Lavigne O.P., 'Antonin des Conseils – un théologien de l'usure au XVème siècle', in *Finance & the Common Good/Bien Commun*, No. 16, *op. cit.*, pp. 60–9, and 'Interdit ou toléré ? – le prêt à intérêt après *Vix Pervenit* (1745)', in *Finance & the Common Good/Bien Commun*, No. 21, *op. cit.*, pp. 85–97.
3 Lahsen Sbail El Idrissi, 'La rémunération du capital en Islam', in *Finance & the Common Good/Bien Commun*, No. 16, *op. cit.*, pp. 16–30.
4 Yehuda Don, 'Some Thoughts about Religious Rulings and Economics', in Jean-Michel Bonvin, *Debt and the Jubilee*, Observatoire de la Finance, 1998, pp. 83–94.
5 Edouard Dommen, 'Calvin et le prêt à intérêt', in *Finance & the Common Good/Bien Commun*, No. 16, *op. cit.*, pp. 42–58 ; André Biéler, *La pensée économique et sociale de Calvin*, Geneva, Georg, 1959, 563 pp.
6 John Micklethwait and Adrian Wooldridge, *The Company: A Short History of a Revolutionary Idea*, New York, Random House, 2003, 215 pp. See also Jean Favier, *op. cit.*, and Mark Achbar, Jennifer Abbott and Joel Bakan's film *The Corporation* (Canada, 2004), reviewed in *Finance & the Common Good/Bien Commun*, No. 23, *op. cit.*, pp. 121–2.
7 Interpersonal relationships are conspicuous by their absence in economics, which treats them simply as a means of exploiting others. This approach emphasizes the form rather than the spirit of relationships, thus blurring the contrast with transactions. See Luigino Bruni, '*Hic sunt leones*: interpersonal relations as unexplored territory in the tradition of economics', in Benedetto Gui and Robert Sugden, *Economics and Social Interaction*, Cambridge, Cambridge University Press, 2005, pp. 206–28. See also Luigino Bruni and Stefano Zamagni, *Civil Economy: Efficiency, Equity, Public Happiness*, Oxford, Peter Lang, 2007, 282 pp.
8 The International Finance Corporation (IFC), the World Bank and the IMF have been almost evangelistic in their efforts to impose this model on developing and transitional countries. Similar changes have taken place in European countries over the same period.
9 This was discussed in depth in Paul H. Dembinski and Alain Schoenenberger, *Financial market: mission impossible?*, *op. cit.*

10. Paul H. Dembinski, 'L'impasse de la séduction financière: l'exclusion par la finance', in Bernard Baertschi, François Dermange and Pierre Dominicé (eds), *Comprendre et combattre l'exclusion: l'exclusion sociale face aux exigences de l'éthique*, Lausanne, Presses Polytechniques et Universitaires Romandes, 1998, pp. 113–29.
11. Michel Albert, *Capitalism Versus Capitalism*, New York, Four Walls Eight Windows, 1993, 260 pp.
12. Paul H. Dembinski (main contributor), *Economic and Financial Globalization: What the Numbers Say*, op. cit.
13. Charles Mackay, *Extraordinary Popular Delusions and the Madness of Crowds*, Amherst, N.Y., Prometheus Books, 2001, 724 pp.; Charles P. Kindleberger, op. cit.; René Girard, op. cit.
14. Nicolas Véron, Mathieu Autret and Alfred Galichon, *L'information financière en crise: Comptabilité et capitalisme*, Paris, Odile Jacob, 2004, 269 pp., reviewed in *Finance & the Common Good/Bien Commun*, No. 21, op. cit., pp. 115–18.
15. Bébéar, Claude, op. cit.
16. George Soros was accused of triggering the Asian crisis by signalling his investment funds to get out of Thailand.
17. Robert J. Shiller, *Irrational Exuberance*, Princeton, Princeton University Press, 2000, 296 pp.
18. John K. Galbraith, *The Great Crash 1929*, London, Penguin Books, 1975, 223 pp.; Werner Abegg, Ernst Baltensperger et al., *The Swiss National Bank 1907–2007*, Zurich, NZZ Libro, 2007, 824 pp.
19. Bank for International Settlements, *BIS 77th Annual Report*, Basle, April 2007, 244 pp. (especially the conclusions).
20. Maurice Allais, *La crise mondiale d'aujourd'hui: pour de profondes réformes des institutions financières et monétaires*, Paris, Ed. Clément Juglar, 1999, 237 pp.
21. Deutsche Bank Research, 19 March 2007.
22. *Financial markets – mission impossible?* (op. cit.) already raised the question of whether this was added value or subtracted value, in the sense of an opportunity cost to other economic activities.
23. Alex Trew, 'Finance and Growth: A Critical Survey', in *The Economic Record*, Vol. 82, No. 259, December 2006, pp. 481–90.
24. SwissBanking (Swiss Bankers Association), *Swiss Banking – Roadmap 2015*, September 2007, p. 8.
25. Following poor stock-market performance in 2001 and 2002, Switzerland's pension fund supervisors reduced the minimum rate of return from 4 per cent to 2.5 per cent. This change led to only a moderate public outcry, even though it meant a reduction in future pensions and just happened to coincide with the start of a debate on whether the contribution period should be extended.
26. The number of enterprises in the twenty-seven countries of the European Union alone has been very roughly estimated at twenty million.
27. The Observatoire de la Finance is grateful to Thomson Financial for granting it special access to its statistical resources. A large number of the analyses presented here have been drawn up in collaboration with the World Business Council for Sustainable Development, a Geneva-based foundation. An earlier version of these analyses has been published in *Economic and Financial Globalization: What the Numbers Say*, op. cit.

28 Paul H. Dembinski, 'The New Global Economy: Emerging Forms of (Inter)-dependence', in *Globalization – Ethical and Institutional Concerns*, Vatican City, Pontifical Academy of Social Sciences, 2001, pp. 83–108; Paul H. Dembinski, *Economic and Financial Globalization: What the Numbers Say, op. cit.*; Charles-Albert Michalet, *Qu'est ce que la mondialisation?*, Paris, La Découverte, 2002, 206 pp.; John H. Dunning, *Multinational Enterprises and the Global Economy*, Reading, Addison-Wesley Publishing Company, 1992, 704 pp.
29 *Enhancing the role of SMEs in global value chains* was the name of a research project conducted by UNCTAD, OECD and the author between 2004 and 2007 (see, in particular, the background document http://www.oecd.org/dataoecd/27/43/38900592.pdf).
30 Franck Cochoy, *Une histoire du marketing: discipliner l'économie de marché*, Paris, La Découverte, 1999, 390 pp. See also Richard S. Tedlow, *New and Improved: The Story of Mass Marketing in America*, New York, Basic Books, 1990, 481 pp.
31 Lutz Kruschwitz and Andreas Löffler, *Discounted Cash Flow: a Theory of the Valuation of Firms*, London/New York, Wiley & Sons, 2005, 178 pp.
32 One situation in which use of the historical cost method led to economic absurdities was the economic transition and subsequent privatization of enterprises in post-communist Europe. See Paul H. Dembinski, *La privatisation en Europe de l'Est*, Paris, Presses Universitaires de France (*Que sais-je?* series), 1995, 127 pp.
33 Deutsche Bank Research, 'Value Intangibles', in *Current Issues*, 19 October 2005.
34 IMF, *World Economic Outlook*, January 2006, p. 150.
35 James Crotty, 'The Neoliberal Paradox: The Impact of Destructive Product Market Competition and "Modern"' Financial Markets on Nonfinancial Corporation Performance in the Neoliberal Era', in G. Epstein, *op. cit.*, pp. 87–91.
36 Henri-Claude De Bettignies, 'The corporation as a "community": an oxymoron? Can business schools re-invent themselves?', in *Concepts and Transformation*, Vol. 5, No. 2, 2000, pp. 165–211.
37 Cf. Alfred D. Chandler, Jr, *Strategy and Structure: Chapters in the History of the American Industrial Enterprise*, Cambridge, Mass, MIT Press, 1962, 480 pp.; Peter Drucker, *Concept of the Corporation*, New Brunswick & London, Transaction Publishers, first published in 1949, third edition 2001, 326 pp.; Edith Penrose, *The Theory of the Growth of the Firm*, Oxford, Blackwells, 1959, new edition 1995, 272 pp.
38 William Lazonick and Mary O'Sullivan, 'Maximizing shareholder value: a new ideology for corporate governance', in *Economy and Society*, Vol. 29, No. 1, 2000, pp. 13–35.
39 For example, the merger of Daimler-Benz and Chrysler in 1998 was followed by the sale of Chrysler in 2007; similarly, Rover was taken over by BMW in 1994, only to be resold in 2000.
40 Sumantra Ghoshal, 'Bad Management Theories are Destroying Good Management Practices', in *Academy of Management Learning and Education*, Vol. 4, No. 1, 2005, pp. 75–92. See also Rakesh Khurana, *From Higher Aims to Hired Hands. The Social Transformation of American Business Schools and the Unfulfilled Promise of Management as a Profession*, Princeton and Oxford, Princeton University Press, 2007, 531 pp.

41 Henry Mintzberg, *Managers not MBAs*, London, FT Prentice Hall, 2004, 450 pp. 'Shareholder value is an antisocial dogma that has no place in a democratic society. It breeds a society of exploitation – of people as well as of institutions. It is bad for business because it undermines its respect and credibility. [...] Of course shareholder value is not promoted as selfishness. Rather it is claimed to be a "rising tide" that lifts all boats. In that convenient twist of dogmas, selfishness becomes altruistic' (p. 154). See also the review of this book in *Finance & the Common Good/Bien Commun*, No. 20, Autumn 2004, pp. 106–8. Issue No. 30 of *Finance & the Common Good/Bien Commun* 'Can Management Survive without Values?' is entirely devoted to this topic (I/2008).

42 Jean-Paul Betbèze, *Les dix commandements de la finance*, Paris, Odile Jacob, 2003, 320 pp. The author's commandments are based on this 15 per cent norm, which was seemingly imposed on the world without further ado in the latter third of the twentieth century. Like revelation, it is self-justifying and self-targeting. See the review of this book in *Finance & the Common Good/Bien Commun*, No. 20, *op. cit.*

43 Paul H. Dembinski and Alain Schoenenberger, 'The Safe Landing of the Financial Balloon is not Impossible', *Finance & the Common Good/Bien Commun*, No. 1, Autumn 1998, pp. 35–41.

44 William Lazonick and Mary O'Sullivan, *op. cit.*

45 International Monetary Fund, *Global Financial Stability Report 2006*, p. 19; Dennis Chung, Du_an Isakov and Christophe Pérignon, 'Repurchasing Shares on a Second Trading Line', in *Review of Finance*, Vol. 11, 2007, pp. 253–85.

46 The International Monetary Fund devoted a whole chapter of its December 2006 *World Economic Outlook* to the question of why enterprises are up to their ears in liquidity. The chapter began with the following quotation: 'Companies, which normally borrow other folks' savings in order to invest, have turned thrifty. Even companies enjoying strong profits and cash flow are building cash hoards, reducing debt and buying back their own shares – instead of making investment bets' (David Wessel, *Wall Street Journal*, 21 July 2005).

47 A fascinating book by Manfred Deselaers (*Und Sie hatten nie Gewissensbisse?*, Leipzig, Benno Verlag, 2001, 424 pp.) analyses, with reference to Hitler's rise to power, how a graven image can take God's place. In an autobiographical work written during the 1930s (*Defying Hitler: a Memoir*, New York, Farrar, Straus and Giroux, 2002, 309 pp.), Sebastian Haffner shows how the rise of Nazism proceeded in tiny stages that were scarcely perceptible in people's daily lives. Despite the very different circumstances, a similar mechanism may well be operating in a present-day society obsessed with financial efficiency.

48 Vincent de Gauléjac, *La société malade de la gestion*, Paris, Seuil, 2005, 275 pp. The subservience of university management courses to the pursuit of efficiency is criticized by Alain-Charles Martinet in *Sciences du management*, Paris, Vuibert, 2007, 304 pp.

49 Jean-Pierre Durand, *La Chaîne invisible*, Paris, Seuil, 2004, 386 pp.

50 Patrick de Varax, 'Les grandes sociétés transnationales en mutation', in *Finance & the Common Good/Bien Commun*, No. 23, winter 2005–6, *op. cit.*, pp. 45–55, and *L'Eglise face aux Grandes Sociétés Transnationales*, Vatican, Lateran Pontifical University, 2004, 124 pp.

51 Barry Lynn, *End of the Line: the Rise and Coming Fall of the Global Corporation*, New York, Doubleday, 2005, 310 pp.

52 A recent (2007) French documentary by Gilles Perret entitled *Ma mondialisation* ('My globalization') very clearly explains the economic and financial dilemmas now facing Western SMEs.
53 James B. Twitchell, *Lead us into Temptation*, New York, Columbia University Press, 1999, 310 pp.; Paul Glimcher, *Decisions, Uncertainty, and the Brain: The Science of Neuroeconomics*, Cambridge and London, MIT Press, 2003, 375 pp.; Wojciech Chudy, *Kłamstwo jako metoda* ('Lying as method'), Vol. 2, Warsaw, Oficyna Naukowa, 2007, 609 pp.
54 Bernard Stiegler, *Mécréance et discrédit*, Paris, Galilée, 3 volumes published between 2004 and 2006. See also Randy Martin, *op. cit.*
55 Marie-Monique Robin, *Le monde selon Monsanto: de la dioxine aux OGM, une multinationale qui vous veut du bien*, Paris, Editions La Découverte, 2008, 254 pp.
56 Hans Blommestein, *The Future of Banking*, Tilburg, Tilburg University Press, 2005, 35 pp.
57 Jeremy Rifkin, *The Age of Access: The New Culture of Hypercapitalism, where All of Life is a Paid-for Experience*, New York, Jeremy P. Tarcher/Putnam, 2000, 311 pp.
58 Randy Martin, *op. cit.*, p. 195.
59 Michel Aglietta and André Orléan first drew attention to this new view of human beings in *La violence de la monnaie* (Paris, Presses Universitaires de France, 1982, 324 pp.).
60 *Critique de l'existence capitaliste: pour une éthique existentielle de l'économie*, Paris, Cerf, 2006, p. 12.

Part III

Finance – What Kind of Society Do We Want?

The previous pages have described the paradoxical situation Western man now finds himself in. In his work he is simultaneously exposed to the pressure of efficiency and the risk of unemployment for the benefit of stock-market prices that he ultimately owns; in his private life, as a consumer, he is harassed by consumerist temptations and payment obligations; and finally, as a human being and in some cases parent, he attempts to resist all these pressures and preserve an area of independence and truth – a haven of humanity, so to speak. Why is there all this pressure, which can sometimes lead to physical or mental violence?

Supposedly, it is all in his best interests! Western man is the ultimate beneficiary of the forthcoming fruits of financialization – provided, of course, that he puts all his daily energies into ensuring the smooth running of the economic machine in which he has invested all his hopes (and all his money). Under the terms of the economic pact that underpins Western society, today's saver/shareholder will, when he retires, enjoy the fruits of his years of work. It is this prospect of a life of leisure that explains the sacrifices free societies accept in order to accumulate financial wealth.

The material progress achieved over the past two centuries owes much to the Western world's ability to save and invest. The industrial revolution took place and has continued in successive waves up to the present day thanks to financial techniques that have enabled savings to be invested on a large scale. Throughout most of this period, savings were used for projects which were certainly profitable but did not have financial performance and returns as their main goal. Finance was a necessary but not sufficient means towards other ends. It thus admitted its inability to determine goals. When infinite multiplication of assets becomes an end in itself, an ultimate goal that predominates over all others, finance becomes a deceiver.

Although fear of the future leads to precautionary behaviour and accumulation of resources, it tells us nothing about how to use these resources (except in emergencies). 'How to spend it?', the title of the glossy supplement to the world's leading economics and finance journal, the London *Financial Times*, reflects this inability of 'assets' to give meaning to existence. The question of how accumulated wealth is to be used cannot be divorced from that of meaning. It is no accident that ostentatious philanthropy and patronage are now so fashionable. It is therefore natural to return to the dilemma expressed in the title 'Finance: Servant or Deceiver?' by asking some questions about meaning.

Is finance a means to an end, or an end in itself? Where are we today, tossed back and forth between the thankless nature of finance as a means and the euphoria of finance as an end? The previous pages have shown that financialization is dragging the West, and with it the rest of the world, into the arms of finance the deceiver. Is this an endless deterministic process guided by the iron hand of human history, a process that contains its own inherent limits – or an open-ended process that can be contained if we have the will and the strength to do so?

Box 3.1 The fecundity of money[1]

'In the pages I was hoping to write in order to round off this study, I will attempt to explain exactly what I mean by this expression. Today, however, I will keep the explanation brief.

Has anyone ever claimed that money is fecund in and of itself? Surely not. On the other hand, is it wrong for money not to remain unproductive? Surely not. That is not what I mean.

In theory and in the abstract, it is easy to conceive of a link between money and productive labour whereby money invested in an enterprise represents a share in the ownership of the means of production and serves as a foodstuff, enabling the enterprise to obtain the equipment and material resources it needs, so that if the enterprise is fecund and profitable, a share of this profit will return to capital. An impeccable arrangement.

Box 3.1 *Continued*

In reality and in practice, this impeccable arrangement operates very differently, and in a pernicious manner. In the human judgements that shape the economic system, the values are inverted, although the basic mechanism has the same configuration. Rather than being seen simply as a foodstuff that enables a living organism – a manufacturing enterprise – to obtain equipment and material resources, money itself is seen as the living organism, and the enterprise, with all its human activities, is seen as its foodstuff and instrument, so that profit is no longer the normal product of an enterprise fed by money, but the normal product of money fed by an enterprise. That is what I mean by the fecundity of money. The first consequence of this inversion of values is that the right to a dividend takes precedence over the right to wages, and that the entire economy is governed by the laws and fluidity of the sign (money) rather than the thing it stands for (goods that are useful to man).'

This concluding part of the report will discuss (i) the three limits inherent in the financialization process; (ii) its external limits; and (iii) possible ways of intervening to curb it.

3.1
Limits Inherent in the Process Itself

The spectre of sterility

As we have seen, financial transactions provide a way for non-captive partners in a relationship to escape from it by objectivizing the value that was hitherto built into it by a transaction oriented price discovery process. It is therefore not surprising that efforts to 'enhance value' are part of the arsenal of those who seek to get out of relationships with a profit and those who make their living from transactions. All the transactional 'noise' is, in principle, external to the actual relationship. The potential, or value, of a relationship is known above all to the partners on whom it depends. They are happy with their relationship and do not need to shout about it from the rooftops. Since the relationship is by definition open to the future and since the future depends (among other things, of course) on the partners' trust, loyalty and commitment, it has no objective value that is independent of the partners. It is thus an untransparent reality, one that is both fertile and fragile. As we have seen, financialization involves large-scale exploitation of relationships for transactional purposes. This situation will have a direct impact on relations between partners in relationships. They will become more cautious, and less willing to commit themselves to new relationships.

What happens in a relationship when one of the partners starts looking for ways to get out of it? As soon as the captive partner becomes aware of this, he will develop a sense of insecurity which will erode trust and may even lead him to adopt cunning retaliatory or countervailing strategies. Such behaviour will deprive the relationship of part of its substance and its development potential. The resulting masquerade will have potentially devastating economic and social consequences and may ultimately destroy the relationship altogether.

The commitment on which fertility, growth and multiplication depend in turn depends on trust. Investment projects presuppose and rely on cooperation and hence trust between the partners – in other words, lasting relationships. The root of all investment is openness, acceptance, trust and even self-denial in the hope of return and profit. All of this is only possible in a lasting relationship. Failing this, distrust of the future, and of the other partner, is likely to prevent cooperation, and creativity, by freezing them into a mechanical sequence of tit-for-tat transactions. This will destroy any potential for cooperation. A relationship is by definition a succession of imbalances which, as in the process of walking, makes it more dynamic and increase its potential. The prospect and fear of transactions makes relationships sterile and deprives economy and society of its adaptive capacity. This is what happens when, instead of trusting the other partner's ability to rebalance the relationship if necessary, each partner is looking for ways to get out of it.

What is the point of establishing new relationships if distrust is growing? When distrust increases, each partner seeks to protect himself and to control the other partner's activities and performance. This makes the relationship economically less efficient, increasing its costs and reducing its productivity. Any relationship that is merely formal will rapidly loose its economic potential. The limit will be reached when the costs of monitoring or supervising each other's approach what the relationship can reasonably be expected to produce. At this point the relationship becomes sterile. When distrust is widespread, there can no longer be any cooperation, or creativity, or innovation. Economic sterility looms. This is the first of the limits inherent in financialization.

Sterility surely reaches its height when financial relationships are established not because of their creative potential but merely so that they can be valued by a market and then resold. Such extreme exploitation of relationships for transactional purposes was condemned in early 2007 by the Bank for International Settlements, which termed it the 'originate and distribute' strategy. Before the subprime crisis of mid-2007 gave it a moral dimension, this condemnation was a purely technical one, on the grounds that purchasers of securities had no knowledge of the underlying relationships. When relationships are established merely to be instrumentalized for transactional purposes, we are dealing with a clear inversion of ends and means. As the subprime crisis and the financial instruments created in its wake make only too clear, a good deal of financial innovation in recent years has involved precisely this kind of inversion.

Complexity

The spread of transactions involving increasingly sophisticated components of economic reality has made the whole system a good deal more complex. Transactions and the underlying relationships are more and more strictly regulated and cannot be understood, or realized, without whole teams of qualified intermediaries.

This increased complexity is due to several factors. Today's computer and database resources make it possible to grasp increasingly refined elements of finance and to carry out sophisticated transactions with almost infinite precision. The handling of vast sums to an accuracy of mere hundredths of a percent requires an extremely complex technological and regulatory apparatus. The fragility of the market mechanism has been discussed at length in the previous pages. To preserve its theoretical efficiency, modern society has hedged it about with an increasingly dense set of rules and procedures.

The difficulty of correctly diagnosing recent upheavals, such as that caused by LTCM, is partly due to the dense network of linkages. So complex has the system become that even the best-informed players, including central banks, are unable to grasp it. The web of risks and conditional contracts is so complicated that global finance is increasingly treated as a compact, total entity – an anonymous process – in which individual players' autonomy is reduced to almost nothing. The second move of the financial crisis of Autumn 2008 has shed full light on the impossibility to mastermind complexity.

Even the most sophisticated player cannot cope with this complexity, and individual operators attempt to mark out the terrain by establishing procedures that will at least enable them to grasp specific segments of finance. Governments do likewise, laying down standards and regulations in specific areas and imposing them on operators. Yet the complexity remains. Mere proceduralization accompanied by strict division of responsibilities cannot cope with it, for finance is an intrinsically innovative activity and markets are not, by definition, open areas. Although proceduralization has revealed its limits, especially in times of crisis, it is still the only method used both at institutional level and throughout the system. Despite attempts to channel developments, the changes described above are inevitably turning modern finance into an anonymous process – a plane with no pilot and a huge number of passengers.

Like distrust, the complexity of modern finance, with its hidden, unpredictable risks and frailties, is the second limit inherent in financialization. Beyond a certain point, growing complexity could plunge financialized societies into chaos – as some of the scenarios in mathematical catastrophe theory indeed suggest. According to this theory, the most complex systems may find themselves out of control as a result of minute changes. Researchers have used such theories of complexity to explain the collapse of various societies in the course of history, suggesting, for example, that excessive complexity was a major factor in the collapse of social orders such as Ancient Rome.[2] On the one hand, complexity is a source of efficiency and precision; on the other, it is a source of fragility and management and monitoring costs. When costs – which today are largely socialized – exceed efficiency gains, financialization will no longer serve any economic purpose. Things will then go into reverse, but the process is likely to be messy. When complexity gets out of hands, and controls and monitoring costs have reached the threshold of sterility, a massive destruction of financial assets looms.

Concentration of economic power

As we have seen, financialization is based on, and in turn amplifies, concentration of economic and financial power. The emergence of savings silos has created mega-players who are able to handle unprecedented sums, thus greatly speeding up the development of financial transactions and so fuelling the financialization process. To control their costs, particularly intermediation and management costs, these mega-players have encouraged the emergence of financial intermediaries of similar size. Liquidity has been channelled towards the largest markets, which are the only ones capable of absorbing it, and stock-market capitalization in the OECD countries has skyrocketed as a result (as has the volume of transactions and commissions). Thus, as we have seen, there has been a consolidation of large intermediaries, and remunerations have been greatly polarized. The same process is equally evident among quoted VLCs, the hubs of the real economy discussed earlier.

It is clear that the moral, technical and social legitimacy currently enjoyed by the principle of remuneration of capital measured in proportion of the sums invested has, for purely mathematical reasons, speeded up the concentration process. Today, this process has been further boosted by financialization, with its vast number of transactions. Ideologically, this trend has been justified by the doctrine of shareholder value. The beneficiaries are financial intermediaries and foremen in enterprises, and only to a marginal extent the final recipients – present and future pensioners. Financialization has not increased their pensions or reduced their contribution periods, but in the meantime some directors and intermediaries have seen their incomes rocket.

This concentration of economic power would seem mainly to involve Northern countries, but appearances are deceiving. The globalization of their supply and distribution networks means that VLCs now influence the economies of both the North and the South. The concentration of resources and the main economic levers in the hands of so few has not gone unnoticed by the starving masses of the South. While the North will soon only be working to guarantee its pensions, the South can still barely earn its daily bread. Although a few Southern countries have managed to keep up with the lead group, such inequality cannot continue to grow without eventually triggering a response of some kind – expulsion, rejection or outright aggression.

The recent and widely noted emergence of sovereign wealth funds has given the North good cause for concern. Massive investment by these funds in banks weakened by the 2007–2008 crisis may herald a new inversion of trends. It may turn out that the new shareholders do not revere shareholder value and intend to use their newly acquired power for purposes other than simply increasing their returns on assets. This may be one way in which other goals, including political ones, will start to challenge and threaten financialization on its own turf.

Concentration of economic power in the hands of a small number of financial players, including sovereign wealth funds, threatens the future of financialization, for it suggests that growing inequality may no longer be tolerated. As the history of the world has shown, the affluence and dogmatic arrogance of the few may eventually become unbearable to the excluded masses.[3] Thus the growth of inequality, as reflected by a large number of national and international measures, should be seen as a possible limit to financialization.

3.2
Limits Inherent in Human Nature

Besides the limits inherent in financialization itself, the process may also run into external obstacles. Three of these deserve brief mention here: (i) the widespread sense that life has lost all meaning; (ii) the erosion of ethical principles and (iii) the sense of ethical alienation and helplessness. These obstacles may well be inherent in human nature.

Transactions: beyond conflicts of interest

Anything goes in the pursuit of financial efficiency, including things which seemed unacceptable only a few years ago. The long list of scandals and dubious practices exposed by the media shows that today's 'winner-take-all society'[4] has less and less time for losers. The struggle for economic survival is almost bestial, sometimes suggesting a Hobbesian war of all against all. In such a society, the weak, the naïve, the gullible, the less well educated and immigrants are not objects of sympathy, but targets for marketing and opportunities for others to make money.

Confrontation and aggressive pursuit of profit are emerging in areas in which trust-based relationships prevailed until recently – areas in which commissioned agents were supposed to act in their clients' best interests in the name of the fiduciary principle. This is the case in all areas in which knowledge is asymmetrical, and hence in most service sectors. Doctors, lawyers, accountants, sales advisors – even asset managers – traditionally had a moral duty to defend their clients' interests, if necessary at the expense of their own monetary interests. This fiduciary obligation was part of their professional ethics and hence was passed on from generation to generation, and at the same time it was founded in the prevailing moral principle that people should not exploit each other. Agents torn between loyalty to their wallets and loyalty to their clients were thus internally equipped to resist temptation. Today, as a brilliant analysis by Tamar Frankel has shown, things are changing: in professions which were until recently based on the fiduciary respect for clients' interests, there is a growing shift towards strictly contractual relationships, which are closer to sell-buy transactions than to genuine relationships. Such a shift towards transactions only makes sense if the partners have equal knowledge – which is clearly not the case with professions specifically based on know-how and expertise. This shift towards contractualization, which is a form of transaction, is part of a wider trend that is pushing relationships into the background.

This trend further strengthens the agent's position, for once the contract is signed his only duty is to perform the tasks specified in it. At that point, the question of whether the client understands its meaning and scope becomes irrelevant. This trend towards contractualization of all services is part of professionals' pursuit of legal cover and their wish to shed the ethically based fiduciary principle that formerly required them to defend their clients' or patients' interests.[5]

This trend leads to situations in which trust-based relationships can be abused quite legally. Trust and service no longer count – only transactions matter. If the trend were to persist, it would erode one of the cornerstones of civilization: the idea that the strong have a moral duty to take care of the weak. This minimum duty of care is the basis for society and for solidarity. As Albert Tévoédjrè has indicated, the rise of transactions may, unless it is contained by ethics, undermine the very foundations of society: 'The ills of the industrial civilization have their origins in the principles applied at grass-roots level in order to increase production and profit: concentration and specialization [...] From the moment industrialization "specializes" the individual, every time the economy switches from use-based to exchange-based, one sees the family reduced to its most simple expression. The accumulative society certainly enjoys an extraordinary ability to take things over [...] But can the society itself be said to truly exist?'[6]

In a book that caused a sensation at the time, George Soros recalled that even the most perfect market could end up destroying the social nexus unless it was embedded in a firm cultural and ethical corset.[7] The previous pages have described the mechanism whereby trust is systematically exploited by transactions performed solely with a view to capital gains. This value-extracting process driven by financialization is having a destructive impact on society. It is feeding an unhealthy self-perpetuating pattern, for no-one wants to lose out. This race for transaction premiums may irreversibly blight the social fabric. From a societal as opposed to purely economic point of view, efficiency gains that can be quantified in terms of increased national product must be set against their destructive effects on society, which are very real, even though unquantifiable and almost invisible. The only way to stop this process of erosion is to take action to put relationships and transactions back where they belong.

Ethical alienation

The spread of procedures and regulations is intended to organize society as rationally and efficiently as possible – to make it predictable, standardized and controllable – and to keep opportunistic behaviours in check. Proceduralization – which simply means chopping up relationships into separate segments, or transactions – is part of an attempt to depersonalize processes and make roles interchangeable. If there is a detailed procedure for everything, it no longer matters whether Tom, Dick or Harriet is pressing the keys or performing the transactions.

Use of procedures also means that responsibility is broken up into pieces for each separate stage of the procedure. All those involved are thus well aware of their 'own' responsibility and feel no need to think about the meaning of what they are doing, i.e. the meaning of the chain of procedures in which they are involved. Ultimately, no-one feels responsible for the overall result, but everyone feels an exaggerated technical responsibility for his or her particular segment. No longer knowing why they are doing what they do, they become mere operatives who simply obey their superiors rather than use their common sense and their instincts. In a compartmentalized world that prevents them from seeing the big picture, they tend to withdraw into themselves and stop thinking, obeying authority either because they are afraid or because they can no longer rely on their own survival instincts.[8] Totalitarian regimes have never demanded that everyone should believe in all their ideas, but have simply required people to obey authority and carry out precisely defined tasks in meticulous detail – a phenomenon described in numerous works on Nazism and Stalinism.[9]

Finance, with its promise of an utterly risk-free society, is not actually totalitarian, but it is certainly 'totalizing'. Its complexity makes it very suitable for division of responsibility, which insulates players from the consequences of their acts. This is because (a) markets dissolve individual operators into the broad mass, which by definition relieves them of responsibility; and (b) finance, which involves manipulation of symbols in its purest form, is kept remote from its consequences by technology and by its language of ratios and percentages. Above all, players are insulated because they work in the closed environment of finance, where they feel more powerful than other economic players.[10] Finance is thus unquestionably a fertile breeding ground for 'ethical alienation'. Like Marx's workers, who are alienated because the pursuit of industrial efficiency denies them contact with the end product of their labour, manipulators of symbols are bound by rigid procedures and can easily become indifferent to the meaning and implications of what they do. In many cases ethical alienation becomes a habit – especially since the rewards are so high.

More than half a century ago, Stanley Milgram showed that ethical abdication is a typical feature of situations in which people obey authority. Yet the market economy is in theory based on free interaction between players, whereas in practice it is the product of free societies. The spread of ethical abdication among people who claim they are acting under the pressure – and in some cases the *authority* – of impersonal forces, and hence of behaviour similar to that analysed with such acuity by Stanley Milgram, is therefore particularly disturbing.

A sense of helplessness

Ethical alienation – the abandonment or loss of criteria other than those of efficiency – leads to a sense of helplessness. This paradoxical feeling is clearly expressed in the French documentary *Ma mondialisation*.[11] In an economy theoretically based on freedom of choice, it is striking to see that all the real-world players present in the film say that they have no choice, and hence that they are acting under duress. This is because the all-out pursuit of efficiency is driven by implacable anonymous processes. It is presented not only as a benefit, but as the sole criterion for behaviour. This piece of sleight-of-hand allows it to take over the area reserved for goals and eventually to be perceived as the only true motive for human activity.

Technology is a field in which the efficiency ethos can easily become entrenched. Yet the implacable logic of technological responses increases people's sense of helplessness. In the same way, markets – the mass of nomadic shareholders – impose their 'sentiment' on individual operators and drag them along with them. The only way to overcome this feeling of helplessness is to reformulate the problem – not just in terms of 'how?' (a purely technical question) but also in terms of 'why?' (a question which takes account of finalities). Although this is not easy, it is essential if we are to escape from the technical totalitarianism that is feeding on this widespread sense of helplessness.

The end of religious and moral control over the economy coincided with Adam Smith's recognition of economics as a separate discipline. The end of social control over the economy was proclaimed by writers such as Karl Polanyi, who described the end of the 'embedding' of the economy in society as a 'great transformation'. In the last quarter of the twentieth century, globalization finally ended political control over the economy and finance. The financialization process analysed here is not only the culminating phase of this development, but also marks the establishment of economic thinking as the predominant paradigm. Today, economics and finance are not only free from metaphysical, societal and political control, but, in the absence of any countervailing forces, have come to prevail over metaphysics, society and politics. Given the current predominance of financialization, calls for political control to be re-established over the economy are little more than pious hopes or idealistic incantations that seem unlikely to be heeded any time soon. This being said, the size of the financial torment in late 2008 shows that tide might be shifting, and politics recovers the importance it had during the Thirty Golden Years.

Yet, however powerful financialization may seem, it is not some deterministic historical 'law' whose progress cannot be halted. People's sense of helplessness is thus not entirely justified, although not everything is possible and what is possible cannot be done at once. In today's world, financialization has solid intellectual, social, institutional and regulatory foundations. Over the past quarter-century it has become an integral part of everyday life in the West, and indeed the whole world – for other cultures have offered no resistance to the efficiency ethos and its battery of statistical indicators.[12] Yet financialization is merely one of many possible organizing principles, and it represents a choice which, if taken to its extreme, is a threat to both humanity and society. As this analysis shows, there are other, currently less prominent principles which could take its place – among them the notion of the common good.

There is a permanent confrontation between various ways of thinking at every level of the social system: at the microsocial level of everyday behaviour and decisions, at the level of established mechanisms and at the level of institutions. Despite appearances, social and economic reality is not fixed, but is influenced at the margin by individuals' day-to-day decisions. The changes that have led to financialization will be halted only if they run into internal resistance or external opposition. Given the current predominance of financial thinking, the only kind of resistance strong enough to undermine it is one based on the question of meaning. The search for meaning as the sole antidote to the implacable but empty logic of technology has been forcefully expressed by Jean-Baptiste de Foucauld in the following terms: 'To opt for meaning [...] is to acknowledge that, available and present within us, there is a spirit, a moral awareness, a wish to love and to give that are peculiar to man – something whose origins and purpose we do not know for certain, but which we must carry, develop and affirm in the face of all opposition, against absurdity, stupidity and injustice and at our own risk, simply in order to be ourselves.'[13] Accordingly, the end of this book will be devoted to the search for ways to resist.

3.3
What is to be Done?

Some fragmentary avenues concerning the various modes of causality whereby financialization has managed to permeate society will be briefly explored here. Perhaps the most powerful and fundamental process analysed here is the slow maturation of ideas. It took more than two centuries for the efficiency ethos to become the dominant, unquestioned paradigm and world view in the modern era. Our first priority for action should therefore be to resist this paradigm's attempt to monopolize meaning – for meaning is first and foremost a question of ends, and only then of means. The aim, then, is not to make financialization more moral, but to make it subservient to ends that respect human dignity and human nature.

Challenge financial ethics

There have been countless ethical initiatives to make finance 'more moral'. They have all resulted in various professional codes of financial ethics, on which a number of now classic books have been published.[14] This approach to the issue of financial ethics – or rather ethics in finance – involves finding methods and regulations that will make financial transactions 'ethical'. The focus is thus on the way in which transactions are performed: measures to combat insider trading and increase transparency, the duty to keep partners informed, and the fight against corruption and trickery (as in the recent option backdating scandal). Each of these problems is important in itself, particularly as regards market organization and regulation and the establishment of compliance procedures within enterprises.[15] This is a key concern for all the institutions whose job is to ensure the integrity of markets and transactions. Yet, as our analysis has shown, the sole purpose of all these measures is to make transactions as mechanically 'flawless' as possible. Most current efforts to promote financial ethics focus on these issues.

In fact, the technical quality of transactions is a side issue. This report has emphasized the risk that the socioeconomic fabric may be undermined by the expansion of transactions at the expense of relationships. Putting too much energy into microregulatory issues may distract attention from the main threat that financialization poses to the system, namely that relationships are becoming sterile, which ultimately will affect the economic growth performance. Microregulation of markets and their environment will not suffice. In a lonely crowd of individuals linked only by transactions, the common good is an irrelevant and meaningless notion.[16] All that politicians have to do at present is regulate more precisely greed, i.e. use procedures to prevent collisions between the countless market players, in much the same way as road traffic is managed.

Encourage long-term relationships

Financialization has become predominant through the gradual replacement of relationships by transactions. This process creates distrust, generates supervision costs and eventually makes cooperation, creativity and long-term commitment almost impossible. Relationships, and the common good, can only exist in the long term. In other words, the pressure of financialization is a threat to relationships. The only way to resist this pressure is to encourage long-term, personal relationships.

Apart from firm individual choices, there are various ways to encourage long-term relationships. The first is to increase transaction costs. Even though such measures clash with the dominant ideology of flexibility, they must be progressively introduced. The first thing that is needed is a tax on financial transactions. James Tobin once suggested 'throwing sand in the wheels of finance' by levying a 'Tobin tax', a concept that has since been taken out of context and – contrary to its originator's wishes – used as a rallying cry for the anti-globalization movement.[17] Tobin was concerned by the predominance of financial transactions over the real economy and was looking for a simple way to reduce their volume by introducing some viscosity in the system. A tax on all financial transactions (not just those involving foreign exchange) would serve this purpose admirably, but is once again at odds with the dominant political creed.

In the case of joint-stock companies, 'golden shares' are under pressure throughout the world because they imply that different groups of shareholders – stable, strategic shareholders on the one hand, and nomadic shareholders looking for a quick killing on the other – should be treated differently. However, the advantage of this arrangement was that it introduced a filter between the real economy and the turmoil of finance, allowing enterprises a degree of strategic independence. The fact that some enterprises are now being 'de-listed' and that others are issuing fewer financial reports suggests that less exposure to stockmarket neurosis may be good for them.

Emphasis on the long term may be reflected in working relationships, remuneration and even rewards for loyalty. Working relationships must involve more than just negotiation of legal conditions. Relationships that are not based on trust will remain hollow in both economic and human terms, and will become mere formal links with little or no potential.[18]

Rather than encourage formal relationships, it is important to develop arrangements that will encourage trust within socioeconomic relationships. There have already been some innovative steps in this direction, from 'solidarity finance' to microfinance projects and responsible investment initiatives based on long-term relationships between shareholders and enterprises.[19]

Lasting relationships are also important when it comes to taxation, which is the material expression of taxpayers' links to particular national as well as local communities. There should be bonuses for staying in one place rather than, as is now the case, for moving around (tax breaks for newcomers). Taxation must break out of the present vicious circle of distrust, in which taxpayers see governments as robbers and governments treat taxpayers as lawbreakers. All initiatives in this area should be reinforced and more firmly tied to their philosophical and ethical underpinnings, which need to be better known and understood. One relationship that should be restored as soon as possible is international solidarity, particularly full-fledged, not linked, no-strings-attached development aid – a topic that has been vanishing from international agendas, at least under that name.

Greater emphasis on long-term relationships does not necessarily require legal or regulatory action. The point is to reward faithfulness and loyalty to places, individuals, projects and ideas, rather than lure people with the prospect of easy pickings. Effective action will depend on individual behaviour based on firm conviction. Transactions reflect a systematic preference for an 'elsewhere' (in time or space) that liquidity can supposedly bring within our reach, at the expense of the here and now. Yet, despite all the achievements of modern communication technology, it is only in the here and now that the human spirit – and, of course, the common good – can truly blossom.

Besides duration, proper relationships depend on the partners not being too far distant from one another – and not just in geographical terms. If relationships are to be strong and fruitful, the partners must know each other personally. This is not the case in many present-day quasi-relationships, in which the links are purely legal ones and the partners cannot see each other's faces. This deprives the relationships of some of their dynamism. If relationships are to predominate once more, they must become literally closer and less anonymous, with a reduced role for intermediaries.

Change the system of remuneration

As this report has made clear, remuneration has been one of the most powerful vehicles for financialization. The number of intermediaries and others keen to earn commissions on transactions has rapidly expanded. This system of remuneration distracts people's attention from the intrinsic quality – including the moral quality – of their work and encourages them to focus instead on how others will see them. It also encourages greed and ruthless pursuit of gain, distracting attention from the quality of people's behaviour and focusing instead on its effects. The 2007–8 financial crisis has shed light on how aggressive remuneration packages have endangered the whole system.

A system of remuneration that will encourage long-term relationships and increase the quality of professional conduct will certainly help reduce the pressure of financialization, particularly where things are being sold.

Revisit financial process

Financialization is driven by a self-accelerating mechanism. The need to maintain the value of savings entrusted to financial assets requires ROE and productivity levels that are predicated on increasing rates of consumption. Financialization has imperceptibly made the present dependent on projections of the future. Paradoxically, it is by consuming today that we are supposed to ensure comfort tomorrow. There are three interrelated ways in which the implacable logic which subordinates the present to a hypothetical future can be halted and the present can cast off the millstone round its neck – improvidence, frugality and the progressive limitation of savings silos.

One-sided focus on transactions and fear of the future have totally obscured the issues of the present – vital issues that depend on deeper and richer relationships, including those with God. 'Open the Scriptures. In both the Old and the New Testament you will see that nothing angers God so much as this preoccupation with accumulating money, this fear of running short; and you will see not only that he does not command us to worry about tomorrow, but that he condemns and expressly forbids this.'[20] Improvidence thus means trusting in the future, abandoning the false haven of market transactions and its promises that future can be 'bought' for the continuing wealth of human relationships, which each of us should discover for ourselves, cherish and cultivate day by day. Rather than expecting to buy a future, we have to admit, despite financial promises, that personal and societal future has to be built by each and everyone. Only then will finance cease to be a deceiver and become a true servant: 'Use money, for it is there to be used – but never be its slave.'[21]

As we gradually discover the freedom of improvidence, we must also discover the virtues of frugality, of self-restraint in the consumption of goods and services. This will help us shrug off economic worries, and hence escape the financialization of society.[22] All we need do is turn the classic definition of economics – maximization of profit with limited resources – on its head, and instead aim to achieve a given goal with the fewest possible resources. If we adopt this approach (as other civilizations did), goals and ends are no longer economic – they are of a quite different order, and economics and management are merely tools that help us achieve them. Whether we are talking about the frugal abundance proposed by Jean-Baptiste de Foucauld or the frugality of Algerian oases, the aim should be to achieve limited goals as efficiently as possible and so leave ourselves time and energy for things that are more important than material survival. 'Here in the oasis there is no consumption. This is the great thing. There is sustenance: bread, tea, coffee. The key to the system is finding an intelligent way to consume; choosing ways of consuming that appropriately reduce the industrial regime; learning to live at certain times of the day without consuming. The oasis replies: I will do only what is necessary to take me from barrenness – the desert, endless land of hunger and thirst – to splendour, from suffering and anguish to well-being, from terror to peace of mind, from emptiness to fullness, from the desert to the oasis, to bliss and nothing more.'[23]

Efforts to be more improvident, to be deliberately frugal and to limit consumption to what is reasonable will have little impact on the system as long as the aforementioned return search of savings silos continue to weigh down on the present and impose their pace on the economy in the name of financial viability of the future. The system of capitalization-based pensions, the masterpiece of financialized providence, is one of the most powerful driving forces behind the changes discussed here. It is because the viability of pensions shares must be reassessed day after day that the world has fallen prey to acute transactionitis. This is a blessing, but it is also a dogma, and a prison. For the sake of the truth, it is therefore essential that we seriously examine the undoubtedly deceptive promises – political and financial – that have been made, their true cost and their implications for the economy and society. This will show us that tying the present to a false future built on financial deals is like building a radiant (and deceptive) future whose sole task, as in Alexander Zinovyev's brilliant analysis of the Soviet 'radiant future', is to maintain the façade even though the interior is on the verge of collapse.

The sooner these deceptive and profoundly influential promises are recognized for what they are, the sooner the Western world will be able to regain control of finance and use it to build, rather than destroy, economic and social relationships without which no future is possible.

Box 3.2   The Observatoire de la Finance

The Observatoire de la Finance is a non-for-profit foundation under Swiss law, based in Geneva. Its mission is to encourage account to be taken of the demands of the common good, both in and through financial activities.

Our work is based on three firm beliefs:

- Financial activities are essential to progress and development, and are a key economic instrument in pursuing these goals, but are not an end in themselves.
- The common good is not a social project, but results from the actions (which need not be concerted) of players concerned with both the good of the individual and that of the community.
- Those who are aware of the demands of the common good can take account of them in every facet of their work as decision-makers or communicators.

The Observatoire published a bilingual review called *Finance & the Common Good/Bien Commun*.

Only then will finance reassumes its natural role as the true servant of human development and the common good.

The feeling that financialization has run its course and that a new transition may be on the horizon is starting to spread, even though there is still no broad diagnosis. This feeling is still largely piecemeal (although that is bound to change) and intuitive, and only seldom reasoned. In any case, there is a strained and potentially explosive relationship between the pursuit of meaning and the pursuit of pleasure. Behind this lies a profound dilemma. Do we want a society that relies on instant, mechanically flawless transactions, or one built on lasting, open human relationships – a society that intends to seek, and promote, the common good?

The manifesto 'For Finance that Serves the Common Good', sponsored by the Observatoire de la Finance (in the appendix) is a call for action and thinking when the means to do so are still around.

Notes

1 'Jacques Maritain en 1930', in *Raison et Culture*, Paris, Desclée de Bouwer, pp. 5–246 (Note 1, p. 214). Maritain's complete works were published in sixteen volumes by the Cercle d'Etudes Jacques et Raïssa Maritain between 1980 and 2000 (*Œuvres complètes de J. & R. Maritain*).
2 Joseph Tainter, *The Collapse of Complex Societies*, New York, Cambridge University Press, 1988, 250 pp.
3 Jean Ziegler, *L'empire de la honte*, Paris, Fayard, 2005, 323 pp., and David Hollenbach, *op. cit.*
4 Robert Frank and Richard Cook, *The Winner-Take-All Society*, New York, Penguin Books, 1996, 288 pp.
5 Tamar Frankel, *Trust and Honesty*, New York, Oxford University Press, 2002, 264 pp., and Paul H. Dembinski, 'Conflits d'intérêts: le déni de l'éthique', in *Rapport Moral sur l'Argent dans le Monde 2003–2004*, Paris, Association d'Economie Financière, 2004, 450 pp.
6 Albert Tévoédjrè, *La pauvreté richesse des peuples*, Paris, Collection Economie et Humanisme, Les Editions Ouvrières, 1978, p. 33.
7 See the review of *The Crisis of Global Capitalism* in *Finance & the Common Good/Bien Commun*, No. 2, Spring 1999, pp. 56–60.
8 Stanley Milgram, *Obedience to Authority: an Experimental View*, New York, Harper and Row, 1974, 224 pp.
9 See, in particular, Sebastian Haffner, *op. cit.* and Manfred Deselaers, *op. cit.*
10 Paul H. Dembinski, Jean-Michel Bonvin, *et al.*, 'Les enjeux éthiques dans les activités financières', in *Finance & the Common Good/Bien Commun*, No. 3, spring 2000, pp. 6–21.
11 Gilles Perret, 2007.
12 Thomas Crump's *The Anthropology of Numbers* (Cambridge, Cambridge University Press, 1990, 197 pp.) shows that extreme quantification is the prerogative of Western culture, and explains that it was able to spread across the globe so easily because other cultures had no 'antibodies' to the invasion of statistics and the concomitant notion of efficiency.

13 Jean-Baptiste de Foucauld, *Les trois cultures du développement humain*, Paris, Odile Jacob, 2002, p. 41.
14 John R. Boatright, *Ethics in Finance*, Boston, Blackwell Publishing, 1999, 224 pp.; Domenec Melé Carné, *Etica en la actividad financiera*, Pamplona, Ediciones Universidad de Navarra (EUNSA), 1998, 250 pp.; Peter Koslowski, *Ethik der Banken und der Börse*, Tübingen, Mohr Siebeck, 1997, 118 pp.
15 Luc Thévenoz and Rashid Bahar, *op. cit.*; John Plender, *op. cit.*
16 David Riesman, *The Lonely Crowd*, New Haven, Yale University Press, 1950, 386 pp.
17 Alex Michalos, *Good Taxes*, Toronto and Oxford, Dundrum Press, 1997, 87 pp.
18 Michel Villette, *Le Manager jetable*, Paris, La Découverte, 1996, 186 pp.
19 See the following issues of *Finance & the Common Good/Bien Commun*: No. 8, autumn 2001, 'Socially Responsible Investment'; No. 20, autumn 2004, 'Solidarity-based Economy and Finance: Mirage or Challenge?'; and No. 25, autumn 2006, 'Europe: La microfinance se fait une place'; also Bernd Balkenhol, 'Microfinance: Performance and Efficiency', in *Finance & the Common Good/Bien Commun*, No. 28–9, III/2007, 'Africa: between ethical tradition and financial attraction', pp. 147–51.
20 Isabelle Rivière, *Sur le devoir d'imprévoyance*, Liège, Pensée catholique, 1946, p. 11.
21 *ibid.*, p. 62.
22 Julie Schor et al., *Do Americans shop too much?*, Boston, Beacon Press, 2000, 96 pp., and other books by the same author.
23 Le Corbusier, quoted by Manuelle Roche in *Le M'zab: cités millénaires du Sahara*, Bez-et-Esparon, Etudes & Communication, 2003, p. 64.

Appendix

For finance that serves the common good

Manifesto of the Observatoire de la Finance

The current financial crisis is systemic in nature. It is a symptom of steadily increasing pressure that is undermining the material, social, and intellectual aspects and ethics of the liberal socio-economic system. In a recent report, the Observatoire de la Finance carried out an extensive analysis of this transformation. More emphasis will deflect the market economy from its principle vocation, that of promoting the dignity and well-being of humankind.

Society is never set in stone; it is characterized by an on-going quest for the arrangements best adapted to a given time. Today is no exception. During the last thirty years, finance has constantly increased not only its share of economic activity but also of people's world view and aspirations. We call the greater practical and conceptual role of finance 'financialization'. The Observatoire de la Finance dedicated its last report1 to the analysis of the multiple dimensions of financialization. The report shows how financialization has transformed both our economy and our society by increasingly organizing it around the search for financial efficiency. Today, pushed to its extremes, this tendency is coming close to its breaking point.

The diagnosis

By the mid-70s, most Western countries had linked their promises of pensions and retirement benefits to investments that depended on sustainable liquidity. The long-term viability of this model is dependent on the profitability of financial instruments. At the same time, other savings instruments were developed. This progressively exposed the rest of the productive economy to the vagaries of finance, thereby producing an increasing need to devote more and more of the added value to the remuneration of the savings thus invested and more and more self-nourishing complexity.

Pressures on the companies from stock exchange and from private equity fund have been translated into other pressures in three complementary directions: on their staff to achieve ever-increasingly improved performance; on consumers, who came under increased pressure from sophisticated marketing techniques; and on the companies' suppliers and larger distributors as well as on many SMEs (small and medium-sized enterprises) in both the North and the South to achieve increasingly unsustainable results.

Though initially financial, the demand for financial results has trickled down through the entire economic system and become an omnipresent part of the culture of everyday life. This evolution has now resulted in a paradoxical situation for Western societies. The system of capitalization and shareholder value, by imposing demands for the future, has compromised the present. This 'radiant future' is proving to be as much of an illusion as the communist utopia.

This process of 'financialization' has been facilitated by the political appeal of deregulation, as well as by 'laws' and other 'theorems' postulated by Nobel prize-winners. The 'ethos of efficiency' has also been allegedly validated by 'scientific' truths, and has progressively overcome moral and ethical resistance.

After over thirty years of 'financialization', the state of the economic and social system is worrying on more than one count:

- 'Financialization' has led to the almost total triumph of transactions over relationships. Contemporary finance has prevailed because it has carried to its ultimate the search for capital gains and instant results. At the same time, patience, loyalty, enduring relationships, and trust have been undermined leading to increased distrust. The liquidity of financial markets is nothing more than a mechanical substitute for interpersonal trust.
- The ethos of efficiency has become the ultimate criterion of judgement. If pushed to the extreme, the preoccupation with efficiency leads to internal procedures that distribute tasks and responsibilities in an increasingly strict manner, until the point of 'ethical alienation' has been reached. Employees lose their sense of meaningful employment and replace it by gainful employment.
- The ethos of efficiency, when disassociated from moral considerations, has led to the increasingly brutal expression of greed. This is obvious in the subservience of trust to transactions. Repeated acts of self-interest can push any society to the breaking point. The free market, based on a sense of responsibility of its actors, is about to be replaced by a 'greed' market – which will require escalating controls and costs, in both public and private spheres. This, in turn, will

breed the unwillingness of the actors themselves to take responsibility for their actions.

Possible lines of action

This analysis suggests that the fundamental values of free judgement, responsibility and solidarity – which form part of the common good, and without which a free and humane society cannot exist – are under threat. The Observatoire de la Finance proposes three lines of action:

- Carry out a critique – in the positive sense of the term – of the world vision underlying contemporary economic and financial theories. This critique would include both their relation to social and economic realities and the conceptual and ethical dimensions of their underlying assumptions. This should lead to a challenge to the dogmatic pre-eminence of the preoccupation with economic and financial efficiency as well as to the reinstatement of ethical concerns and of the primacy of common good.
- Encourage the development of long-term commitments in all aspects of financial life. Such commitments would slow or even reverse the destruction of relationships due to the current focus on extracting surplus through ill-considered transactions. This would be a huge undertaking with implications in several different fields: finance, taxation, salaried work, local development, etc.
- Loosen the stranglehold which the unrealistic promise of retirement benefits currently brings to bear on productive activity. This will require great political courage, since the professional interests of financial intermediaries could be at stake. However, it is crucial since it is increasingly obvious that pension promises will prove unrealistic, and that the pursuit of strategies to earn the returns demanded are undermining the ethical basis of capitalism. But the work must be undertaken before the threatened breakdown of the current saving and pensions system becomes a reality.

Appeal

The above text aims to alert men and women of goodwill to a serious threat to the economic and political freedom we treasure. This threat is the result of having succumbed to the illusion that private greed could contribute to the common good. While private greed may give the impression of increasing economic efficiency, this is at the cost of the very basis of society: trust, respect and solidarity. It has now become indispensable to take our future in hand – to walk out, to slam the door of the apparently golden prison of financial promises, to free humankind from the illusions of 'financialization', and to set it to work for the betterment and dignity of all.

The *Finance & the Common Good/Bien Commun* reviews, as well as the Observatoire de la Finance's website, are at your disposal.

Please send your contributions to manifeste@obsfin.ch.

Observatoire de la Finance (www.obsfin.ch), April 2008

References

Werner Abegg, Ernst Baltensperger et al., *The Swiss National Bank 1907–2007*, Zurich, NZZ Libro, 2007, 824 pp.

Mark Achbar, Jennifer Abbott and Joel Bakan, *The Corporation* (movie), Canada, 2004.

Michel Aglietta and André Orléan, *La violence de la monnaie*, Paris, Presses Universitaires de France, 1982, 324 pp.

Michel Aglietta and Antoine Rebérioux, *Dérives du capitalisme financier*, Paris, Albin Michel, 2004, 394 pp.

Michel Albert, *Capitalism Versus Capitalism*, New York, Four Walls Eight Windows, 1993, 260 pp.

Maurice Allais, *La crise mondiale d'aujourd'hui: pour de profondes réformes des institutions financières et monétaires*, Paris, Ed. Clément Juglar, 1999, 237 pp.

Christian Arnsperger, *Critique de l'existence capitaliste*, Paris, Le Cerf, 2006, 205 pp.

Raymond Aron, *Eighteen Lectures on Industrial Society*, London, Weidenfeld & Nicolson, 1968, 264 pp.

Philip Augar, *The Death of Gentlemanly Capitalism*, London, Penguin Books, 2001, 416 pp.

Bernd Balkenhol, 'Microfinance: Performance and Efficiency', in *Finance & the Common Good/Bien Commun*, No. 28–9, III/2007, 'Africa: between ethical tradition and financial attraction', pp. 147–51.

Bank for International Settlements, *Ageing and pension system reforms: implications for financial markets and economic policies*, drawn up by a group of experts led by I. Visco, Basle, September 2005.

Bank for International Settlements, *BIS 77th Annual Report*, Basle, April 2007, 244 pp.

Claude Bébéar, *Ils vont tuer le capitalisme*, Paris, Plon, 2003, 222 pp.

Ulrich Beck, *Risk Society: Towards a New Modernity*, London, Sage Publications Ltd, 1992, 272 pp.

Philippe Bernoux and Jean-Michel Servet, 'De la foi publique', in *La construction sociale de la confiance*, Paris, Monchrestien, 1997, pp. 45–72.

Peter L. Bernstein, *Against the Gods: the remarkable story of risk*, New York, John Wiley and Sons, 1996, 382 pp.

Alain Besançon, *Anatomie d'un spectre : l'économie politique du socialisme réel*, Paris, Calmann-Lévy, 1981, 169 pp.

Jean-Paul Betbèze, *Les dix commandements de la finance*, Paris, Odile Jacob, 2003, 320 pp.

Jacques Bichot, *Huit siècles de monétarisation*, Paris, Economica, 1984, 238 pp.

Jacques Bichot, 'La personne humaine aux prises avec les structures de péché', in Paul H. Dembinski, Nicolas Buttet and Ernesto Rossi di Montelera, *op. cit.*

André Biéler, *La pensée économique et sociale de Calvin*, Geneva, Georg, 1959, 563 pp.

John R. Boatright, *Ethics in Finance*, Boston, Blackwell Publishing, 1999, 224 pp.

Tito Boeri, Arij Lans Bovenberg, Benoît Coeuré and Andrew Roberts, *Dealing with the New Giants*, Geneva Reports on the World Economy, Geneva, International Centre for Monetary and Banking Studies, 2006, 140 pp.

Hans Blommestein, *The Future of Banking*, Tilburg, Tilburg University Press, 2005, 35 pp.

Fernand Braudel, On History, Chicago, University of Chicago Press, 1982, 236 pp.

Luigino Bruni, '*Hic sunt leones*: interpersonal relations as unexplored territory in the tradition of economics', in Benedetto Gui and Robert Sugden, *Economics and Social Interaction*, Cambridge, Cambridge University Press, 2005, pp. 206–28.

Luigino Bruni and Stefano Zamagni, *Civil Economy: Efficiency, Equity, Public Happiness*, Oxford, Peter Lang, 2007, 282 pp.

Frances Cairncross, *The Death of Distance*, Boston, Harvard Business School Press, 1997, 302 pp.

Capgemini and Merrill Lynch, *World Wealth Report 2006*.

Cercle d'Etudes Jacques et Raïssa Maritain, *Œuvres complètes de J. & R. Maritain*, 6 Volumes, between 1980 and 2000.

Alfred D. Chandler, Jr, *Strategy and Structure: Chapters in the History of the American Industrial Enterprise*, Cambridge, Mass, MIT Press, 1962, 480 pp.

Wojciech Chudy, *Klamstwo jako metoda* ('Lying as method'), Vol. 2, Warsaw, Oficyna Naukowa, 2007, 609 pp.

Dennis Chung, Dušan Isakov and Christophe Pérignon, 'Repurchasing Shares on a Second Trading Line', in *Review of Finance*, Vol. 11, 2007, pp. 253–85.

Gordon Clark, *Pension Fund Capitalism*, Oxford, Oxford University Press, 2000, 342 pp.

Harlan Cleveland, *Birth of a New World*, Hoboken (NJ), Jossey-Bass, 1993, 292 pp.

Franck Cochoy, *Une histoire du marketing : discipliner l'économie de marché*, Paris, La Découverte, 1999, 390 pp.

André Comte-Sponville, *Le capitalisme est-il moral ?*, Paris, Albin Michel, 2004, 237 pp.

Andrew Crockett, Trevor Harris, Frederic Mishkin and Eugene White, *Conflicts of Interest in the Financial Services Industry: What Should We Do About Them?*, Geneva/London, Centre International d'Etudes Monétaires et Bancaires and Centre for Economic Policy Research, 2003, 119 pp.

James Crotty, 'The Neoliberal Paradox: The Impact of Destructive Product Market Competition and "Modern" Financial Markets on Nonfinancial Corporation Performance in the Neoliberal Era', in G. Epstein, *Financialization and the World Economy*, Cheltenham & Northampton, Edward Elgar, 2005, pp. 87–91.

Michel Crozier and Erhard Friedberg, *Actors and Systems: The Politics of Collective Action*, Chicago, University of Chicago Press, 1981, 333 pp.

Thomas Crump, *The Phenomenon of Money*, London, Routledge and Kegan Paul, 1981, 366 pp.

Thomas Crump, *The Anthropology of Numbers*, Cambridge, Cambridge University Press, 1990, 197 pp.

Philip E. Davis, *Pension Funds, Retirement-Income Security and Capital Markets: An International Perspective*, Oxford, Clarendon Press, 1997, 337 pp.

Henri-Claude De Bettignies, 'The corporation as a "community": an oxymoron? Can business schools re-invent themselves?', in *Concepts and Transformation*, Vol. 5, No. 2, 2000, pp. 165–211.

Jean-Baptiste de Foucauld, *Les trois cultures du développement humain*, Paris, Odile Jacob, 2002, p. 41.
Vincent de Gauléjac, *La société malade de la gestion*, Paris, Seuil, 2005, 275 pp.
Paul H. Dembinski, *L'endettement international*, Paris, Presses Universitaires de France (*Que sais-je?* series), 1989, 128 pp.
Paul H. Dembinski, *The Logic of the Planned Economy: the Seeds of the Collapse*, Oxford, Clarendon Press, 1991, 246 pp.
Paul H. Dembinski, *La privatisation en Europe de l'Est*, Paris, Presses Universitaires de France (*Que sais-je?* series), 1995, 127 pp.
Paul H. Dembinski, 'Le piège de l'économisme: quand l'arithmétique remplace l'éthique', in Beat Sitter-Liver and Pio Caroni (eds), *Der Mensch – ein Egoist?*, Fribourg, Universitätsverlag Freiburg, 1998, pp. 227–45.
Paul H. Dembinski, 'L'impasse de la séduction financière : l'exclusion par la finance', in Bernard Baertschi, François Dermange and Pierre Dominicé (eds), *Comprendre et combattre l'exclusion: l'exclusion sociale face aux exigences de l'éthique*, Lausanne, Presses Polytechniques et Universitaires Romandes, 1998, pp. 113–29.
Paul H. Dembinski, 'The New Global Economy: Emerging Forms of (Inter)-dependence', in *Globalization – Ethical and Institutional Concerns*, Vatican City, Pontifical Academy of Social Sciences, 2001, pp. 83–108.
Paul H. Dembinski (leading contributor), *Economic and Financial Globalization: What the Numbers Say*, New York and Geneva, United Nations, 2003, 160 pp.
Paul H. Dembinski, 'Conflits d'intérêts: le déni de l'éthique', in *Rapport Moral sur l'Argent dans le Monde 2003–2004*, Paris, Association d'Economie Financière, 2004, 450 pp.
Paul H. Dembinski, 'Towards a Multimodal Causation Framework of Entrepreneurship', in *Estudios de Economía Aplicada*, Vol. 24, 2006, pp. 339–58.
Paul H. Dembinski, Jean-Michel Bonvin, *et al.*, 'Les enjeux éthiques dans les activités financières', in *Finance & the Common Good/Bien Commun*, No. 3, spring 2000, pp. 6–21.
Paul H. Dembinski, Jean-Michel Bonvin, Andrew Cornford and Carole Lager, *Enron and World Finance: a Case Study in Ethics*, London, Palgrave, 2005, 320 pp.
Paul H. Dembinski, Nicolas Buttet and Ernesto Rossi di Montelera, *Car c'est de l'homme qu'il s'agit : défis anthropologiques et enseignement social chrétien*, Paris, Desclée de Brouwer, 2007, 326 pp.
Paul H. Dembinski and Christophe Perritaz, 'Towards the break-up of money: when reality, driven by information technology, overtakes Simmel's vision', in *Foresight*, Vol. 2, No. 5, October 2000.
Paul H. Dembinski and Alain Schoenenberger, *Financial markets: mission impossible?*, Paris, Charles-Léopold Mayer Foundation for Human Progress, 1993, 94 pp.
Paul H. Dembinski and Alain Schoenenberger, 'The Safe Landing of the Financial Balloon is not Impossible', *Finance & the Common Good/Bien Commun*, No. 1, Autumn 1998, pp. 35–41.
Paul H. Dembinski and Patrick Vauthey, 'La bourse dans la transition: l'expérience de Varsovie', in *Revue d'études comparatives Est-Ouest*, Vol. 25, No. 1, 1994, pp. 59–79.
Théodore de Régnon, *La métaphysique des causes*, Paris, Victor Retaux, 1906, 663 pp.

Manfred Deselaers, *Und Sie hatten nie Gewissensbisse?*, Leipzig, Benno Verlag, 2001, 424 pp.

Patrick de Varax, *L'Eglise face aux Grandes Sociétés Transnationales*, Vatican, Lateran Pontifical University, 2004, 124 pp.

Patrick de Varax, 'Les grandes sociétés transnationales en mutation', in *Finance & the Common Good/Bien Commun*, No. 23, winter 2005–6, 'The Enterprise: Matter and Form(s)', pp. 45–55.

Jean-Loup Dherse and Hugues Minguet, *L'éthique ou le chaos?*, Paris, Presses de la Renaissance, 1999, 381 pp.

Deutsche Bank Research, 'Value Intangibles', in *Current Issues*, 19 October 2005.

Yehuda Don, 'Some Thoughts about Religious Rulings and Economics', in Jean-Michel Bonvin, *Debt and the Jubilee*, Observatoire de la Finance, 1998, pp. 83–94.

Edouard Dommen, 'Calvin et le prêt à intérêt', *Finance & the Common Good/ Bien Commun*, No. 16, autumn 2003, 'Interest Rates and Moral: Religious Perspectives'.

Peter Drucker, *Concept of the Corporation*, New Brunswick & London, Transaction Publishers, first published in 1949, third edition 2001, 326 pp.

Dany-Robert Dufour, *Le Divin Marché: La révolution culturelle libérale*, Paris, Denoël, 2007, 342 pp.

John H. Dunning, *Multinational Enterprises and the Global Economy*, Reading, Addison-Wesley Publishing Company, 1992, 704 pp.

Jean-Pierre Durand, *La Chaîne invisible*, Paris, Seuil, 2004, 386 pp.

Paul Einzig, *The Euro-dollar System*, Basingstoke, MacMillan, 1977, 132 pp.

Jacques Ellul, *The technological system*, New York, Continuum, 1980, 362 pp.

Gerald A. Epstein, *Financialization and the World Economy*, Cheltenham & Northampton, Edward Elgar, 2005, 425 pp.

Jean Favier, *De l'or et des épices: naissance de l'homme d'affaires au Moyen Age*, Paris, Fayard, 1995, 380 pp.

Finance & the Common Good/Bien Commun, No. 4, summer 2000, 'The Break-up of Money'.

Finance & the Common Good/Bien Commun, No. 8, autumn 2001, 'Socially Responsible Investment'.

Finance & the Common Good/Bien Commun, No. 9, winter 2001–2, 'Will the Euro shape Europe?'.

Finance & the Common Good/Bien Commun, No. 15, summer 2003, 'Globalization in Crossfire'.

Finance & the Common Good/Bien Commun, No. 18–9, spring/summer 2004, 'Enron and the World of Finance'.

Finance & the Common Good/Bien Commun, No. 20, autumn 2004, 'Solidarity-based Economy and Finance: Mirage or Challenge?'.

Finance & the Common Good/Bien Commun, No. 21, spring 2005, 'From Bretton Woods to Basel II'.

Finance & the Common Good/Bien Commun, No. 22, summer 2005, '*Homo oeconomicus*. Le mal-compris et le mal-aimé'.

Finance & the Common Good/Bien Commun, No. 23, winter 2005–6, 'The Enterprise: Matter and Form(s)'.

Finance & the Common Good/Bien Commun, No. 25, autumn 2006, 'Europe: La microfinance se fait une place'.

Finance & the Common Good/Bien Commun, No. 30, I/2008, 'Can Management Survive without Values?'.

Viviane Forrester, *The Economic Horror*, Oxford, Blackwell, 1999, 156 pp.

Robert Frank and Richard Cook, *The Winner-Take-All Society*, New York, Penguin Books, 1996, 288 pp.

Tamar Frankel, *Trust and Honesty*, New York, Oxford University Press, 2002, 264 pp.

Francis Fukuyama, 'The End of History?', in *The National Interest*, summer 1989, and *The End of History and the Last Man*, London, Penguin Books, 1992, 328 pp.

John K. Galbraith, *The New Industrial State*, London, Pelican Books, 1967, 288 pp.

John K. Galbraith, *The Great Crash 1929*, London, Penguin Books, 1975, 223 pp.

John K. Galbraith, *A Short History of Financial Euphoria*, New York, Viking Penguin, 1993, 113 pp.

René Girard, *I See Satan Fall Like Lightning*, London, Orbis Books, 2001, 199 pp.

Jean-Noël Giraud, *Le commerce des promesses*, Paris, Seuil, 2001, 370 pp.

Sumantra Ghoshal, 'Bad Management Theories are Destroying Good Management Practices', in *Academy of Management Learning and Education*, Vol. 4, No. 1, 2005, pp. 75–92.

Paul Glimcher, *Decisions, Uncertainty, and the Brain. The Science of Neuroeconomics*, Cambridge and London, MIT Press, 2003, 375 pp.

Charles Goldfinger, *La géofinance*, Paris, Seuil, 1986, 422 pp.

Michaël Gonin, *The Social Disembedding of Business Theory and Practice*, Lausanne, University of Lausanne, HEC, 2008, 127 pp.

Augustin Gonzalez Enciso, *Valores burgueses y valores aristocraticos en el capitalismo moderno: una reflexion historica*, Cuadernos Empresa y Humanismo, Pamplona, Instituto Empresa y Humanismo – Universitad de Navarra, Vol. 78, 2000, 45 pp.

Marion Gräfin Dönhoff, *Zivilisiert den Kapitalismus: Grenzen der Freiheit*, Stuttgart, Deutsche Verlagsanstalt, 1997, 222 pp.

Thomas Guggenheim, *Preclassical monetary theories*, London, Pinter Publishers, 1989, 199 pp.

Sebastian Haffner, *Defying Hitler: a Memoir*, New York, Farrar, Straus and Giroux, 2002, 309 pp.

Jean Halpérin, 'La prohibition de l'usure et la naissance de l'assurance', in *Finance & the Common Good/Bien Commun*, No. 16, autumn 2003, 'Interest Rates and Moral: Religious Perspectives'.

Charles Handy, *The Empty Raincoat*, New York, Random House, 1995, 288 pp.

Albert Hirschman, *The Passions and the Interests*, Princeton, Princeton University Press, 1997, 180 pp.

David Hollenbach, *The Common Good and Christian Ethics*, New Studies in Christian Ethics, Vol. 22, Cambridge, Cambridge University Press, 2002, 270 pp.

Samuel Huntington, *The Clash of Civilizations and the Remaking of World Order*, New York, Simon & Schuster, 1996, 367 pp.

IMF, *World Economic Outlook*, January 2006, p. 150.

Institut für Finanzdienstleistungen, *Access to Financial Services: Strategies towards Equitable Provision*, Final study (5th International Conference on Financial Services, Gothenburg, 22–23 September 2000), Hamburg, 2001, 220 pp.

Giorgio Israel, *La mathématisation du réel*, Paris, Seuil, 1996, 350 pp.

Kevin R. James, *The Price of Retail Investing in the UK*, London, Financial Services Authority, Occasional Paper Series No. 6, February 2000.

Michael Jensen and William Meckling, 'The Nature of Man', in *Bankamerica*, Vol. 7, No. 2, summer 1994, pp. 4–19.

Rakesh Khurana, *From Higher Aims to Hired Hands. The Social Transformation of American Business Schools and the Unfulfilled Promise of Management as a Profession*, Princeton and Oxford, Princeton University Press, 2007, 531 pp.

Charles P. Kindleberger, *Manias, Panics and Crashes*, London, Macmillan, 1989, 288 pp.

János Kornai, *Economics of Shortage*, Amsterdam, Elsevier, 1980, 316 pp.

Peter Koslowski, *Ethik der Banken und der Börse*, Tübingen, Mohr Siebeck, 1997, 118 pp.

Alexandre Koyré, 'Sens et portée de la synthèse newtonienne', in *Etudes Newtoniennes*, Paris, Gallimard, 1968, pp. 27–43.

Greta Krippner, 'The financialization of the American economy', in *Socio-Economic Review*, No. 2, Vol. 3, 2005, pp. 173–208.

Lutz Kruschwitz and Andreas Löffler, *Discounted Cash Flow: a Theory of the Valuation of Firms*, London/New York, Wiley & Sons, 2005, 178 pp.

Christian Laval, *L'homme économique*, Paris, Gallimard, 2007, 396 pp.

Jean-Claude Lavigne OP, 'Antonin des Conseils – un théologien de l'usure au XVème siècle', in *Finance & the Common Good/Bien Commun*, No. 16, autumn 2003, 'Interest Rates and Moral: Religious Perspectives', pp. 60–9.

Jean-Claude Lavigne OP, 'Interdit ou toléré ? – le prêt à intérêt après *Vix Pervenit* (1745)', in *Finance & the Common Good/Bien Commun*, No. 21, spring 2005, 'From Bretton Woods to Basel II', pp. 85–97.

Raquel Lázaro, *La sociedad comercial en Adam Smith: Método, moral, religión*, Pamplona, Ediciones Universidad de Navarra (EUNSA), 2002, 355 pp.

William Lazonick and Mary O'Sullivan, 'Maximizing shareholder value: a new ideology for corporate governance', in *Economy and Society*, Vol. 29, No. 1, 2000, pp. 13–35.

Jonathan Lear, *Aristotle: the Desire to Understand*, Cambridge, Cambridge University Press, 1988, 352 pp.

Bernard Lecomte, *La vérité l'emportera toujours sur le mensonge*, Paris, Editions J.-Cl. Lattès, 1990, 370 pp.

Jacques Le Goff, 'The Usurer and Purgatory', in *The Dawn of Modern Banking*, Centre for Medieval and Renaissance Studies, University of California, New Haven & London, Yale University Press, 1979, pp. 25–52.

Jacques Le Goff, *La naissance du Purgatoire*, Paris, Gallimard, 1981, 500 pp.

Jean-Louis Le Moigne, *Théorie du système général*, Paris, Presses Universitaires de France, 1990, 330 pp.

Jacques Le Mouël, *Critique de l'efficacité*, Paris, Seuil, 1991, 184 pp.

Arthur Levitt (with Paula Dwyer), *Take on the Street: What Wall Street and Corporate America don't want you to know. What you can do to fight back*, New York, Pantheon Books, 2002, 338 pp.

Lisbon Group, *Limits to competition*, Cambridge, MIT Press, 1996, 189 pp.

Bryan Lowell and Diana Farrell, *Market Unbound: unleashing global capitalism*, New York, John Wiley & Sons, 1996, 268 pp.

Barry Lynn, *End of the Line: the Rise and Coming Fall of the Global Corporation*, New York, Doubleday, 2005, 310 pp.

Alasdair MacIntyre's book *After Virtue*, Notre Dame, University of Notre Dame Press, 1984, pp. 22–35.

Charles Mackay, *Extraordinary Popular Delusions and the Madness of Crowds*, Amherst, N.Y., Prometheus Books, 2001, 724 pp.

Harry Markowitz, 'Foundations of Portfolio Theory', in *Nobel Lectures, Economics 1981–1990*, Karl-Göran Mäler (ed.), Singapore, World Scientific Publishing Co., 1992, p. 279.

Randy Martin, *Financialization of Daily Life*, Philadelphia, Temple University Press, 2002, 220 pp.

Alain-Charles Martinet, *Sciences du management*, Paris, Vuibert, 2007, 304 pp.

Domenec Melé Carné, *Etica en la actividad financiera*, Pamplona, Ediciones Universidad de Navarra (EUNSA), 1998, 250 pp.

Charles-Albert Michalet, *Qu'est ce que la mondialisation ?*, Paris, La Découverte, 2002, 206 pp.

Alex Michalos, *Good Taxes*, Toronto and Oxford, Dundrum Press, 1997, 87 pp.

John Micklethwait and Adrian Wooldridge, *The Company: A Short History of a Revolutionary Idea*, New York, Random House, 2003, 215 pp.

Stanley Milgram, *Obedience to Authority: an Experimental View*, New York, Harper and Row, 1974, 224 pp.

Hyman Minsky, 'The financial-instability hypothesis: capitalist processes and the behaviour of the economy', in *Financial crises*, Charles P. Kindleberger and Jean-Pierre Laffargue (eds), Cambridge, Cambridge University Press, 1982, pp. 13–39.

Henry Mintzberg, *Managers not MBAs*, London, FT Prentice Hall, 2004, 450 pp.

Miklos Molnar, *La démocratie se lève à l'Est : société civile et communisme en Europe de l'Est*, Paris, Presses Universitaires de France, 1990, 360 pp.

Douglass North, *Institutions, Institutional Change and Economic Performance*, Cambridge, Cambridge University Press, 1990, 159 pp.

Miroslav Novak, *Du printemps de Prague au printemps de Moscou : les formes de l'opposition en Union soviétique et en Tchécoslovaquie depuis 1968*, Geneva, Georg Editeur, 1990, 470 pp.

Richard O'Brien, *Global Financial Integration: The End of Geography*, New York, Council on Foreign Relations, 1992, 120 pp.

OECD, *Institutional Investors in the New Financial Landscape*, Paris, OECD Publications, 1998, 488 pp.

Tommaso Padoa-Schioppa, *Regulating Finance, Balancing Freedom and Risk*, Oxford, Oxford University Press, 2004, 147 pp.

Robert W. Parenteau, 'The Late 1990s' US Bubble: Financialization in the Extreme', in Gerald A. Epstein, *Financialization and the World Economy*, Cheltenham & Northampton, Edward Elgar, 2005, pp. 111–48.

Harold Parrish, 'Thoughts on the Path Forwards for Financial Services Regulation', *Finance & the Common Good/Bien Commun*, No. 4, summer 2000, 'The Break-up of Money'.

Frank Partnoy, *Infectious greed: how deceit and risk corrupted the financial markets*, London, Profile Books, 2003, 474 pp.

Edith Penrose, *The Theory of the Growth of the Firm*, Oxford, Blackwells, 1959, new edition 1995, 272 pp.

Bernard Perret, *Les nouvelles frontières de l'argent*, Paris, Seuil, 1999, 296 pp.

Gilles Perret, *Ma mondialisation* (movie), France, 2007.

Etienne Perrot, *Le Chrétien et l'argent*, Paris, Assas Editions, 1994, 122 pp.
Etienne Perrot, 'L'homo financiarius dans son environnement culturel', in *Finance & the Common Good/Bien Commun*, No.30, I/2008.
Jean Peyrelevade, *Le capitalisme total*, Paris, Seuil, 2005, 95 pp.
Denis Piveteau and Jean-Baptiste de Foucauld, *Une société en quête de sens*, Paris, Odile Jacob, 1995, 300 pp.
John Plender, *Going off the Rails*, London, John Wiley & Sons, 2003, 282 pp.
Theodore Porter, *Trust in Numbers: The Pursuit of Objectivity in Science and Public Life*, Princeton, Princeton University Press, 1996, 324 pp.
Edward Prescott and Ellen R. McGrattan, 'Is the Stock Market Overvalued?', in *Federal Reserve Bank of Minneapolis Quarterly Review*, Vol. 24, No. 4, 2000, pp. 20–40.
Profile Business Intelligence Ltd., *Sending Money Home? A Survey of Remittance Products and Services in the United Kingdom*, 2005, 42 pp.
Hélène Rainelli-Le Montagner, *Nature et fonctions de la théorie financière*, Paris, Presses Universitaires de France, 2003, 225 pp.
Ayn Rand, *The Virtue of Selfishness*, London, Signet, 1964, 172 pp.
Ayn Rand, *Capitalism: the Unknown Ideal*, London, Signet, 1967, 348 pp.
Robert Reich, *The Work of Nations: Preparing Ourselves for 21st-Century Capitalism*, New York, Random House, 1991, 340 pp.
David Riesman, *The Lonely Crowd*, New Haven, Yale University Press, 1950, 386 pp.
Jeremy Rifkin, *The Age of Access: the New Culture of Hypercapitalism, where All of Life is a Paid-for Experience*, New York, Jeremy P. Tarcher/Putnam, 2000, 311 pp.
Isabelle Rivière, *Sur le devoir d'imprévoyance*, Liège, Pensée catholique, 1946, 132 pp.
Marie-Monique Robin, *Le monde selon Monsanto: de la dioxine aux OGM, une multinationale qui vous veut du bien*, Paris, Editions La Découverte, 2008, 254 pp.
Manuelle Roche, *Le M'zab: cités millénaires du Sahara*, Bez-et-Esparon, Etudes & Communication, 2003, p. 64.
Ernesto Rossi di Montelera, Ernesto, 'Epargne: entre l'exigence de libéralité et la quête de sécurité', in *Finance & the Common Good/Bien Commun*, No. 4, summer 2000, 'The Break-up of Money'.
Lahsen Sbail El Idrissi, 'La rémunération du capital en Islam', in *Finance & the Common Good/Bien Commun*, No. 16, autumn 2003, 'Interest Rates and Moral: Religious Perspectives', pp. 16–30.
Catherine Sauviat in *Finance & the Common Good/Bien Commun*, op. cit., pp. 65–6.
Julie Schor et al., *Do Americans shop too much?*, Boston, Beacon Press, 2000, 96 pp.
Michael Sherwin, 'Une anthropologie dissidente dans une théologie johannique: La vérité et la liberté dans la pensée de Jean Paul II', in *Car c'est de l'homme qu'il s'agit: défis anthropologiques et enseignement social chrétien*, edited by Paul H. Dembinski, Nicolas Buttet and Ernesto Rossi di Montelera, Paris, Desclée de Brouwer, 2007, pp. 37–56.
Robert J. Shiller, *Irrational Exuberance*, Princeton, Princeton University Press, 2000, 296 pp.
Georg Simmel, *The Philosophy of Money*, London, Routledge and Kegan Paul, 1978, 512 pp.
Werner Sombart, *The Quintessence of Capitalism*, London, Unwin, 1915 (originally published in German as *Der Bourgeois*, Munich and Leipzig, Duncker and Humblot, 1913, 540 pp.).

George Soros, *The Crisis of Global Capitalism*, New York, Public Affairs, 1998, 288 pp.
George Soros, *The New Paradigm for Financial Markets: The Credit Crash of 2008 and What It Means*, New York, Public Affairs, 2008, 208 pp.
Bernard Stiegler, *Mécréance et discrédit*, Paris, Galilée, 3 volumes published between 2004 and 2006.
Joseph Stiglitz, *Globalization and its discontents*, London, Penguin Books, 2002, 288 pp.
Maja Svilar, *Concepts of human freedom: Festschrift in honour of André Mercier on the occasion of his 75th birthday*, Frankfurt am Main, Lang, 1988, 227 pp.
SwissBanking (Swiss Bankers Association), *Swiss Banking – Roadmap 2015*, September 2007, p. 8.
SwissRe, 'World insurance in 2005', in *Sigma*, No. 5, 2006.
Joseph Tainter, *The Collapse of Complex Societies*, New York, Cambridge University Press, 1988, 250 pp.
Richard S. Tedlow, *New and Improved: The Story of Mass Marketing in America*, New York, Basic Books, 1990, 481 pp.
Albert Tévoédjrè, *La pauvreté richesse des peuples*, Paris, Collection Economie et Humanisme, Les Editions Ouvrières, 1978, 206 pp.
Luc Thévenoz and Rashid Bahar (eds), *Conflicts of Interest: Corporate Governance & Financial Markets*, Leiden, Kluwer Law International, 2007, 416 pp.
Jean-Marie Thiveaud, 'Fait financier et instrument monétaire entre souveraineté et légitimité : l'institution financière des sociétés archaïques', in Michel Aglietta and André Orléan, *La monnaie souveraine*, Paris, Odile Jacob, 1998, pp. 85–126.
Jean-Marie Thiveaud, 'La gestation séculaire et l'Etat dépositaire dans l'Europe des Lumières', in *Caisse des Dépôts et Consignations – 175 ans*, a special issue of *Revue d'Economie Financière*, Paris, 1999, pp. 9–31.
Philippe Thureau-Dangin's *La concurrence et la mort*, Paris, Editions Syros, 1995, 215 pp.
Alex Trew, 'Finance and Growth: A Critical Survey', in *The Economic Record*, Vol. 82, No. 259, December 2006, pp. 481–90.
James B. Twitchell, *Lead us into Temptation*, New York, Columbia University Press, 1999, 310 pp.
Hélène Vérin, *Entrepreneurs, entreprises: Histoire d'une idée*, Paris, Presses Universitaires de France, 1982, 262 pp.
Nicolas Véron, Mathieu Autret and Alfred Galichon, *L'information financière en crise: Comptabilité et capitalisme*, Paris, Odile Jacob, 2004, 269 pp.
Michel Villette, *Le Manager jetable*, Paris, La Découverte, 1996, 186 pp.
Michel Villette and Catherine Vuillermot, *Portrait de l'homme d'affaires en prédateur*, Paris, La Découverte, 2007, 294 pp.
Christian Walter and Eric Brian, *Critique de la valeur fondamentale*, Paris, Springer, 2007, 200 pp.
Max Weber, *General Economic History*, New York, Greenberg, 1927, 425 pp.
George Weigel, *Witness to Hope: The Biography of Pope John Paul II*, New York, Cliff Street Books, 1999, 1040 pp.
Paul Windolf (ed.), *Finanzmarkt-Kapitalismus*, Wiesbaden, VS Verlag für Sozialwissenschaften, 2005, 516 pp.
Jean Ziegler, *L'empire de la honte*, Paris, Fayard, 2005, 323 pp.

Index

Accounting 51, 56
  company 5
  standards 88
  creative 112
Actuarial
  calculations 42
  utopia 18, 136
Advertising 126
Alienation
  diagnosed 131
  ethical 156, 168
Anthropology 8, 136
Anticipation 88
Anxiety 136–7
Assets 113, 133
  asset management 27, 46, 101
  portfolio of assets 114, 134
Authority 156
  supervisory 41
Autonomy 133

Bank 27, 46, 76, 84, 93, 101, 132
  -based economy 84
  central 21, 52
  commercial 21
  for International Settlements 38, 40, 90, 149
  global 42
  supervision 40
Basel II 23, 124
Benchmarking 48
Berlin Wall 13, 15–16
Bonds 103
Bonuses 161
Bretton Woods 18–20, 22
Business school 115

Calvin 75
Capacity
  earning 115
  productive 45
Capital 57, 123
  account 19–20
  financial 134

gains 113, 130–1, 135–6, 154
  mobility of 21
  remuneration of 116
  return on 58
  venture 77
Capitalism 3, 57
  free–market 34
  mature 58
Cash flow 29–30, 121
Causality 11
  Aristotle 6, 11
  mechanical 66
  multi-modal 138
Chrematistic 74
Churning 49
Cold War 14
Commissions 27, 49
Common
  good 8, 65, 160, 162, 165, 167
  sense 155
Complexity 66, 150–1
Corporation *see* Enterprise 16, 105
  joint-stock 77
  quoted 105
  very large corporation (VLC) 105, 108, 113, 118, 120, 125–7, 134, 151
Corruption 159
Credit 53, 74, 132
  -based 76
  relationships 77
Crisis
  Asian and Russian 99
  financial 2
  Latin America 99
  subprime 134, 149
Cumulative return 104
Customers 128–9, 133

Debt 53, 87
  financing 116
  international 21
  national 52

Dematerialization   29
Derivative   38, 79
Discounted cash flow   111
Distrust   8, 130, 135, 149–50, 160
  spiral of   135
Diversification   63

Economic
  growth   43, 100
  international order   18
  mainstreams   4
  man   17
  neoclassical   16
  paradigm   3
  rationality   136
  thinking   98
  vulnerability   14
Economy   56
  bank-based   84
  financial-market   85
  real   99
  regulation of the global   18
Efficiency   100, 119–20, 130, 145, 151, 156, 167
  ethos   56, 62–4, 83, 136, 159, 168
  financial   57, 115, 120
  gains   155
  ideal of   37
  technical   55, 56, 110
Enron   99
Enterprise *see* Corporation   57, 118, 129, 135
  financial structure   115
  quoted   102, 103
  small and medium-sized   121
  value of   111
Equity
  funds   122
  private-   77
  return on (ROE)   115
Ethics   153–4, 161, 167, 169
  abdication   156
  alienation   8, 168
  financial   159
  initiatives   159
Ethos   5, 12
  aristocratic   57
  efficiency   56, 62–4, 83, 136, 159, 168

Euphoric years   13–14, 16, 34, 62, 83, 98, 111
Eurodollars   21, 25
Exchange floating   23
Existential anxiety   136

Family   17, 134
Fiduciary obligation   153–4
Finance   3, 5, 17, 20, 23, 29, 30, 33, 37, 60, 84, 99, 103, 145
  a means to an end   146
  a project   78
  as organizing principle   6
  as pattern of behaviour   6
  as rationality   6
  as tyranny   99
  becomes a deceiver   146
  behavioural   90
  contribution to national product   100
  governance of global   22
  modern science of   138
  neuro-   127
  private   22
  purpose of   61
  spirit of   11
  to be servant or deceiver?   100
Financial
  asset   22, 30, 43, 48, 59–61, 80, 132, 151
  capital   134
  crises   36
  depending   100
  efficiency   57, 115, 120
  engineering   122
  ethics   159
  euphoria   85, 104, 120
  innovation   27
  institutions   27
  intensity   98
  intermediaries   25, 151
  investors   59, 116
  market   22, 25, 37, 61, 84, 86, 118, 119
  -market economies   85
  products   27
  relationships   74, 77, 79, 81, 83, 94, 123

Financial – *continued*
    return   101
    sector   100
    system   37
    thinking   6
    transactions   81, 83, 92, 151
Financialization   2, 5, 6, 12, 13, 18, 28, 34, 43, 44, 54, 57, 63, 65, 73, 79, 86, 89, 100, 106, 112, 113, 118–20, 123, 126, 130, 134, 138, 145, 148, 152, 162, 167
    of growth   114
    of society   163
    process   104
Frugality   162, 163
Funds
    equity   49
    hedge   35, 37, 40, 49, 77
    investment   48, 49
    pension   48, 93, 131, 134
    private equity   35
    sovereign wealth   152
Future
    fear of the   163
    radiant   164
    societal   163

Global value chains   108
Globalization   107, 111, 114, 152
Gold   20, 22
Government   37, 50, 53, 150
Greed   64, 130, 137, 162, 168–9
    infectious   64
    precisely   160
Growth
    reasonable   104

Hedge funds   35, 37, 40, 49, 77
Herd behaviour   88
High-net-worth individuals   44
Homo
    financiarius   69, 72
    oeconomicus   17, 69
Human
    beings   134
    nature   55

ICT – information and communication technology *see* technology   23
Improvidence   162, 163
Inequalities in income   44
Inflation   51
Information   87
    confidential   36
Innovation   30, 126, 127
Insurance   42, 43, 62
    private   93
Intangible assets   111, 112, 125, 134, 135
Interest   64, 75, 85, 132
    conflicts of   46
    private   37
    public   37
    rates   78–9, 116
Intermediaries   46, 50, 99
    financial   151
Internal rate of return   116
International
    debt   21
    economic order   18
    liberalization   27
    regulation   20
    trade   15, 19
Investment   76, 84, 119, 149
    foreign direct   108
    funds   48, 49
    stock-market   102

Labour   123
    remuneration of   117
Legitimacy   151
Leverage   110, 114, 116
Liberalization   14, 27
Liquidity   21, 35–6, 38, 51–2, 59, 84, 101, 167
Loans
    standardized   47
Long-Term Capital Management (LTCM)   37–8, 99, 150
Loyalty   2, 128, 130, 135, 148, 154, 161, 168

Man
    economic   17
    picture of   16
Management   113–15

Manufacturing   111, 121
Market   3, 14, 22, 25, 43, 49, 50, 66, 110, 128
  financial   61, 84, 86, 118–19
  free   54
  imperfection   38
  integrity   36, 41
  mark to   88
  mechanism   37
  organized   35, 86–7, 91
  panic   39
  perfect   154
  price   88
  process   87
  sentiment   87
  stock *see* Stock-market   85, 94, 97, 101, 114, 122, 145
  value   89
Marketing   110–11, 125, 127
  neuro-   127
Marxism   3, 66
Master/slave paradox   80
Materialism   16, 64
Mathematization   60
Metaphysical   16, 157
Method
  cumulative return   101
  Methodenstreit   3–4
  multimodal causality   7, 11
Monetary
  policy   27
  resources   84
  standard   52
  system   28–9, 31, 34, 50
Money   23, 29, 37, 81
  accounting   30
  accumulating   163
  as information   29
  as means of payment   29
  break-up of   27
  creating   52
  dual anchor of trust in money hypothesis   28
  essence of   27
  fecundity of   146
Moral   136, 151, 153, 157
  dimension   149
  duty   76, 153
  justification   58

Organizing principle   5, 8–9, 33, 41, 54, 56, 65, 73, 100, 119, 157
Outsourcing   118, 121
Over the counter (OTC)
  transactions   35–6, 40, 50, 87, 98

Panic   88
Paradigm   3–4
  dominant   9
  scientific   62
Pension   42, 116, 152, 164, 167, 169
  funds   48, 93, 131, 134
  individualization of   42
  promises   34, 43
Portfolio theory   46, 59, 136
Positivism   17
Precautionary   146
Price
  manipulation   37
  market   88
  market-stock   101
  insurance   93
Private equity funds   87, 122
Privatization   14
Proceduralization   150, 155
Process
  anonymous   150
  concentration   111
Productivity   24, 53, 68, 107, 111, 117, 132–3, 159, 172
Products' cycle life   125
Professional codes   159
Profit   79, 147, 149
Public
  deficit   21, 50
  virtues   137

Rate
  exchange   20, 22
  of interest   78–9, 116
Rating agencies   35, 49, 89
Rationality   5, 16, 55
Regulation   41, 81, 89
  international   20
  self-   40

Relationships 2, 8, 85, 125, 129–30, 135, 138, 149, 154, 163, 168
  asymmetrical 76
  credit 77
  financial 74, 77, 79, 81, 83, 94, 123
  property 131
  trust-based 153
Religion 75, 157
  Calvin 75
  Christian view 15
  Judaism 75
  Koran 75
Remuneration 78, 136, 161–2
  of the savings 167
Responsibility 155, 169
Return 42, 149
  ROE (return on equity) 115, 121–2, 135, 162
Risk 58, 78, 85, 87–8, 91, 124, 133, 150
  -cover 63
  -free society 63, 155
  and return 61
  control 62
  demutualization of 42

Savings 29, 42, 44, 47, 84–6, 90, 101, 138, 145
  forced 43
  remuneration of the 167
  silos 45, 104, 138, 151, 162, 164
  yield 42
Scientific paradigm 62
Securities 80–1, 85
  selling the 87
Selfishness 64
Self-referential 23
Servant 163
Shareholder 115–16
  nomadic, anonymous 85, 105
  value 113–15, 118, 151
Small and Medium Enterprises (SME) 122
Social
  exclusion 14
  fabric 64
  institutions 33
  phenomenon 28

  sciences 3
  welfare system 17
Society
  economy-based 13, 15, 17, 23
  foundations of 154
  industrial 15
  international 161
  market-based 16
  risk-free 63
Sovereignty 19
Speculators 60
Spirit of finance 33
Standardization 25, 33, 35
  loans 47
Strategies
  strategic games 135
  originate and distribute 90
Stock-market *see* Market 85, 94, 97, 104, 114, 122, 145
  -capitalization 112
  -index 103
  -prices 101
  -value 127
Subprime
  crisis 134, 149
  mortgage crisis 37
  mortgage loans 2
SWIFT 25, 29
System 89
  analysis 5
  driven by impersonal logic 120
  organizing principle 5, 8–9, 33, 41, 54, 56, 65, 73, 100, 119, 157
  systemic approach 6, 66
  viscosity 160

Tax 161
  breaks 53
  on all financial transactions 160
  Tobin 160
Technical efficiency 55–6, 110
Technology 9, 13, 15–16, 23, 55, 156, 162
  information and communication (ICT) 18
Term
  long 90, 135, 160–1
  short 90

Theory
  economic and financial   169
  portfolio   46, 59
Thirty Golden Years   13, 15, 42–3, 55, 114, 119–20, 138
Trade   64
  flows   20
  insider   89
  international   15, 19
Transactions   8, 27, 43, 80, 85, 113, 123, 128–9, 131, 135, 138, 148, 154, 160, 163, 168
  costs   160
  financial   81, 83, 92, 151
  foreign-exchange   98
  mechanically flawless   165
  over-the-counter (OTC)   87
  strategy   63
  towards   2
  transactionitis acute   164
Transparency   88, 159
Trust   28–9, 34, 56, 75, 123, 148, 154, 161, 168
  -based relationships   153
  between people   68
  distrust   130
  in external   77
  in institutions   68
  public   50

Uncertainty   58
Unemployment   14, 145

United States
  dollars   20
  GDP   101
  monetary policy   20
  Treasury   102
Utilitarianism   55

Valuation   122
Value
  added   98, 100, 123
  book   112
  global value chains   108, 110, 124
  hierarchy of   14
  market-stock   127
  resale   90
  shareholder   113–15, 118, 151
  true   90
Values   147
  ethical   54
  inversion of   147
  market   89
Viscosity   160
Very large corporations (VLC)   108, 113, 118, 120, 125–7, 134, 151

Wages   116, 120
Wealth   30
  accumulated   146
  accumulation of   58

Zeitgeist   55